PROJECT
SMOKE

Also by
STEVEN RAICHLEN

The Barbecue! Bible®

Barbecue! Bible Sauces, Rubs, and Marinades, Bastes, Butters & Glazes

How to Grill

Beer-Can Chicken

BBQ USA

Indoor! Grilling

Barbecue! Bible Best Ribs Ever

Planet Barbecue!

Man Made Meals

Miami Spice

PROJECT SMOKE

SEVEN STEPS *to* SMOKED FOOD NIRVANA, PLUS
100 IRRESISTIBLE RECIPES *from* **CLASSIC** (SLAM-DUNK BRISKET)
to **ADVENTUROUS** (SMOKED BACON-BOURBON APPLE CRISP)

STEVEN RAICHLEN

WORKMAN PUBLISHING
NEW YORK

Library of Congress Cataloging-in-Publication Data is available.

Paperback ISBN 978-0-7611-8186-6
Hardcover ISBN 978-0-7611-8923-7

Cover and interior design: Becky Terhune
Original photography: Matthew Benson
Food styling: Nora Singley
Prop styling: Sara Abalan
Additional photo credits on page 281

Steven Raichlen is available for select speaking engagements. Please contact speakersbureau@workman.com.

Workman books are available at special discounts when purchased in bulk for premiums and sales promotions as well as for fund-raising or educational use. Special editions or book excerpts can also be created to specification. For details, contact the Special Sales Director at the address below or send an email to specialmarkets@workman.com.

Workman Publishing Company, Inc.
225 Varick Street
New York, NY 10014-4381

workman.com

Printed in the United States of America
First printing April 2016

10 9 8 7 6 5 4 3 2 1

To Ella, Mia, and Julian, who light my fire.

ACKNOWLEDGMENTS

It gives me great pleasure to thank all the people on team *Project Smoke*.

Editorial and Production: Sarah Brady, Kate Karol, Suzanne Fass, Barbara Peragine, and Claire McKean

Design: Becky Terhune

Photography: Anne Kerman, Matthew Benson, Nora Singley, Sara Abalan, Bobby Walsh, Angela Cherry, and Lena Diaz

Publicity and Marketing: Selina Meere, Rebecca Carlisle, Jessica Wiener, and Lauren Southard

Sales: All the members of the great Workman sales team

Website: Molly Kay Upton and Joanna Eng

Recipe Testers: Rob Baas, Chris Lynch, Denise Swidey, and Ashley Archibald

Project Smoke TV: Matt Cohen, Gwenn Williams, Richard Dallett, Ryan Kollmorgan, John Pappalardo, Patrick Shea, Jillian Kuchman, Michael Orsborn, Jon Nichols, Paul Stapleton-Smith, Emily Belleranti, Michael Cottrel, and John Dietz

Maryland Public Television: Steven Schupak, Jay Parikh, Stuart Kazanow, Frank Batavick, and Donna Hunt

Additional Support: Chuck Adams, Ron Cooper, Sam Edwards, Ole Hansen, Patrick Martini, Matthias Messner, Helle Mogenson, and Nathan Myhrvold

Gear: All-Clad, BBQ Guru, Big Green Egg, Bradley Smoker, Camerons Products, Carolina Cookwood, Hasty-Bake, Horizon Smokers, Kalamazoo Outdoor Gourmet, Kai USA, Ltd. (Shun Cutlery), Kamodo Kamados, Kingsford, Landmann, Lodge Manufacturing, Maverick Housewares, Memphis Wood Fire Grills, Nordic Ware, Weber, The Pit Barrel Cooker Co., Polyscience, Royal Oak, Smoke Daddy, Spitjack, ThermoWorks, and Yoder Smokers

Food Companies: Alaskan Seafood Marketing Institute, The Green Grape Provisions, Heritage Foods USA, Melissa's, Strauss Brands, Tecumseh Farms, and Trivento

Finally, a huge *Project Smoke* thanks to my indefatigable assistant, Nancy Loseke, my extraordinary editor, Suzanne Rafer, and my amazing wife Barbara, who's behind all the good things that happen in my life.

CONTENTS

INTRODUCTION
A CRASH COURSE IN SMOKING

There are many places I could start this book. On Bornholm, Denmark, where at the height of the smoked herring industry in the 1930s, this small island in the Baltic Sea boasted more than 120 active smokehouses, their whitewashed brick chimneys still punctuating the landscape today.

Or in the Italian Alps, where salt-cured hams are smoked with juniper wood for two weeks to make a smoky prosciutto called speck. A similar scene takes place in Surrey, Virginia, where the Edwards family has been smoking hams since 1926.

Or on Islay Island in Scotland, where barley is smoked over peat to make Scotch whisky, or on the rugged hillsides around Oaxaca, Mexico, where agave cactus hearts are smoke-roasted in fire pits to prepare a unique smoky spirit called mezcal.

Or closer to home, at the American Royal World Series of Barbecue in Kansas City, where for three days and nights, barbecue teams from all over the world—more than 600—gather to compete, sending fragrant clouds of wood smoke over Arrowhead Stadium.

But the best place to begin might be my backyard, where as I write these words, salmon, scallops, and beef jerky—not to mention ricotta, mustard, and hot sauce—are smoking in a cedar smokehouse I built with my neighbor Roger Becker.

Smoke. Few words have such power to make you hungry. Think of some of the world's most pleasurable foods: ham, bacon, pastrami. All owe their distinctive flavor and character to smoke.

Smoke is the subject of this book. Hot-smoked foods like kippers and ham. Cold-smoked foods like *mozzarella affumicata* and Scandinavian *lax*. American barbecue, from Texas brisket to Carolina pulled pork to Kansas City ribs. Smoked foods from around Planet Barbecue like Jamaican jerk chicken and Chinese tea-smoked duck.

So you might ask: How does this book differ from all my other *Barbecue! Bible* cookbooks? While it's true that most of my books touch on smoking, particularly as practiced in the American barbecue belt, this book focuses exclusively on smoke—from smoked meats and seafood to smoked cocktails, condiments, and desserts. You'll learn how to smoke the icons *and* the foods you'd never dream of smoking, including cheesecake, ice cream, mayonnaise, butter, and ice.

So fire up your smokers. *Project Smoke* is about to begin.

THE SEVEN STEPS TO SMOKING NIRVANA

Smoking is easy but it isn't always simple. There are hundreds of smokers to choose from and each type operates differently. You can spend a few hundred dollars on a smoker—or thousands—and the price doesn't always predict performance.

Then there's the wood: hickory, oak, apple, or mesquite, to mention just a few of the dozens of fuels used for smoking. Each has its partisans, and that's *before* you start talking green or seasoned; dry or soaked; logs, chunks, chips, or pellets.

Next come the meats: prime or choice; organic or heritage; not to mention seafood (wild or farmed, whole or filleted), vegetables, cheese, eggs, and desserts.

And once you build your fire—believe me, there's a lot of debate about the best way to do that—you have to choose the smoking method: hot-smoking or cold-smoking; smoke-roasting or with a handheld smoker. How long the various foods smoke and how you know they're done.

Does it sound complicated? It is (a little), but I've broken the process into seven easy steps. Follow them and you'll master smoking in no time, and you'll have a lot of fun—and satisfaction—in the process.

STEP 1
CHOOSE YOUR SMOKER

Your first step is to select the right smoker for *you*. There are dozens of types and hundreds of individual models. So read this section and The Various Types of Smokers on page 261.

The right smoker for you depends on your experience, goals, and how many people you usually cook for—collectively called your smoker personality.

Beginner: You want a smoker that's affordable and easy to operate, and that doesn't take up a lot of space. Good bets include: a kettle-style charcoal grill or other grill with a tall lid; a water smoker; a ceramic cooker; and an upright barrel smoker.

Grilling enthusiast who wants to explore smoking: Grilling is your first love, but you want to do smoking, too. Check out a kettle grill or front-loading charcoal grill; a wood-burning grill; a ceramic cooker; or an offset smoker with a firebox that comes with a grate.

Convenience- and results-oriented smoker: You love smoked and barbecued foods, but want the push-button convenience of a gas grill. Consider electric or gas smokers or pellet grills.

Process-oriented smoker: You embrace not just the results, but the process of smoking—building and maintaining a fire, adjusting the air vents, and so on. A water smoker or an offset smoker would be right for you.

Smoked food addict: You love smoked and barbecued foods—the smokier the better. An offset smoker, water smoker, or even a home-built smokehouse would be a perfect match.

Competition or commercial barbecuer: Your TV is tuned to *BBQ Pitmasters* and you want to compete against other barbecue fanatics. You often cook for a crowd. Look for a big rig offset smoker (preferably on a trailer) or a carousel-style commercial smoker.

Apartment- or condo-bound smoker: You love the flavor of smoked food but live in an apartment or condo or in a dense urban environment where you can't grill or smoke outdoors. Get yourself a stovetop smoker or a handheld smoker.

TYPES OF SMOKERS

 Kettle-style charcoal

 Ceramic cooker

 Front-loading charcoal grill

 Stovetop smoker

 Water smoker

 Upright barrel smoker

Electric or gas smoker

 Handheld smoker

 Wood-burning grill

 Offset smoker

 Pellet grill

  Home-built smokehouse

Big rig offset smoker

 Carousel-style commercial smoker

ANATOMY OF A SMOKER

Smokers range in size from handheld smokers to monster rigs trailered around the competition barbecue circuit. They can be as simple as a 55-gallon steel drum or as elaborate as a high-tech Enviro-Pak you literally can drive a truck through. Some smokers burn wood or charcoal; others run on propane or electricity.

Despite the wide range of shapes, sizes, and configurations, most smokers share a similar construction. Understand how the various parts function and you're on your way to becoming a master smoker.

At one end or the bottom of the smoker, you find the **firebox**, where you burn wood or wood products to generate smoke. At the other end you find the **chimney**, which creates a draft to pull the smoke through and out of the smoker.

Between them you find the **smoke chamber** and **heat diffuser**. The smoke chamber—sometimes called the **cook chamber**—is where the food smokes and often cooks at the same time. The smoke chamber can be located adjacent to the firebox or directly above it. (With handheld smokers, you use a separate container, such as a bar shaker or plastic wrap-covered bowl, to serve as a smoke chamber.) On one end of the smoke chamber you sometimes find a **grease drain** with a small bucket to collect the fat and drippings.

Fire produces heat, yet most smoked foods are cooked at a low temperature. The **heat diffuser** shields the food from the full force of the fire. In a water smoker, it's a shallow **water pan** filled with liquid and positioned between the fire and the smoke chamber. In a ceramic cooker, it's a **convection plate** (sometimes called a **plate setter**), positioned between the embers and the rack. In an offset barrel smoker, it's a sliding metal plate, often perforated, positioned under the cooking rack.

The **vents** are a small but essential feature on a smoker. The intake vent on the firebox controls the airflow entering the smoker. The chimney vent, located at the end of the smoke chamber, regulates the escape of hot air and smoke. Some vents are rotating disks; others, sliding metal panels. All control the airflow—and thus the heat—in the smoker. Remember these simple formulas:

• Greater airflow equals higher heat.

• Reduced airflow equals lower heat.

So open or close the vents to control the airflow and the heat.

Electric smokers (including pellet grills) use an **electric heating element** to burn the wood and a **thermostat** to control the heat. Gas smokers also have a thermostat to control the heat. Just set the temperature and let the thermostat do the rest. When working with pellet grills, remember:

• Lower heat gives you more smoke.

• Higher heat gives you less smoke.

In fact, that's true for most smokers.

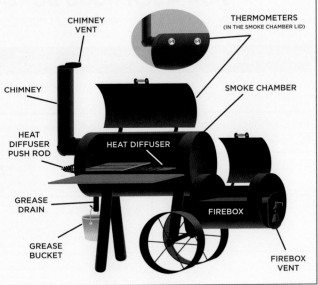

STEP 2
SOURCE YOUR FUEL

Wood is the premier fuel for smoking, whether you burn hickory to smoke ribs in Kansas City, alder to smoke salmon in Alaska, or pimento (allspice) wood to cook authentic Jamaican jerk.

A lot of ink has been spilled about which wood smoke goes best with particular meats or seafood. Some people go to great lengths to match particular woods to specific foods—for example, apple with pork or cherry with chicken—the way oenophiles match wines to specific foods.

So I'm about to make a heretical statement: The wood variety matters less than how you burn it. And while each wood variety produces smoke with a *slightly* different color and flavor, if you're new to smoking, the major hardwoods (hickory, oak, apple, cherry, and maple) all work equally well.

Carolina Cookwood's owner Bud Williford groups woods into two broad categories: **forest woods** and **orchard woods**. The former includes nut woods like hickory, pecan, and oak, and wild woods like maple and alder. The latter includes fruit woods like the already popular apple and cherry, and the up-and-coming peach, pear, and mulberry. To this list you could add **exotic woods** like camphor wood, used for smoking in China, and pimento wood from the allspice tree, which produces the intensely aromatic smoke responsible in part for the unique taste of Jamaican jerk.

These diverse woods share one point in common: All come from deciduous trees (trees that shed their leaves annually) and are classified as hardwoods. You don't normally smoke with soft woods like pine, spruce, and other evergreens, which produce a dark sooty smoke full of harsh oily flavors. There are exceptions here, too: Canadians, for example, smoke-grill steaks over fresh branches of spruce. The French smoke mussels over dry pine needles to make a remarkable dish called *éclade de moules*. Elsewhere on Planet Barbecue, people smoke with tea (in China; see page 168), with herbs and spices, such as allspice berries and cinnamon (see Jamaican Jerk Chicken on page 154). But the strangest smoking fuel? That would be dried sheep dung, used for smoking mutton and horsemeat in Iceland.

HOW MUCH WOOD DO YOU NEED FOR SMOKING?

How much wood do you need for your smoker? Read the manufacturer's instructions. Here's a rough guide.

FORM OF FUEL	SMOKER TYPE	AMOUNT
Logs	Large offset smokers	1 to 3 split logs every hour, once you have a good bed of embers
Wood chunks (added to charcoal embers)	Charcoal grills, water smokers, ceramic cookers, upright barrel smokers	2 to 4 chunks or so every hour
Wood chips	Charcoal grills, water smokers, ceramic cookers, upright barrel smokers	2 handfuls (1½ to 2 cups) every 30 to 40 minutes
Pellets	Pellet smokers	About 2 pounds per hour on high, 1 to 1½ pounds on medium, ½ pound on the smoke setting
Sawdust	Stovetop smokers, handheld smokers	1 to 2 tablespoons for the former; 1 teaspoon for the latter

A WORD ON CHARCOAL

Large competition and commercial smokers burn only wood. But most of us will fuel our smokers with a combination of charcoal and wood chunks or chips. Charcoal comes in two basic types: **lump** and **briquette**.

Lump charcoal is made by charring logs in a low oxygen environment in a kiln. It's a pure wood fuel with no additives. Lump charcoals vary depending on the base wood: Mesquite, for example, burns hot with a lot of sparking. Maple and oak charcoal (my favorites) produce a clean steady heat. When buying lump charcoal, look for brands that sell irregular jagged chunks. Straight edges or square corners suggest charcoal made from lumber or flooring scraps—not my first choice. Lump charcoal burns clean and hot when first lit, but the temperature drops off more quickly than with briquettes and the burn time is shorter. But you know you're burning a pure wood product and you can add fresh lump charcoal directly to the fire without producing an unpleasant-tasting smoke.

Briquettes are a composite fuel, a mixture of wood scraps, coal dust, borax, petroleum accelerants, and sometimes sand stamped into pillow-shaped nuggets. You can also buy "natural" briquettes made solely with wood or coconut shells and starch binders. The advantage of briquettes is that they burn at a consistent temperature for longer than lump (typically, a chimney-full maintains a 600°F fire for 1 hour). On the down side, when first lit, briquettes release an acrid-tasting smoke. For this reason, when refueling a smoker with briquettes, I recommend lighting them in a chimney starter instead of directly on the existing coals.

NOTE: Most charcoal produces heat, not wood smoke, so you can't really smoke foods with charcoal alone. However, some manufacturers, like Kingsford, embed tiny pieces of mesquite or hickory wood in some of their briquettes. These will give you a mild smoke flavor when grilling, but you really need to add wood to generate smoke.

Charcoal briquettes (left) come uniformly shaped. Lump charcoal (right) comes in irregular chunks.

A BRIEF SCIENCE LESSON—WHAT IS SMOKE (AND WHY DOES IT TASTE SO GOOD?)

Before we dive into the specifics, a general word about smoke. You know it when you see it. You certainly recognize it when you smell it and taste it. It's the soul of barbecue, not to mention the essence of some of the world's greatest foods and drinks, from bacon to kippers to Scotch whisky.

But what exactly is smoke, how does it flavor foods, and why does it taste so good?

Smoke is a vaporous by-product that results from burning wood and other organic materials. It contains:

- Solids (in the form of tiny carbon particles called soot)

- Liquids (such as tars and oils)

- Gases (responsible for most of the flavors we prize in smoked foods)

All three contribute to the look, aroma, and taste of smoked foods.

Smoke results when you burn wood, but not all wood smokes or tastes the same. Hardwoods (from deciduous trees like hickory and apple, which shed their leaves once a year) produce the best-tasting smoke. Many other plant fuels are used for smoking, from hay to smoke cheese in Italy to corncobs to smoke bacon in the Midwest.

Wood goes through three stages when you burn it:

- Desiccation/dehydration

- Pyrolysis (decomposition by heat)

- Combustion

In other words, the fire first dries out the wood, then breaks it down, and finally ignites it. Each stage produces a different type of smoke and releases a different cluster of smoke flavors.

In his visionary book *Modernist Cuisine*, food scientist Nathan Myhrvold breaks the smoking process into six key temperature phases.

- **At 212°F** the water in the wood boils, releasing steam and carbon dioxide. The latter reacts with the charred wood, producing carbon monoxide and nitrogen dioxide—compounds responsible for the formation of the iconic smoke ring (see page 127) in briskets and other smoked meats.

- **At 340°F** pyrolysis begins, releasing formic acid, acetic acid, and other acidic compounds. These provide some of the tart flavors in smoke and help color and preserve the food.

- **At 390°F** the smoke flavor mellows as pyrolysis begins producing carbonyls—aromatic molecules responsible for the appetizing yellow, brown, and dark red colors of smoked foods. One carbonyl, formaldehyde, acts as an antimicrobial and preservative.

- **At 570°F** the smoke develops a more complex flavor, as pyrolysis produces aromatic compounds called phenols. These include creosol (responsible for a peatlike flavor one associates with Scotch whisky); isoeugenol (responsible for the clove and other spice flavors in smoke); and vanillin (source of a vanilla-like sweetness). Other inviting compounds produced at this stage include sweet maltitols, nutty lactons, and caramel-tasting furans.

- **At 750°F** the wood blackens and smoke production peaks. This is your smoking sweet spot, with the highest concentration of phenols, plus liquid droplets of tar and oil that add color and taste to the food.

- **At 1,800°F** the wood ignites and the flavor-producing compounds cease. The burning wood becomes an agent for cooking, no longer for smoking.

FORMS OF WOOD AND HOW TO USE THEM

FORM OF WOOD	SIZE	EQUIPMENT BEST USED IN	ADVANTAGES	WATCH POINTS
Logs	12-18 inches long	Large offset smokers (stick burners), commercial smokers	Generates both heat and smoke.	You need a big smoker with good airflow. It takes at least an hour to burn logs down to a hot bed of embers.
Chunks	1½-4 inches across	Small offset smokers, water smokers, ceramic smokers, upright barrel smokers, gas smokers, gas grills	Sold in hardware stores and supermarkets. Portable and easy to store and quick to produce smoke.	No need to soak before adding to a charcoal fire. One way to smoke on a gas grill is to place chunks beneath the grate or on or between the metal heat deflectors or ceramic briquettes or bricks (see page 21).
Chips	½-1 inch wide and long, ¼ inch thick	Small offset smokers, water smokers, ceramic smokers, upright barrel smokers, gas smokers, gas grills	Sold in hardware stores and supermarkets. Portable and easy to store. Wood chips produce smoke quickly.	Soak in water for 30 minutes, then drain. This slows down the rate of combustion.
Sawdust	Wood in powdered form	Electric smokers, stovetop smokers, handheld smokers	Heated sawdust starts to smoke almost instantaneously.	Do not soak.
Disks	Small puck-shaped disks of compressed sawdust	Electric smokers	Convenient, easy to use, and quick to produce smoke.	Do not soak (will disaggregate if exposed to moisture).
Pellets	Tiny cylinders of compressed sawdust	Pellet smokers, under-grate smoker boxes, smoking tubes	Convenient and easy to use and quick to produce smoke.	Do not soak (will disaggregate if exposed to moisture).

TYPES OF WOODS USED FOR SMOKING

The asterisks in this chart note all-purpose woods that are good for smoking a wide variety of foods. Make it a point to try all of them.

WOOD	SMOKE FLAVOR	WHERE USED	TRADITIONALLY USED TO SMOKE
FOREST WOODS			
Alder	Full-flavored	Pacific Northwest, Alaska	Salmon and other seafood
Beech	Full-flavored	Scandinavia, Germany	Pork and poultry
Hickory*	Full-flavored	American South and Midwest	All meats, seafood, and vegetables
Juniper	Aromatic	Europe	Herring, salmon, and other fish; speck
Maple	Mild	New England, Quebec	Poultry and pork
Mesquite	Strong	Texas and the American Southwest	Beef
Oak*	Full-flavored	California, Texas, Europe, South America	All meats, seafood, and vegetables
Pecan	Full-flavored	American South	Pork and poultry
Walnut	Full-flavored	California, Eastern US	Pork and other meats
ORCHARD WOODS			
Apple*	Full-flavored	Across the United States	All meats (especially bacon), seafood, and vegetables
Apricot	Full-flavored	California	Poultry and pork
Cherry*	Full-flavored	Pacific Northwest, the Upper Midwest	All meats, seafood, and vegetables
Orange	Mild, even faint	Florida, California	Poultry and pork
Mulberry	Mild	American South	Poultry and pork
Peach	Full-flavored	American South	Poultry and pork
Pear	Mild	California, New England	Poultry and pork
Plum	Full-flavored	California	Poultry and pork

EXOTIC WOODS			
Buttonwood	Full-flavored	Florida Keys	Seafood
Camphor wood	Intense, aromatic	China	Poultry and pork
Guava	Full-flavored	Philippines	Poultry and pork
Olive	Mild, a little citrusy	California, the Mediterranean	Pork, veal, poultry, seafood, and vegetables
Palochina	Full-flavored, piney	Philippines	Used by the popular Bacolod Chicken Inasal restaurant chain to smoke pork
Pimento	Intense, aromatic	Jamaica	Jerk pork and chicken
Tangatanga	Intense, aromatic	Guam	Beef, pork, and chicken
Whiskey barrel chips	Mild and sweet	Kentucky, Tennessee	All meats, seafood, and vegetables
EXOTIC SMOKING FUELS (NONWOOD)			
Allspice berries	Aromatic, spicy	Jamaica	Jerk pork and chicken
Cinnamon sticks	Aromatic, spicy	Jamaica, China	Pork and poultry
Hay	Full-flavored, herbaceous	Italy, United States	Cheese, poultry, burgers
Pine or spruce needles	Aromatic	France, Canada	Mussels
Rice	Pungent	China	Duck
Rosemary and other herbs	Aromatic, herbal	California, the Mediterranean	All meats, seafood, and vegetables
Sugarcane pressings	Aromatic	French West Indies	Chicken
Tea	Pungent	China	Duck

WOOD CONTROVERSIES AND CONSIDERATIONS

Few cooking techniques inspire more, er, heated debate than smoking, and the controversy starts with the wood. Green or seasoned? Bark on or off? To soak or not to soak? Here are my personal preferences, plus some additional considerations when smoking with wood.

Green or seasoned? A freshly cut tree contains about 60 percent moisture. Season (dry) it in the open air (my preference) or in a kiln and you reduce the moisture content to 15 to 20 percent. Green wood is difficult to light and puts out a dense pungent smoke once it smolders. Sometimes that pungency borders on acrid. Smoke with seasoned (dry) wood.

Bark on or bark off? Straight tree bark produces a thick, often bitter smoke—especially if from green logs. And bark is where insects dwell if they find their way into an outdoor woodpile. But split logs with an edge of bark still intact are what most of the world's smoke masters burn throughout North America and Europe. It's fine to use logs or wood chunks with an edge of bark attached. Go easy on straight wood bark.

Whole logs or split? That's easy: split. They light quicker and burn easier.

To soak or not to soak?
Advocates argue that soaking wood chips or chunks slows the rate of combustion, giving you a slower, steadier smoke. And evidence suggests that soaked wood chips release more nitrogen dioxide, which may help produce a more pronounced smoke ring in the cooked meat. Opponents maintain that soaking simply delays pyrolysis (decomposition by heat) and the consequent release of smoke flavor. For a slower, steadier burn, soak wood chips in water to cover for 30 minutes before smoking, then drain before adding to the fire. But don't freak out if you forget to soak them—you can add dry chips directly to the coals. You'll just need more. Soak wood chunks or not—the final taste will be the same. I don't bother.

I'm just starting out with smoking; is there any particular wood I should use or avoid?
I'd go for the classics—and what's readily available in your area.
- alder (the Pacific Northwest)
- hickory or pecan (the South)
- oak (Texas and Europe)
- apple (the Midwest and the Pacific Northwest)
- cherry (Michigan and the Pacific Northwest)
- maple (New England)
- mesquite (Texas and the Southwest—but use sparingly and mainly for beef)

Is blending or sequencing woods a good idea? If you're just starting out with smoking, stick with one wood variety to get a feel for its color and flavor properties. Once you've mastered that, you can experiment.

How long should you smoke during cooking? Some smoke masters burn wood throughout the entire smoking process. Others argue that meat gradually loses its ability to absorb smoke, especially during the second half of the cook. Many meats like brisket or pastrami call for wrapping during the final hours of cooking. Continue smoking until you wrap the meat. At that point, you don't need to add wood (unless you're using a wood-burning smoker). Let the heat of the charcoal finish the cooking.

How much wood should I add to the fire and when should I add it? Smoking is like the old fable about the tortoise and the hare. Slow and steady wins the race. It's better to add a little wood every hour than pile it on all at once. On page 6, you'll find rough guidelines on how much wood to add to each type of smoker.

SOME FINAL THOUGHTS ON WOOD

- Store logs outdoors off the ground in a cool, dry, covered, well-aerated area. Damp wood can get moldy and wet wood eventually rots.
- Do not use moldy or bad-smelling wood for smoking. I live in Miami, where wood—even a bag of wood chips—left outdoors during the rainy season often acquires a musty smell. You might think the moldy smell would burn away in the fire. It doesn't.
- Drain any leftover soaked wood chips in a colander and let them dry completely in the sun before reusing. Prolonged soaking diminishes a wood's ability to produce a good-flavored smoke.

STEP 3
ASSEMBLE YOUR TOOLS

You can smoke with little more than a kettle grill and a set of tongs. But having the right tools definitely makes the job easier. I've grouped them by task.

TOOLS FOR HANDLING WOOD, CHARCOAL, AND HOT ASH

Metal trash cans with tight-fitting lids: For storing charcoal, wood chunks, and pellets. Also use for disposing of spent coals and ash. Have several small ones.

Firewood rack: For storing logs outdoors above ground so they won't rot or attract insects. Also, a cover or tarp to keep the wood dry in inclement weather.

 Ax, maul, or hatchet: For splitting logs.

Leather work gloves: For handling logs without getting splinters.

Shovel or metal scoop: For moving hot embers and cleaning out ash.

Shop vacuum: An even more efficient tool for cleaning out ash. Just be sure the ash is completely cold before vacuuming.

TOOLS FOR STARTING THE FIRE

Fireplace matches: Long-stem matches that reach deep into the firebox.

Butane match or lighter: Lights your fire with the click of a switch.

Paraffin fire starter: A small cube or block of paraffin or other flammable material used for starting a fire.

Sugarcane fire starter gel: Like lighter fluid, only plant-based.

Chimney starter: The most efficient way to light charcoal. See the lighting instructions on page 27.

Electric fire starter: Plug-in wand with a looped heating element. Often used to light ceramic cookers. Requires a power outlet, of course.

Looftlighter: A Swedish fire starter that directs a blast of superheated air at charcoal or wood.

Blowtorch: The ultimate tool for lighting a wood or charcoal fire. Use a workbench model for lighting small quantities of charcoal or invest in a roofer's torch, which has an arm-length wand you hook up directly to a propane cylinder (note I said *cylinder*, not canister). Fires a 50,000-plus-BTUs blast of heat at your wood or charcoal.

TOOLS FOR HANDLING YOUR SMOKER

 Insulated suede gloves, welder's gloves, or fireplace gloves: Choose long ones to protect your forearms.

Grill hoe or garden hoe: For raking hot coals.

 Grate grabber or grid lifter: Helps you lift a hot grill grate or smoker rack to add fresh wood or coals.

SMOKE GENERATORS AND GRILL INSERTS

These devices help you pump extra wood smoke into smokers, grills, and smokehouses. Recommended brands are listed in Additional Smoking Essentials beginning on page 278.

Charcoal smoke generator: Comprised of a metal canister with a burn chamber to hold smoldering wood chips and an electric blower to pump the smoke.

Electric smoke generator: Has a hopper to hold sawdust, disks, pellets, or wood chips and an electric heating element for slow-burning them to produce wood smoke.

Charcoal grill smoking insert: Turns your charcoal kettle grill into a smoker by corralling the embers in one section and creating a separate smoke chamber for the food. Look for a model with a built-in water pan to add moisture as well as smoke.

Note: Smoker tubes, pouches, and under-grate smoker trays that hold wood chips or pellets are covered on pages 21 and 22.

THERMOMETERS

Instant-read thermometer:

Essential for checking the doneness of smoked foods. Insert the probe deep in the meat or fish (but not touching the bone) and leave it for about 30 seconds.

Remote digital thermometers:

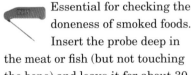

One probe goes in the meat or fish, with a wired or wireless connection to a display unit outside the smoker. Some models broadcast the temperature to your smartphone; check the broadcast range before buying. Advanced models come with multiple probes for the various foods you're smoking and to monitor the internal temperature of the smoker.

TEMPERATURE AND DRAFT CONTROLLERS

The key to great smoked foods is a long slow burn at a consistent low temperature. Enter the draft controller, a device that links a thermocouple inside the cook chamber to a tiny electric fan mounted over the bottom vent to regulate the airflow and consequently, the heat.

1. To use a temperature controller, attach the fan socket to the bottom vent of a ceramic cooker or charcoal smoker or grill.

2. Clip the thermocouple to a rack inside the smoker.

3. Set the digital controls to the desired temperature; the fan will control the airflow and heat.

TRAYS AND CONTAINERS FOR SEASONING, CURING, AND DRYING THE MEAT AND SEAFOOD

- Large rimmed baking sheets
- Large stainless-steel or glass mixing bowls
- Large durable food-safe containers for brining and other food preparation uses
- Heavy-duty resealable plastic bags in an assortment of sizes
- Wire racks or grids (preferably footed)
- Nonstick silicone mesh mats for smoking and indirect grilling small, delicate, or fragile foods that would stick to or fall through the bars of the grate or rack. They also come in handy for wrapping fatties (page 143) and meatloaf.

TOOLS FOR GETTING FLAVOR INTO MEAT AND SEAFOOD

Injectors: Oversize hypodermic needles for injecting flavorful liquids or pastes deep into large hunks of meat. See page 164 for more on injecting.

Vacuum marinating canisters: Some home vacuum sealers, such as the popular FoodSaver, can be used to accelerate the marinating process. Place the food with your favorite marinade in the polycarbonate canister, then activate the system to pump out the air. This cuts marinating

time to as little as 12 minutes. Alternatively, use a manual system with a hand-operated plunger in the top to help you remove the air in the container.

Vacuum tumblers: Another device for accelerating the marinating process. Meats are tumbled in a vacuum-sealed rotating cylinder. This separates and abrades the meat fibers, tenderizing the meat and accelerating the absorption of the brine or marinade. Most supermarket hams are cured in this manner.

TOOLS FOR APPLYING FLAVOR DURING SMOKING

Basting brushes: Buy an assortment of silicone basting brushes (which are easy to clean in the dishwasher) or natural bristle paintbrushes (available at your local hardware store and inexpensive enough to discard after using). Some brushes come with a custom saucepot.

Barbecue mops: These look like miniature cotton floor mops and are often sold with plastic-lined buckets. Look for a mop with a detachable head you can run through the dishwasher. When cooking for large crowds, a full-size cotton floor mop (brand new and never previously used, of course) comes in handy.

Spray bottle or barbecue sprayer: Indispensable for spraying apple cider, wine, and other flavorful liquids on meats and seafood during smoking.

SMOKER AND GRILL TOOLS

Grill brush: For cleaning the grate or smoker racks. Preferably long-handled with twisted stiff wire bristles that won't shed during use.

Tongs: Preferably long-handled and spring-loaded with a locking mechanism.

Spatula: With a wide metal head and beveled leading edge. Extra-wide heads (6 to 8 inches) come in handy for fish.

Grill humidifiers: Metal boxes with perforated tops that hold water, wine, or other liquid. Place on the grate of your charcoal or gas grill directly over the fire. The resulting steam creates a moist environment for smoking.

Rib rack: Holds racks of ribs upright so you can cook up to 4 racks of spareribs or baby backs in a smoker with limited space, such as a water smoker or kettle grill.

Beer-can chicken roaster: Holds the bird upright without tipping. Fill the stainless steel canister with wine, fruit juice, or beer.

MISCELLANEOUS SUPPLIES

Disposable rubber or plastic food gloves: Keeps your hands clean and your food safe when rubbing or handling meat.

Insulated food gloves: Indispensable for handling whole hogs or pulling pork shoulders. Some pit masters like the agility of wearing cotton gloves for heat protection with rubber or plastic gloves over them to keep out the grease.

Meat claws (for shredding pulled pork): Recommended brands include Bear Paws and Best of Barbecue.

Butcher paper (sometimes called pink paper): Indispensable for wrapping briskets. Be sure to buy unlined butcher paper (without a plastic lining).

Logbook: For recording the details of your smoke sessions (see below). Only by recording what works and what doesn't will you improve your skills as a smoke master. Important details include:

- Date
- Weather (ambient temperature)
- Meat to be smoked (kind, weight, etc.)
- Cure or seasoning
- Wood (type and how much used)
- Temperature in the smoker
- Internal temperature of the meat
- How you liked it

STEP 4
FLAVOR YOUR FOOD

Wood smoke has such an intense flavor on its own that some foods are smoked with no other flavoring added—for example, the Cherry-Smoked Strip Steak on page 83.

But more often, you combine smoking with other flavoring techniques, such as brining or curing, to boost taste and prevent spoilage. Traditional American barbecue often receives multiple layers of flavor—you might start with an injector sauce or rub, then apply a mop sauce, then a glazing of barbecue sauce—in addition to the actual smoke from the pit.

When it comes to flavoring smoked foods, you have three windows of opportunity: before, during, and after smoking.

FLAVORING THE RAW FOOD

Pre-smoke flavoring techniques include salting, curing, brining, rubbing, marinating, and injecting.

Salting: Early on—likely in Stone Age times—our forebears learned that salting food before smoking not only delayed spoilage by dehydrating the meat and preventing the growth of harmful bacteria, but also added extra flavor. We use this technique to make Nova Scotian or Scandinavian-style smoked salmon (page 183). To salt food,

you sprinkle it with or sandwich it between layers of salt; depending on the size of the food, salting might last a few hours (for small fish fillets) or a few weeks (for large hams). Typically, you rinse off the salt before smoking.

Curing: Almost as early on, people observed that salts from certain subterranean sources preserved food longer and better, adding an appetizing pink color and umami-like flavors. Those salts contained traces of naturally occurring food preservatives called sodium nitrate or sodium nitrite. A single oxygen molecule differentiates them, but sodium nitrate ($NaNO_3$) is used to slow-cure foods that are served raw (like dry-cured sausages and country hams), while sodium nitrite ($NaNO_2$) goes into foods that will be cooked further. In this book we use only sodium nitrite, which works much faster than sodium nitrate. A cure contains salt and often sodium nitrite, plus optional sugar, pepper, and other spices. Curing is responsible for some of the world's great smoked sausages, bacons, and hams, such as Tennessee bacon and Virginia ham. Sometimes water or other liquid is added to the dry ingredients to make a wet cure.

Brining: Add enough water or other liquid to salt or a salt cure and you get a saline solution called brine. Brines have the advantage of penetrating deeper and more evenly into meats than dry cures. They also help keep inherently dry meats like turkey and pork chops moist during the smoking process. Popular brined foods include cooked ham, Canadian bacon, and smoked turkey.

Rubs: A unique American contribution to the world of smoked foods, rubs are mixes of spices and seasonings applied to the exterior of meats, and often "rubbed" in by hand, before they go in the smoker. Most American rubs start with salt, pepper, paprika, and brown sugar, with additional spices and flavorings that reflect the region where they developed. For example, cumin and chili powder give you a Texas-style rub; dry mustard

5-4-3-2-1 Rub (brown sugar, salt, five-spice powder, salt, pepper; page 100)

and hot red pepper flakes evoke the barbecue of South Carolina. Rubs differ from cures in that they don't contain sodium nitrite. Add mustard or a little liquid like water or vinegar and you get a wet rub. There are two ways to apply a rub: as a seasoning just prior to smoking, or the day or night before to both cure and season the meat. Rubs help define some of America's greatest barbecue, from Memphis dry ribs to Texas brisket.

Marinades: A marinade is an intensely flavored liquid seasoning often comprised of an oil (like olive or sesame), an acid (vinegar or citrus juice), condiments (soy sauce or Worcestershire sauce), and aromatics (onion or garlic). If the essence of brine is saltiness, the essence of a marinade is its aromatic flavor. Smoked marinated foods include Jamaican Jerk Chicken (see page 154) and Smokehouse Char Siu (see page 107).

Injection: A combination of broth, melted butter, and/or other flavorful liquids that is forced deep into the meat with an oversized syringe. Competition barbecue teams often inject whole hogs and pork shoulders for extra flavor and moistness.

Pull back the plunger to load the injector with melted butter, broth, or liquid flavorings.

FLAVORING THE FOOD WHILE IT COOKS IN THE SMOKER

The second opportunity to add flavor is during the actual smoking and cooking process. Flavorings added while the food cooks include mop sauces, sprays, bastes, glazes, and barbecue sauces.

Mop sauce: An aromatic liquid sauce traditionally swabbed on the meat with a barbecue mop or basting brush to provide extra flavor and moistness. Unlike barbecue sauces, mop sauces aren't particularly sweet. (Sugars in them would burn with prolonged cooking.)

Sprays: Another way to build layers of flavor and keep the food moist is to spray it with apple cider or wine while it smokes. Use a barbecue sprayer or food-safe spray bottle.

Bastes: Bastes often start with fat, like melted butter or meat drippings, and they tend to be savory rather than sweet. Brush them on with a silicone basting brush or natural bristle paintbrush.

Glazes: Similar to bastes but sweetened and thickened with sugar, honey, jam, or other sweeteners. Glazes bestow a sheen on the meat; apply at the end of smoking so you don't burn the sugar.

Barbecue sauces: One of the best ways to finish ribs is to paint them with barbecue sauce and direct-grill them to sear the sauce into the meat. As with all sweet condiments, apply barbecue sauce toward the end of smoking so the sugar caramelizes without burning.

UPGRADE YOUR INGREDIENTS

Barbecue originated, in part at least, to make inexpensive, less desirable cuts of meat palatable. But inexpensive doesn't need to mean mediocre. One of the biggest revolutions in American barbecue in recent years is the rise of organic and grass-fed beef, heritage pork, wild seafood, and organic produce at new-school barbecue restaurants.

Or as I like to say: "What your food eats and how it's raised matters as much as how you smoke it." I have certainly changed the way I shop for a smoke session and I urge you to join me.

- Beef: Seek out organic, hormone-free, antibiotic-free, or grass-fed. Grass-fed beef is leaner than industrial corn-fed beef, so you'll need to add more fat to the preparation.

- Pork: Choose a heritage breed like Berkshire, Duroc, Mangalitsa, or Red Wattle. These hog varieties are bred for flavor, not growth speed—you'll be amazed by their rich porky taste.

- Chicken: Buy small farm and/or organic. You don't want to know what happens at an industrial poultry plant.

- Seafood: Buy wild whenever possible. The quality difference between wild Pacific Northwest salmon and commodity farm-raised salmon is enormous.

- Produce and eggs: Buy organic. You get enough flavor from the rub and smoke. You don't need pesticides.

Other things to look for when shopping:

- Shop at farmers' markets when possible. Local food is fresher, tastes better, encourages us to eat seasonally, and helps support local farmers and the local economy. Another option is to buy a share from a local CSA (Community Supported Agriculture) farm, which entitles you to periodic deliveries of locally raised food. (To find out what's available in your area, go to localharvest.org.)

- Look for Animal Welfare Standards ratings, which indicate how naturally and humanely the animals that provide our meat were raised. (Whole Foods, for example, puts this rating on every cut of meat.)

- Ignore the word *natural* when it appears on labels. It's a marketing term with no legal standards to back it up.

FLAVORING THE FOOD AFTER IT'S SMOKED

The final flavoring for smoked foods comes with the condiments you serve with it. The sharp flavor of mustard works particularly well with smoked meats; so do horseradish and barbecue sauces.

Barbecue sauce: Mix thin barbecue sauces, like the Carolina Vinegar Sauce on page 91, directly into chopped or shredded meat. Brush thick barbecue sauces, like the Beijing Barbecue Sauce on page 101, on the meat just prior to direct-grilling, or serve in a bowl on the side.

Dill sauce and tartar sauce: Mayonnaise-based dill and mustard sauces, like the ones served with the Smoked Shrimp on page 180, are classic accompaniments to smoked fish and shellfish. For an even more outrageous flavor, start with the smoked mayonnaise on page 204.

Condiments: Smoked pork and ham demand mustard; check out the Mustard Seed Caviar on page 106. Smoked beef begs for horseradish. Serve smoked ketchup (see page 204) with the Hay-Smoked Hamburgers on page 136. And when serving the reverse-seared Smoked Tri-Tip (page 81), don't forget the Smoked Tomato-Corn Salsa (page 39).

PUTTING IT ALL TOGETHER

Many smoked foods involve a layering of flavors. To make pastrami, for example, you start by brining a beef navel or brisket, then crust it with a peppercorn and coriander seed rub before smoking. To smoke a whole hog (page 92), you might inject it first with an injector sauce (page 164), then apply a rub, then mop it during cooking, baste it with melted butter, and finally shred it and mix it with vinegar-based barbecue sauce.

STEP 5
SELECT YOUR SMOKING METHOD

Smoking is practiced by most of the world's great food cultures, but the techniques vary widely from region to region and dish to dish. Smoking represents a continuum that uses several methods, including cold-smoking, hot-smoking, and smoke-roasting. Despite what you may read, there's no one "right" method. Here are the major smoking methods and what each is used for.

Cold-smoking: Smoking food at a low temperature so it acquires a smoke flavor *without* actually cooking. Cold-smoking is done at less than 100°F (typically between 65° and 85°F). Classic cold-smoked foods include Scandinavian and Scottish smoked salmon, and Italian speck and other cured and smoked hams. See page 22 for more on cold-smoking.

Hot-smoking: Smoking food at

Pork Shoulder (page 88)

a high enough temperature so that it cooks in addition to acquiring a smoke flavor. Hot-smoked foods include everything from Kippered Salmon (page 187) to Slam-Dunk Brisket (page 66) to Chinese Tea-Smoked Duck (page 168). Hot-smoking is done at a wide range of temperatures, each suited to particular foods and dishes. Hot-smoking further divides into:

- **Warm-smoking (aka hot-smoking at a low temperature),** which is done around 165°F and only minimally cooks the food. Warm-smoking is used to make bacon (where you don't want the heat to melt out too much of the fat) and beef jerky (where you want to dry the meat without cooking it too much).
- **Classic smoking (aka "low and slow"),** which is done between 225° and 275°F. Used to smoke pastrami, cooked ham, kippered salmon, and other hot-smoked fish.
- **Barbecuing,** a type of hot-smoking done at temperatures ranging from 225° to 300°F. Texas brisket, Kansas City ribs, and North Carolina pulled pork are examples of true barbecue.
- **Smoke-roasting,** Raichlen-speak for smoking done at a high temperature, typically between 350° and 400°F. Smoke-roasting is great for chicken and other poultry when you want to crisp the skin. (Low-and-slow smoking produces moist meat but rubbery skin.) Also good for smoking and crisping vegetables like the hash browns on page 212.

SPECIALIZED SMOKING TECHNIQUES

In addition to the universally practiced methods described above, you should know a few specialized smoking techniques.

Smoke-braising: Smoking foods in an open pan of simmering liquid. Smoke-braising works great with tough extremity cuts like pigs' trotters and lamb shanks (page 128).

Rotisserie-smoking: Smoking chickens, ducks, turkey breasts, or fat-sheathed roasts like prime rib on a charcoal-burning rotisserie, such as a Weber kettle grill fitted with a rotisserie ring, or on a wood-burning grill, such as the Kalamazoo Gaucho. Smoke-roasting on the rotisserie gives you the advantages of spit-roasting (even heat, internal and external basting) with the flavor-enhancing properties of smoking.

Ember- or burner-smoking (aka, "caveman" smoking): A technique for smoking eggplants, peppers, and other vegetables, popular throughout North Africa and the Middle East. Basically, you roast whole eggplants, peppers, onions, sweet potatoes, and so on directly on a bed of hot embers. The skin chars, driving a pronounced smoke flavor deep into the flesh. (You may recognize this as a variation on the "caveman grilling" found in my earlier books.) The indoor version of this technique involves charring the eggplants or peppers directly on the gas or electric burner of your stove. The classic Middle Eastern dip baba ghanoush uses this technique.

Hay-smoking: Developed by cheesemakers in Italy to flash-smoke mozzarella (page 42), scamorza, and other cheeses with smoldering hay. Hay-smoking works great with delicate foods you want to smoke but not melt or cook, such as cheese or ground beef. A French variation of the technique is *éclade*—think mussels smoke-roasted on a bed of dry pine needles.

Plank-and-stick smoking: Planked salmon is a classic of American grilling. By tweaking the technique, you can turn the plank into a smoking agent. The secret? Don't soak the plank in water to prevent it from catching fire, as most recipes call for. Instead, you encourage smoldering by first charring the plank on the fire, then allowing it to burn in a controlled way during cooking (see planked Camembert on page 41 and planked trout on page 191). Jamaicans use a variation of this technique to smoke jerk chicken (page 154) and pork on pimento (allspice) wood sticks over a fire.

Smoked Planked Trout (page 191)

Tea-smoking: A traditional Chinese technique for smoking duck in a covered wok over a mixture of black tea, rice, brown sugar, orange or tangerine peel, cinnamon sticks, star anise, and other spices. On page 168, you'll find my version of tea-smoked duck.

Stovetop smoking: An indoor method for smoking foods with

Salmon ready for smoking in a stovetop smoker.

hardwood sawdust in a tightly covered metal box or pot on the stove (page 275).

Smoking with a handheld smoker (page 276): Another indoor method for smoking foods in a glass, jar, or bowl covered with plastic wrap or under a cloche, using smoke generated by burning sawdust. Handheld smokers are great for smoking cocktails.

SMOKING ON A GAS GRILL

How do you smoke on a gas grill? My advice: don't. Gas grills work well for direct grilling, indirect grilling, and spit-roasting, but most do a poor job with smoking. (One exception is the high performance Kalamazoo Hybrid Fire Grill.) The problem is the wide venting in the back of most gas grills, which allows the smoke to escape before it has a chance to flavor the food. Gas grills simply don't give you the crusty bark, crimson smoke ring, and rich smoke flavor characteristic of meats smoked on a wood- or charcoal-burning smoker.

However, there are some devices and techniques that will give you a *partial* smoke flavor on a gas grill.

Built-in smoker box: Many higher-end gas grills come with a smoker box, a metal tray with a perforated lid and a dedicated gas burner beneath it to heat the wood to smoldering. You fill the box with wood chips or pellets and light the burner. The smoke emerges from

Adding soaked drained chips to a gas grill's smoker box.

the holes in the lid and, in theory at least, gives your food a mild smoke flavor.

Freestanding smoker box: Works like a built-in smoker box, but you position it on the grate over one of the burners. Again, the smoke flavor is mild.

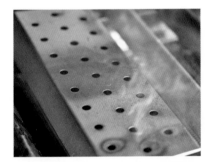
Smoke rising from a freestanding smoker box loaded with wood chips or pellets.

Wood chunks under the grate: This is one of the simplest and most effective ways to smoke on a gas grill. Remove the grate and lodge a half dozen or so wood chunks between the heat diffuser bars (Flavorizer Bars if using a Weber grill) or on the ceramic briquettes. Once you see wisps of smoke, position the food on the grate over the wood.

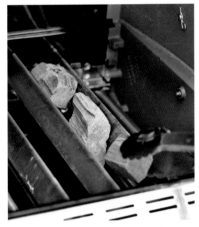
Arrange the wood chunks on the heat diffuser bars below the grate and under the food.

Under-grate smokers: Available in reusable metal or disposable aluminum foil, these V-shaped smoker boxes and cups hold wood chips, sawdust, or pellets and fit between the heat diffuser bars of your gas grill. Because you position them directly under the food, you get a more pronounced smoke flavor than with a smoker box off to the side.

Aluminum foil smoker pouch: Wrap 2 cups wood chips in a large sheet of heavy-duty aluminum foil to make a pillow-shaped pouch. Poke a series of holes in the top and you get a smoker pouch. Position it under the grate directly over one of the burners. Place a second pouch at the opposite end of the grill. Run the grill on high until you see smoke, then reduce the heat to the desired temperature.

1. Place 2 cups wood chips in the center of a sheet of heavy-duty aluminum foil.

2. Bring two sides of the foil up over the top of the chips and fold it closed.

3. Pinch closed the 2 sides.

4. Pierce the top of the smoking pouch with a sharp implement to make a series of holes to release the smoke.

Over-grate smokers: These are smokers you place directly on the grill grate. Some are metal mesh pouches or perforated tubes you fill with wood pellets. Others are shallow metal trays you fill with wood chips (see page 278).

Place the wood chips in the metal box under the grilling platform. Place the smoker on the grate over one of the burners.

COLD-SMOKING

If you're reading this book, chances are you have done some smoking already: hunky proteins like ribs, brisket, pork shoulder, turkey, ham, and so on. All are examples of hot-smoking, in which you both smoke *and* cook the meat.

But there's another type of smoking without which we wouldn't have Virginia ham, Nova Scotia-style salmon, or Italian smoked cheeses. That technique is cold-smoking, which uses smoke to flavor food but not cook it.

As noted earlier, cold-smoking is done at temperatures no higher than 100°F and more often between 65° and 85°F. The smoking time can be a few minutes, as in the case

of Italy's *mozzarella affumicata*, or several days, as in the case of Scandinavian *lax* (smoked salmon).

Cold-smoking is sometimes combined with hot-smoking, like the smoked ham on page 120, which is cold-smoked overnight to imbue it with smoke flavor, then hot-smoked to cook it through.

How did cold-smoking develop? I imagine our prehistoric forebears gathered around the primeval campfire. Someone noticed how the smoke seemed to repel mosquitoes, flies, and other pests. Someone else had the idea to hang strips of meat on sticks or wooden racks next to that smoky fire to dry. These foods didn't spoil as quickly as fresh meat and, in addition, they acquired a delectable smoky flavor.

When you burn wood, two byproducts result: smoke and heat. Smoking food without heat may seem paradoxical, but some of the world's most prized foods result. There are six basic ways to smoke without heat.

1. Distance the fire from the smoke chamber. That is, burn the wood at a distance from the food, channeling the smoke via a tube, pipe, or underground trench.

2. Use a smoker generator (like a Smoke Daddy or Smoke Chief). Pump the resulting smoke into a smokehouse, conventional smoker, or kettle grill.

3. Use a commercial cold-smoker or a cold-smoking attachment for your Bradley or Traeger smoker. The Oklahoma-based company Horizon includes a vertical cold-smoke chamber on its mighty Ranger model.

4. Use a handheld smoker, such as a Smoking Gun or Aladin. Have the food in a glass bowl or jar covered with plastic wrap and pump in the smoke via a rubber tube. Let the food absorb the smoke for several minutes, then stir to mix. Repeat as necessary.

1. Use an electric cold-smoker, which puts out smoke but no heat. 2. Or attach a charcoal smoke generator to your smoker and place a lit coal at the bottom of it. 3. Add unsoaked wood chips to the smoke generator. 4. The generator pumps in a steady stream of smoke.

THE SMOKING PROCESS HOUR BY HOUR

Grilling is a high-heat cooking method defined by its speed and efficiency. It's perfect for a quick meal after work. Smoking is the very antithesis, requiring patience, persistence, and above all, time. Even relatively fast-smoked foods, like chicken or ribs, smoke for several hours. And smoked cured foods like pastrami or ham need to be salted or brined for up to two weeks before you fire up your smoker. Here's your timetable.

BEFORE SMOKING

- 1 to 2 weeks ahead of your smoke session: Brine or cure large pieces of meat like pork bellies or raw hams, turning the meat every 24 hours.

- 24 to 48 hours ahead: Salt or cure whole salmon fillets.

- 12 to 24 hours ahead: Marinate the meat, or rub it if you plan to use the rub as a cure. This is also when to brine or cure small or thin pieces of meat or seafood, like chicken pieces or salmon fillets.

- 2 to 4 hours ahead: Prepare your mop sauce, glaze, and/or barbecue sauce. Inject the meat, if using this technique (see page 164).

- 1 to 2 hours ahead: Drain, rinse, and dry your food. Place it on a footed wire rack on a rimmed baking sheet in the refrigerator. Dry until a pellicle (skin) forms and the surface feels tacky (papery and a little sticky). Smoke adheres better to a tacky surface.

- ½ to 1 hour ahead: Light your smoker and heat to the desired temperature. Soak your wood chips.

- Just prior to smoking: Salt and pepper your meat. (Or rub it now if using rub as a seasoning.)

DURING SMOKING

- Allow enough time for smoking—this can be a few hours or the better part of a day, or even a few days for cold-smoking.

- Every hour: If burning charcoal or wood, replenish the fuel as needed, usually once an hour. Replenish the logs, chunks, or wood chips as needed, usually every half hour to an hour.

- After the first hour: Start applying the mop sauce or spray, if using. Mop or spray once an hour up to the last hour of cooking.

- The last two hours of cooking: If wrapping your brisket or other food in butcher paper or aluminum foil, this is the time to do it.

AFTER SMOKING

- For 10 to 20 minutes: Rest tender smoked meats like pork shoulder, spareribs, prime rib, and beef tenderloin on a cutting board, *loosely* tented with aluminum foil.

- For 1 to 2 hours: Rest tougher smoked meats, like brisket and beef plate ribs, in an insulated cooler.

KEY SMOKING TEMPERATURES

TECHNIQUE	TEMPERATURE	USE FOR
Cold-smoking	Below 100°F; typically between 65° and 85°F	Seafood (especially salmon and herring), cured ham and sausages, cheese, butter, mayonnaise, and other condiments
Warm-smoking	165°-180°F	Bacon, jerky
Hot-smoking	225°-275°F	Fish, shellfish, cooked ham
True barbecue	225°-300°F	Brisket, ribs, pork shoulder, mutton
Smoke-roasting	350°-400°F	Poultry, tender fat-sheathed meats like prime rib, pork rib roast, or rack of lamb
Smoke-roasting on a rotisserie	350°-400°F	Chicken, duck, and other poultry, pork loin, prime rib

Top left: Load the chamber of a handheld smoker with sawdust. Bottom left: Turn on the smoker's fan and light the sawdust. Right: Insert the smoking tube into a pitcher or bowl covered with plastic wrap. Let the smoke infuse the food or drink.

5. Smoke the food over and/ or sandwiched between pans of ice. This is an excellent way to cold-smoke on a conventional charcoal grill. See the Hay-Smoked Hamburgers on page 136.

6. Smoke the food in a refrigerated smoke chamber. This is the technology used by high-tech smoker companies like Enviro-Pak. Some people make smokers from old but still functioning refrigerators, achieving the same effect.

Because the meat or fish remains essentially raw, cold-smoking is generally done in conjunction with another form of food preservation like salting or curing. Scandinavian smoked salmon and Italian smoked prosciutto (speck), for example, are

THE IMPORTANCE OF MOISTURE IN SMOKING

Moisture is an essential component of successful smoking. According to Justin Fourton (who with his wife, Diane, owns the popular Pecan Lodge in Dallas), a 600-pound load of meat puts out 200 pounds of water. Hugh Mangum of Mighty Quinn's Barbeque in New York City won't even open his pit for the first 12 hours of smoking brisket for fear of drying out the meat.

So how do you keep the smoking environment moist in your smoker or pit?

• Place a bowl of water in the smoke chamber.

• Spray the food with apple cider or wine.

• Mop the food with a mop sauce.

---

cured with salt—and sometimes sugar, pepper, and sodium nitrite or sodium nitrate. Cold-smoking often involves a third food preservation technique: drying. Jerky was traditionally dried and smoked next to the fire.

The last phase in cold-smoking is resting the food in the refrigerator to set the smoke flavor and firm up the meat.

How do you know when cold-smoked foods are ready to eat?

• The food will have a handsome brown patina of wood smoke.

• The surface will feel leathery.

• The internal texture will be semi-soft and velvety, not squishy and raw.

STEP 6
LIGHT YOUR FIRE

You've chosen your smoker, gear, flavorings, and wood. The next step is to light your fire. You can channel your inner Scout by using kindling and matches, or fire up a lighting device like a Looftlighter (see page 13) or blowtorch (see page 13). In the following pages, you'll learn how to light a wood

or charcoal fire and maintain it during your smoke session.

HOW TO LIGHT A WOOD FIRE

Teepee method: Crumple a sheet of newspaper into a loose ball the size of an orange. Alternatively, use a paraffin fire starter (see page 13). Steeple small sticks around and over the paper or fire starter like a teepee. Arrange larger sticks around and over these—again, like a teepee. Finally, arrange 3 small

Left: Over crumpled newspaper, arrange sticks and split logs like the poles of a teepee. Right: Light the paper to start your fire.

THE COLOR OF SMOKE

Smoke comes in many colors—cottony white, gray blue, oily black—and the color changes during the burn. White smoke tends to occur just after ignition. It contains acidic compounds that in limited doses help build the overall flavor and act as a preservative. But too much white smoke will make the food bitter.

If you build your fire right and have a good strong airflow, gradually the smoke will become hazy and pale, with just the faintest tinge of blue. This is the **blue smoke** so prized among barbecue geeks: Think of it as your smoking sweet spot.

Too much wood in the firebox, green or wet wood, or excess bark produce a dark—even black—oily smoke loaded with tar and soot. Black smoke makes food taste like you smoked it in a burning building. Avoid it.

---

logs over the larger sticks. Light the paper with a long match. Note: Split logs light and burn better than whole logs.

Log cabin method: Crumple a sheet of newspaper into a loose ball the size of an orange. Alternatively, use a paraffin fire starter. Place small sticks on either side of the ball so they're parallel to each other. Arrange 2 sticks on top, perpendicular to the first two. Arrange 2 larger sticks on top, perpendicular to the second set of sticks. Repeat with 2 more sticks. The process is like assembling a Lincoln Log cabin. Arrange two levels of small split logs in a box shape just outside this box. Arrange a parallel row of large sticks across the top. Light the paper with a long match. As the smaller sticks catch fire, push the small logs in around them. Once they're lit, lay more logs on top.

Charcoal method: Place a bed of lit charcoal embers in the firebox of your smoker. Arrange a few logs on top: small split ones first, then larger split ones on top, perpendicular to the small logs, leaving a couple inches between the logs in each layer. What's convenient about this method is that you can start smoking with logs right away.

HOW TO SMOKE WITH STRAIGHT WOOD

Smoking with wood alone is the Bentley ride of barbecue—the only fuel serious smoke masters use. And there's no doubt that meat tastes better and fish tastes smokier when smoked over pure wood. However, burning only wood requires a substantial pit—offset, brick, or commercial.

Light the wood using one of the methods above. Add a few logs and

Arrange sticks and split logs in a log cabin fashion around and over crumpled newspaper.

let them burn down to embers. Once you have a hot bed of embers, add logs one or two at a time to keep a consistent temperature and constant flow of pale-blue smoke. This may be as few as one log or as many as three, and you may need to add fresh logs every half hour to hour. Leave plenty of space (at least 2 inches) between the logs so they ignite cleanly on all sides.

Layering fresh logs on top of wood embers.

1. Place a crumpled sheet of newspaper or a paraffin fire starter in the bottom compartment of a chimney starter. 2. Fill the top section with charcoal (preferably lump). 3. Place the chimney on the lower grate of your grill or smoker box and light the newspaper or paraffin. 4. When the coals glow red (after 15 to 20 minutes), dump them into the firebox.

HOW TO LIGHT A CHARCOAL FIRE

Chimney method: A chimney starter lights your charcoal (lump or briquettes) quickly and evenly—without the need for petroleum-based lighter fluid. You can also light wood chunks in a chimney starter, but burn them to glowing embers before placing them in your smoker or grill. If you add them sooner, you'll get too much smoke.

Electric starter method: Place the heating coil at the bottom of the firebox. Add the charcoal. Plug in the fire starter; the red hot heating element will ignite the coals in 15 to 20 minutes. Note: This method is often used with ceramic cookers.

Looftlighter/blowtorch method: Arrange the charcoal in the firebox. Point a lit Looftlighter (see page 13) or roofer's blowtorch (see page 13) toward the charcoal to ignite it.

Lighter fluid: I personally don't use lighter fluid, but if you do, squirt it evenly over the coals, light with a match, and be sure it's completely burned off and the coals glow red before you start smoking the food.

HOW TO SMOKE BY ADDING WOOD TO A CHARCOAL FIRE

The Wood Direct on Coal Method: Once you have a hot bed of coals (glowing red), gently place the logs, chunks, or chips on top using tongs. (See page 12 for the dry-versus-soaked debate.) Avoid tossing or throwing the wood on the coals—you'll stir up ash that could land on the food.

How much wood should you add? If using chunks, 2 to 4 per hour; for chips, 1½ to 2 cups every 30 to 40 minutes; and 1 to 3 logs per hour in a larger smoker. Follow the manufacturer's instructions and the chart on page 6.

The Ember Spread Method: Intersperse wood chips among the charcoal. Place a paraffin starter in the center and 3 coals over it. Light the starter. Once the three pieces of charcoal are lit, close the lid and damper down the vents to obtain a temperature of 225° to 250°F. The lit embers will gradually ignite the unlit coals and wood next to them and so on, giving you a slow, steady burn and hours of smoke.

The Top-Down Burn Method: Here's another great way to achieve a long, slow burn, and it works with both lump charcoal and

Adding lit embers to unlit coals.

briquettes. Arrange three quarters of your charcoal in the firebox, interspersing it with wood chunks or chips. Light the remaining coals in a chimney starter. Pour the lit coals on top of the unlit coals, arranging a few more wood chunks or chips on top. The lit embers will gradually light the remaining coals from top to bottom, giving you a slow, steady burn and hours of smoke.

The Minion Method: This is a variation of the top-down method, associated with a competition barbecuer named Jim Minion. Fill the firebox with unlit coals, interspersing them with wood chips or chunks. Place just a few (four to six) lit embers on top and look forward to a long, slow burn.

The Snake Method: Arrange your charcoal in a thick C-shaped coil around the periphery of the lower grate of your kettle grill or water smoker. The coil should be about 3 coals thick. Sprinkle the top of the coil with wood chips. Using a blowtorch, light 3 or 4 coals at one end (or place 3 or 4 lit coals at one end). These coals will gradually light the ones next to them and so on, giving you a long, low-heat burn. A variation on the snake method is the **domino method**, wherein you make a circle or coil of briquettes in a single row, each stood on end and leaning against the one next to it (a little like a row of dominos), with wood chips sprinkled on top.

This produces a slow, very low-heat burn for cold-smoking on a charcoal grill.

MAINTAINING YOUR FIRE

Most smoking is done at low temperatures for an extended period. You'll need to refuel charcoal or wood-burning smokers every hour or so.

- When smoking with lump charcoal plus wood, add 8 to 16 lumps to the existing fire. Leave the firebox door or grill lid open for a few minutes to give the charcoal a chance to ignite.
- When smoking with charcoal briquettes plus wood, I recommend fully lighting the briquettes in a chimney starter (they should begin to ash over) before adding them to the firebox. Unlit briquettes on a hot fire can produce an acrid-tasting smoke.
- Add wood as needed to maintain a light flow of smoke from the smoker. The smoke should be pale with just the slightest tinge of blue. Don't overdo it.

EXTINGUISHING YOUR FIRE

Let the wood fire or coals burn out after your smoke session. Shovel the ash—it may still be hot—into a *metal* trash can. Douse with water to extinguish any lingering embers, or cover the can and let the coals extinguish themselves. Never put hot ash into a plastic trashcan or paper bag.

THE TEN COMMANDMENTS OF SMOKING

1. Know the difference between barbecue and smoking. All barbecue is smoked, but not all smoked foods are barbecue. Texas brisket, Carolina pork shoulder, and Kansas City ribs are barbecue. Virginia ham, Irish smoked salmon, and Wisconsin smoked cheddar are smoked, but they're not barbecue.

2. Understand the flavor of smoke. Think of it as the umami of barbecue. Smoke has a unique ability to endow familiar foods, from sausage to steaks, with an otherworldly quality that is simultaneously familiar and exotic.

3. Smoke everything. Really. Meat, poultry, and seafood, of course, but also cocktails, vegetables, cheeses, fruits, and desserts.

4. Buy organic, heritage, heirloom, grass-fed, and local. What your meat eats and how it's raised matters as much as how you smoke it.

5. Low and slow is the way to go. Ribs, shoulders, and briskets need a slow cook at a low temperature to achieve smoky perfection.

6. Wrap it up. Wrap brisket and beef ribs in unlined butcher paper the last two hours of smoking. This seals in moisture without making the bark (crust) soggy.

7. Give it a rest. Once brisket, pork shoulder, and other large cuts of meat are smoked, transfer them to an insulated cooler to rest for 1 to 2 hours. Your meat will be juicier and more tender.

8. It's okay to overcook your meat. It's essential to overcook your meat. Shoulders, bellies, brisket, and ribs need to be cooked to 195° to 205°F to achieve the proper tenderness.

9. Remember this simple rule: More air equals higher heat; less air equals lower heat. Adjust the vents accordingly to control the airflow and thus the cooking temperature.

10. Remember this other simple rule: Lower heat produces more smoke; higher heat produces less smoke.

STEP 7
KNOW WHEN YOUR FOOD IS DONE

The last skill to master is recognizing when your smoked food is properly cooked. The cues are many—visual (does it look done?), olfactory (does it smell done?), and tactile (does it feel done?)—as well as more precise tests including checking the internal temperature.

SUBJECTIVE TESTS

You've probably watched an old-timer poke a brisket to check the doneness by how it jiggles. Or pull a blade bone out of a pork shoulder with just the right force to make sure the meat is cooked. The following tests rely on your senses, especially touch.

Jiggle test: For brisket. Poke the meat with your finger. If it jiggles, almost Jell-O-like, it's done.

Pull test #1: For pork and lamb shoulders. Grab the end of the blade bone and tug. If it pulls out easily, the meat's done.

Pull test #2: For pork, chicken, and mutton. If you can pull the meat into meaty shreds easily with your fingers or a fork, it's cooked.

Pierce test: For long-cooked meats like brisket or pork shoulder. Poke the meat with the handle end of a wooden spoon or a gloved finger. If it pierces the meat easily, it's done.

Break test: For ribs. Lift a rack of ribs, holding it in the center with tongs. When properly cooked, it will bend like a bow and start to break and tear at the top of the arc.

Shrink test: For ribs. When the meat has shrunk back from the ends of the bones, the ribs are done: ¼ to ½ inch for a rack of baby back ribs; ½ to 1 inch for spareribs; 1 to 1½ inches for beef ribs.

Flake test: For fish, especially salmon. Press the top of the fish

The flake test.

with your forefinger. If it breaks into clean flakes, it's cooked.

Skewer test: For onions, potatoes, and other dense vegetables. Insert a slender bamboo skewer. If it pierces the food easily, it's cooked.

"Charmin" test: For onions, potatoes, cabbage, and other vegetables. Pinch between your thumb and forefinger. If "squeezably soft," the food is cooked.

TEMPERATURE TESTS

The most accurate way to assess the doneness of smoked foods is to check the internal temperature with an instant-read thermometer. Even the pros do it. *Especially* the pros do it. Insert the probe deep into the meat, not touching the bone, and wait 30 seconds or the interval recommended by the manufacturer.

Use the chart below as your basic guide.

WHEN IS IT DONE?		
DEGREE OF DONENESS	**INTERNAL TEMPERATURE**	**APPROPRIATE FOR**
Rare (beef, lamb)	120°-125°F	Reverse-seared steaks and tri-tip, prime rib, beef tenderloin
Medium-rare (beef, lamb)	130°-135°F	Reverse-seared steaks and tri-tip, prime rib, beef tenderloin
Medium (seafood)	140°-145°F	Fish, shellfish
Medium (beef, lamb, pork)	145°-150°F	Beef, pork loin, chops, tenderloin, leg and rack of lamb
Medium (ground meat, pork)	160°F	Hamburgers, sausage, bratwurst, pork roast
Medium (poultry, pork ribs)	165°F	Chicken, turkey, duck, ground poultry
Medium-well (poultry, pork)	170°-180°F	Chicken, turkey, duck, goose, pork ribs
Well	195°-205°F	Brisket, pork or lamb shoulder, any meat you plan to pull or shred

CLEANING YOUR SMOKER

When it comes to cleaning a smoker, I take a commonsense approach: Burnt-on smoke and grease add to a smoker's performance and beauty. Perishable pieces of food left on the grate offend the eye and endanger health.

- Immediately after smoking: Brush the rack clean with a heavy-duty grill brush.

- A few hours after smoking: Scrape out any congealed fat in the bottom of the smoke chamber. Empty the drip pan or grease bucket.

- The next morning: Clean out the spent ash. Shovel it into a metal trash can, not plastic or paper. (Even if the ash looks dead, it may still have some live embers.)

- Hose and brush off the outside of your smoker.

- Periodically check the inside of the hood on your smoker. By-products of the smoking process—tar, creosote, and so on—can build up to the point where they flake off onto your food. Scrape this scaly stuff with a stiff wire brush or paint scraper. (To be really thorough, clean it out with a shop vacuum.)

- Once a season: Clean the smoker inside and out using an environmentally friendly cleanser like Simple Green.

STARTERS

Smoked chicken wings. Smoked poppers. Smoked Sriracha Beef Jerky. Some of the world's best bar food emerges from a cloud of wood smoke. Equally essential is salt: Many smoked appetizers start with a spice rub or brine, and as bartenders have long known, well-salted food prompts you to reach for a cocktail. In this chapter, you'll learn to smoke eggs, Camembert and mozzarella cheeses, jalapeño poppers (here stuffed with crabmeat and cream cheese), and everything from salsa to nachos. Smoking makes for equally awesome dips and spreads like the Smoked Seafood Dip, popular on both coasts of the United States, or the smoked turkey liver pâté served at Raichlen Thanksgiving dinners. Want a new perspective on soup? Try cold-smoking the tomatoes, peppers, and onions the next time you make gazpacho. Or build a soulful chowder with smoked salmon or other smoked fish. You'll even learn how to smoke bread for dipping, spreading, and dunking.

SMOKED EGGS

Eggs may be late-comers to America's barbecue repertory. But elsewhere on the world's barbecue trail, grilled and smoked eggs are common currency. Cambodians grill cilantro- and chili-stuffed eggs on bamboo skewers over charcoal braziers. The chef at the Auberge Shulamit in Rosh Pina, Israel, smokes eggs to make the most remarkable egg salad you'll ever taste, served on, what else, grilled bread. Smoke takes the commonplace egg in gustatory directions you've never dreamed of. Hard-boiled egg? Okay. Smoked hard-boiled egg? Inspired.

INGREDIENTS

12 large eggs, preferably organic

Vegetable oil, for oiling the wire rack or grate

1. To hard-cook the eggs, place them in a large saucepan with cold water to cover by 3 inches. Bring to a boil over high heat, then reduce the heat and simmer the eggs for 11 minutes (a few minutes longer if you live at a high altitude). Drain the eggs and fill the pan with cold water. Cool the eggs in the pan until they're easy to handle but still warm. Peel the eggs. (It's easier to peel them while they're still warm.) Return the eggs to the cold water to cool completely, then drain well and blot dry with paper towels. The eggs can be cooked and peeled up to 48 hours ahead, stored in a container covered with plastic wrap, and refrigerated.

2. Set up your smoker following the manufacturer's directions and preheat to 225°F. Add the wood as specified by the manufacturer.

3. Place the eggs on a lightly oiled wire rack placed over an aluminum foil pan filled with ice (the eggs should not touch the ice). Place in the smoker, and smoke the eggs until bronzed with smoke, 15 to 20 minutes. Let cool to room temperature. Store, covered, in the refrigerator for up to 3 days. Eat as you would hard-cooked eggs or use to make deviled eggs (page 36) or egg salad.

Variation
COLD-SMOKED EGGS

If you'd like to cold-smoke the eggs, you'll need enough fuel for 1½ hours of smoking time. Preheat the cold smoker to 100°F or less. Place the eggs in the smoker and smoke until they're bronzed in color, 1 to 1½ hours.

YIELD: Makes 12 eggs; can be multiplied or reduced as desired

METHOD: Hot-smoking

PREP TIME: 11 minutes

HOT-SMOKING TIME: 15 to 20 minutes

FUEL: Hickory, apple, or hardwood of your choice—enough for 20 minutes of smoking (see chart on page 6)

GEAR: A wire rack; an aluminum foil roasting pan

SHOP: Organic eggs when possible

WHAT ELSE: You have two options for smoking eggs: hot-smoking or cold-smoking. The former is faster, but you have to smoke the eggs over a pan of ice or the whites will become rubbery. Cold-smoking eliminates this risk, but takes longer. For even more smoke flavor, cut the hard-cooked eggs in half before smoking, as pictured on the facing page.

DEVILED SMOKED EGGS

YIELD: Makes 24 halves • **PREP TIME:** 20 minutes (plus egg smoking time)

These may be the most flavorful deviled eggs you will ever experience (see photo on page 34)—thanks to an invigorating blast of wood smoke. For even more flavor, top them with bacon, brisket, or smoked seafood.

INGREDIENTS

FOR THE FILLING

12 Smoked Eggs (page 35)

⅓ cup mayonnaise (preferably Hellmann's or Best Foods), or to taste

1 tablespoon Dijon mustard

1 teaspoon sriracha, Tabasco sauce, or other favorite hot sauce, or to taste

1 teaspoon Worcestershire sauce

FOR THE TOPPINGS (OPTIONAL)

Chopped chives

Spanish smoked paprika (pimentón)

Regular or smoked salmon caviar

Fried bacon slivers

Finely shredded smoked beef brisket (page 66) or pulled pork (page 88)

1. Cut the eggs in half lengthwise. Cut a thin slice off the bottom of each half so it won't wobble. Pop out the yolks and place them and the egg white trimmings in a food processor. (Alternatively, you can mash the yolk mixture with a fork.)

2. Add the mayonnaise, mustard, sriracha, and Worcestershire sauce, and process to a thick puree. For a creamier filling, add more mayo.

3. Spoon the mixture back into the egg white halves or pipe it in with a pastry bag or a resealable plastic bag with a lower corner clipped off. Top the eggs, if desired, with a sprinkling of chives and/or smoked paprika, or a dollop of salmon caviar, bacon, or shredded brisket or pork. Refrigerate in a covered container or loosely covered with plastic wrap until serving.

LIQUID SMOKE AND BEYOND

INGREDIENTS THAT ADD SMOKE FLAVOR, EVEN IF YOU DON'T OWN A SMOKER

Want to boost the smoke flavor—even if you don't have time to fire up your smoker? Add one of the following smoked ingredients.

Bacon: Everything tastes better with bacon. Wrap lean foods, such as shrimp or chicken breasts, in bacon for grilling. Grill or pan-fry bacon until crisp and crumble it over whatever you're serving. Use bacon fat for sautéing or basting. In the best of all worlds, you'd make your own bacon (page 113) or use a good artisanal brand like Nueske's. Most inexpensive bacon uses injected smoke flavoring, not real wood smoke.

Chipotle chiles: Smoked jalapeños from Mexico. This is one of the rare foods I prefer to buy canned. Canned chipotles come in a spicy marinade called *adobo*. A teaspoon of adobo in addition to the minced chiles will electrify any dish.

Ham: Like bacon, smoked ham is a great way to add rich, smoky, meaty umami flavors to any dish you can think of. Wrap asparagus stalks in speck (Italian smoked prosciutto) for grilling. Add diced cooked smoked ham to mac and cheese. And slivers of smoky Virginia ham in red-eye gravy.

Lapsang souchon: Tea leaves are dried over pinewood fires to make this smoked black tea from the Wuyi region in Fujian, China. Use for tea-smoking (page 168); add to brines and marinades. Makes great smoky iced tea. Freeze that tea with a little lemon and sugar, then scrape it with a fork to make a refreshing granita.

Liquid smoke: There's no substitute for wood smoke, of course, but liquid smoke—a natural flavoring made by condensing real wood smoke in a sort of still—does give you a distinctive smoke flavor. Available in several flavors, such as hickory and mesquite, it's especially useful for barbecue sauces. Use sparingly—a dash or two goes a long way.

Mezcal: Tequila's cousin, mezcal is made from fire-roasted agave cactus hearts in the hills around Oaxaca. It gives any cocktail an instant smoke flavor (see recipes on pages 244, 251, and 254). Sprinkle a few drops on grilled oysters or in smoked tomato salsa (page 39).

Pimentón: Use this smoked paprika from Spain to add a smoke flavor to dishes not easily cooked on a grill—scrambled eggs, for example. I also like to substitute *pimentón* for the paprika in barbecue rubs.

Rauchbier: Smoked beer is traditionally from Bamberg, Germany. To make it, the malted barley is dried over a wood fire. Makes interesting beer-based cocktails and barbecue sauces. Melt grated smoked cheese in *rauchbier* for the ultimate cheese fondue.

Scotch whisky: One of the world's most distinctive whiskies, Scotch is made by drying malted barley over a smoky peat fire. The best single-malt Scotches come from Islay Island off Scotland's western coast. My favorite brands are Laphroaig (the smokiest), Lagavulin (distinguished by its finesse), and Bowmore (remarkable for its caramel sweetness). Indispensable in a Blood and Sand cocktail (page 258). Add a few drops to heavy cream with confectioners' sugar to make a smoky whipped cream.

Smoked cheese: The best grilled cheese I ever tasted was smoked mozzarella grilled in lemon leaves at the restaurant Bruno in Positano, Italy. I like to grate smoked cheddar into mashed potatoes and mac and cheese. Popular smoked cheeses include cheddar, Gouda, and mozzarella. Learn how to hay-smoke mozzarella (page 42) and cold-smoke ricotta (page 203).

Smoked salt: A no-brainer seasoning for steaks, chops, and other grilled meats, and a great way to put extra smoke flavor into barbecue rubs. Two brands I like are dark Danish Viking Smoked Salt and Alaska Pure Alder Smoked Sea Salt.

PICKLED SMOKED QUAIL EGGS
IN THE STYLE OF NOMA

YIELD: Makes 24 quail eggs, enough to serve 4 to 6

METHOD: Hot-smoking

PREP TIME: 10 to 15 minutes

SMOKING TIME: 8 to 12 minutes

PICKLING TIME: 10 minutes

FUEL: 2 cups hay or straw plus 1 cup birch or other hardwood chips

GEAR: A wire rack; an aluminum foil pan

SHOP: Quail eggs are available at Whole Foods, farmers' markets, Asian markets, and some supermarkets. Look for hay at garden centers or tack shops. Quail eggs and hay can both be ordered online from amazon.com.

WHAT ELSE: Quail eggs are easier to peel if they are closer to their "use by" dates. Can't find or don't want to bother with quail eggs? You can certainly smoke and pickle full-size chicken eggs. Boiling time will be 11 minutes. Quarter the eggs before pickling them.

In 2014, San Pellegrino ranked Noma in Copenhagen the best restaurant in the world, its fourth first-place win. Its founder-chef, René Redzepi, achieved this remarkable feat by imposing a restriction most chefs would find impossibly limiting: to use only ingredients found within a fifty kilometer radius of Copenhagen. While Denmark offers a wealth of fruits, vegetables, and seafood in the summertime, the winter larder is spare—even Spartan. Smoking and pickling—the techniques used in this recipe—served not only to flavor foods, but also to preserve them in the age before refrigeration. And while pickled eggs are a common bar snack around Europe and North America, smoking them adds a wondrous new dimension. Redzepi smokes the eggs with two fuels, hay and birch chips, and serves them on a nest of smoking hay.

INGREDIENTS

Ice water

24 quail eggs

Vegetable oil, for oiling the wire rack

1½ cups warm water

⅔ cup fruit vinegar (Redzepi uses rosehip vinegar; alternatively, use pear or another mild vinegar)

1 teaspoon salt, or to taste

1. Have ready a large bowl of ice water. Bring a large saucepan of water to a boil over high heat. Add the quail eggs and boil for 90 seconds. Transfer the eggs to the ice water with a slotted spoon; keep the saucepan of water at a boil. Let the eggs sit in the ice water for 2 minutes, then return them to the boiling water for 6 minutes. Remove them again to the ice water. (This two-step boiling process makes the quail eggs easier to peel.)

2. Tap each egg at the broad end to crack the shell, then peel, taking care not to crush the egg. It will still be a little soft in the center—it's supposed to be.

3. Set up your smoker following the manufacturer's instructions and preheat to 225°F. Add hay and birch chips as specified by the manufacturer.

4. Place the eggs on a lightly oiled wire rack placed over an aluminum foil pan filled with ice (the eggs should not touch the ice). Place in the smoker and smoke the eggs until lightly bronzed with smoke, 8 to 12 minutes.

5. Combine the warm water, vinegar, and salt in a nonreactive bowl. Add the smoked eggs and pickle for 10 minutes, then drain. Cover and refrigerate the eggs if preparing them ahead.

6. Serve the eggs in dark bowls or on plates or on a "nest" of fresh hay.

SMOKED TOMATO-CORN SALSA

Sometimes the difference between great and extraordinary turns on a whiff of wood smoke. Case in point: salsa. You start with the usual ingredients—ripe tomatoes, sweet onions, jalapeños—plus another great summer vegetable: fresh corn. You smoke the ingredients before dicing and mixing—just long enough to impart a smoke flavor but briefly enough to retain a fresh raw vegetable crunch. The salsa tastes best made no more than three hours ahead of serving.

INGREDIENTS

4 luscious ripe red tomatoes (about 2 pounds), cut in half widthwise

4 jalapeño peppers, stemmed and cut in half lengthwise (seeded for a milder salsa; seeds left in for hotter)

2 ears sweet corn, shucked

1 small sweet onion, peeled and quartered

½ cup chopped fresh cilantro

¼ cup fresh lime juice (2 to 3 limes), or to taste

Coarse salt (sea or kosher)

Tortilla chips (smoked or not; see Note), for serving

YIELD: Makes 4 cups, enough to serve 6 to 8

METHOD: Hot-smoking

PREP TIME: 15 minutes

SMOKING TIME: 15 to 20 minutes

FUEL: I like hickory for this salsa. You'll need enough for 15 minutes of smoking (see chart on page 6).

SHOP: As with all salsas, this one flies or dies by the quality of the veggies. Summer corn. Farmstand or garden tomatoes. You get the idea.

WHAT ELSE: You can also smoke the salsa ingredients in a stovetop smoker. This may be the most singular salsa you'll ever serve.

1. Set up your smoker following the manufacturer's instructions and preheat to 225°F. Add the wood as specified by the manufacturer.

2. Place the tomatoes and jalapeños (both cut side up), corn, and onion in the smoker. Smoke the vegetables long enough to impart a smoke flavor (but

not so long that you cook them), 15 to 20 minutes. Transfer the vegetables to a platter and let cool to room temperature.

3. Lay the corn flat on a cutting board and slice the kernels off the cob using broad strokes of a chef's knife. Transfer the corn kernels to a large bowl.

4. Coarsely chop the tomatoes, jalapeños, and onion by hand or in a food processor. Add to the corn and stir in the cilantro, lime juice, and salt to taste. The salsa should be highly seasoned. Transfer the salsa to a serving bowl. Serve with chips alongside.

NOTE: To take this salsa over the top, serve it with tortilla chips smoked with a handheld smoker. Place the chips in a large glass bowl and cover tightly with plastic wrap, leaving one edge open. Fill and light the smoker following the manufacturer's instructions. Insert the tube of the smoker, fill the bowl with smoke, withdraw the tube, and tightly cover the bowl with the plastic wrap. Let infuse for 4 minutes. Repeat a couple of times or until the chips are smoked to taste.

SMOKED PLANKED CAMEMBERT
WITH JALAPEÑOS AND PEPPER JELLY

This simple smoked Camembert delivers big flavors (and great looks) by combining two distinctly American live-fire cooking techniques: planking and smoking. The former imparts the aromatic taste of charred cedar; the latter endows the cheese with complex smoke flavors undreamed of by French cheesemakers. The prep time is a couple of minutes; the wow power is off the charts.

YIELD: Serves 4

METHOD: Smoke-roasting

PREP TIME: 10 minutes

SMOKING TIME: 10 minutes

FUEL: Hardwood of your choice—enough for 10 minutes of smoking on a grill or 30 to 45 minutes in a smoker (see chart on page 6).

INGREDIENTS

1 Camembert or small Brie cheese (8 ounces)

3 tablespoons pepper jelly, tomato jam, or apricot jam

1 large jalapeño pepper, stemmed and thinly sliced crosswise

Grilled or toasted baguette slices or favorite crackers, for serving

GEAR: 1 cedar plank or other wood plank, such as hickory, oak, or alder, preferably 6 inches square, available at grill shops and most supermarkets. I'm partial to my Best of Barbecue brand, available at amazon.com. Note: You can also buy cedar boards at a lumberyard, but make sure they're untreated.

SHOP: My cheese of choice is French Camembert or a small (5- to 6-inch) Brie cheese.

WHAT ELSE: I like to smoke-roast the cheese at a high temperature (400°F), but you can also smoke it low and slow at 250°F.

1. Set up your grill for smoke-roasting (indirect grilling, see page 262) and preheat to medium-high (400°F).

2. If you're charring the plank (this step is optional, but it gives you a lot more flavor), place it directly over the fire and grill until singed on both sides, 1 to 2 minutes per side. Set aside and let cool.

3. Place the cheese in the center of the plank. Spread the top with pepper jelly using the back of a spoon. Shingle the jalapeño slices on top so they overlap in a decorative pattern.

4. Place the plank on the grill away from the heat and toss the wood chips or chunks on the coals. Smoke-roast the cheese until the sides are soft and beginning to bulge, 6 to 10 minutes.

5. Serve the cheese on the plank, hot off the grill, with a basket of grilled baguette slices or your favorite crackers.

HAY-SMOKED MOZZARELLA

YIELD: Makes 1 ball mozzarella, enough to serve 2 or 3

METHOD: Hay-smoking (hot-smoking with hay)

PREP TIME: 5 minutes

SMOKING TIME: 2 to 4 minutes

FUEL: About 3 quarts hay

SHOP: For cheese, you want a fresh mozzarella, the sort that comes packed in water or dripping with whey. Extra points if it's made with tangy buffalo's milk. You can find hay at garden centers or tack shops.

Long before hipster chefs in Brooklyn took to serving hay-smoked chicken and rib eyes, cheesemakers in Paestum, Italy, bronzed fresh buffalo milk mozzarella and other cheeses with fragrant clouds of hay smoke. They'd place the cheese in the top of a smoker (sometimes little more than an old refrigerator or a metal box). They'd pile dry hay at the bottom and set it ablaze. The hay erupted in a cloud of fire and smoke, adding an intense smoke flavor in a couple of minutes. Which comes in handy when you're smoking a delicate food like fresh mozzarella, which would melt if exposed even briefly to moderate heat. Hay-smoking delivers high drama—it looks cool and it leaves you feeling the sort of "Why didn't I think of this sooner?" satisfaction you get from mastering a revolutionary and exceedingly effective technique.

WHAT ELSE: Hay-smoking is a great technique for smoking in a hurry, and once you master it, you can use it for a number of melt-prone or otherwise fragile foods. Other cheeses come to mind (Scamorza, Taleggio, fontina, Gouda, and Camembert, for example), but the technique also works for smoking steak tartare, burgers, and racks of lamb before grilling.

INGREDIENTS

Vegetable oil, for oiling the grate

1 ball (8 to 12 ounces) fresh mozzarella, patted dry

Extra virgin olive oil (optional)

Coarse salt (sea or kosher) or fleur de sel (optional)

Place a small mound of charcoal in the smoker firebox or to one side of a kettle grill and light it. Brush and oil the grate. When the coals glow red, place the cheese in the smoke chamber (or on the side of the kettle grill opposite the embers), as far away as possible from the fire. Toss the hay on the coals and close the smoker or cover the grill. Smoke the cheese until it's colored with smoke (but not long enough to melt it), 2 to 4 minutes.

Slide a spatula under the cheese and transfer it to a plate to cool. Do not grab it when hot, or the deposit of smoke will come off on your fingers. Serve once it has cooled to room temperature, or refrigerate until serving. (For maximum flavor, let the cheese warm to room temperature before serving.) Drizzle with olive oil and/or salt, if desired, and serve.

THREE COOL THINGS TO DO WITH HAY-SMOKED MOZZARELLA
(BESIDES EATING IT SLICED OR DICED AT THE END OF A TOOTHPICK)

Smoked Caprese Salad: Thinly slice the smoked mozzarella and arrange on a platter with thinly sliced smoked tomatoes. Strew with torn fresh basil leaves, drizzle with extra virgin olive oil and balsamic vinegar, and season with salt and pepper.

Smoked Mozzarella Panini: Place sliced smoked mozzarella and thinly sliced speck (Italian smoked ham—page 119), prosciutto, or tomatoes in a square of focaccia (slice it in half through one side) to

make a sandwich. Brush the outside with olive oil and toast on the grill (place a grill press on top) or in a sandwich press until crusty and brown and the cheese starts to melt.

Smoked Eggplant Parmigiana: Place slices of smoked mozzarella atop slices of grilled or fried eggplant. Top with tomato sauce and grated Parmigiano-Reggiano cheese. Indirect-grill or bake until browned and bubbling.

SMOKED SEAFOOD DIP

"Claire unpacked the grocery bags and the menu began to take shape. She'd whirl the smoked clams and mussels with mascarpone cheese in the food processor to make a dip to eat by the fire."

The scene comes from my novel, *Island Apart*, but a similar action takes place in some form in summer cottages from Maine to the Puget Sound. The smoked seafood varies from bluefish (favored by Martha's Vineyarders) to salmon (popular in the Pacific Northwest) to clams and oysters (extraordinary when freshly smoked—page 174). Here's the basic blueprint, with a variety of flavorings to help you make the recipe yours.

INGREDIENTS

8 ounces smoked bluefish, salmon, clams, oysters, or other seafood (drained if canned)

8 ounces mascarpone or cream cheese, at room temperature

Coarse salt (sea or kosher) and freshly ground black pepper

Crackers, breadsticks, or slices of grilled or toasted Smoked Bread (page 56), for serving

SUGGESTED FLAVORINGS

Minced sweet onion or shallot

Finely chopped chives or scallion greens

Freshly grated lemon or lime zest

Freshly grated or prepared horseradish

Thai or Chinese chili paste

Worcestershire sauce

Hot sauce

Fresh lemon juice

1. Flake the fish into a food processor, discarding any skin or bones, or add the clams or oysters. Coarsely or finely chop (your choice) by running the processor in short bursts. Add the mascarpone or cream cheese, salt and pepper to taste, and any of the flavorings, and process just to mix. If you like a more coarsely textured pâté, mash the ingredients with a fork in a bowl. Taste and correct the seasoning; the dip should be highly seasoned.

2. Transfer the dip to a serving bowl. Serve with crackers or grilled or toasted bread.

YIELD: Makes 2 cups, enough to serve 6 to 8

PREP TIME: 20 minutes

SHOP: When possible, use fish or shellfish you've smoked yourself. Otherwise, source from a good smokehouse or fishmonger. Mascarpone is a thick Italian cream cheese similar to English clotted cream. Look for it at high-end supermarkets.

WHAT ELSE: To smoke your own fish and shellfish, see the recipes in the Seafood chapter beginning on page 173. To reinforce the smoke flavor, serve the dip with slices of grilled or toasted Smoked Bread (page 56).

SMOKED CHICKEN LIVERS

YIELD: Makes 1 pound, enough to serve 4 as a starter, 2 or 3 as a light main course

METHOD: Hot-smoking

PREP TIME: 15 minutes

BRINING TIME: 3 hours

SMOKING TIME: 30 to 40 minutes

FUEL: Hardwood of your choice—enough for 40 minutes of smoking (see chart on page 6)

GEAR: A wire rack

WHAT ELSE: Smoking adds a great flavor, but leaves the outside of the chicken livers soft and rubbery. They're fine this way for pâté, but if you like your livers with a little snap, undercook them during smoking, then brown them in hot butter or bacon fat in a skillet. And if you think rumaki (bacon-wrapped chicken livers with water chestnuts) is good, wait until you try it with smoked chicken livers.

Maybe you like chicken livers, in which case the following recipe needs no sales pitch. Maybe you don't, in which case I hope you'll reconsider, for smoking accentuates the virtues of liver—that rich cluster of minerally meat flavors. A quick white wine brine mellows any livery unpleasantness and, as always, smoke frames the flavor debate in an interesting, unexpected way. Serve these smoked chicken livers at the end of a toothpick (the Beijing Barbecue Sauce on page 101 makes an awesome dip), or chopped in an amazing smoked liver pâté (recipe follows).

INGREDIENTS

1 pound chicken or turkey livers

1 cup hot water

1½ tablespoons coarse salt (sea or kosher)

1 teaspoon black peppercorns

½ teaspoon fresh or dried thyme leaves

1 cup ice water

½ cup dry white wine

Vegetable oil, for oiling the rack

About 1 tablespoon extra virgin olive oil

1 tablespoon butter or bacon fat, for pan-frying (optional)

1. Trim any green or bloody spots off the livers.

2. Make the brine: Place the hot water, salt, peppercorns, and thyme in a deep bowl and whisk until the salt dissolves. Whisk in the ice water and wine. When the mixture is cold, stir in the chicken livers. Brine, covered, in the refrigerator for 3 hours.

3. Drain the livers in a colander and blot dry with paper towels. Oil a wire rack and arrange the livers on it. Let dry in the refrigerator for 30 minutes. Lightly brush the livers with olive oil on both sides.

4. Meanwhile, set up your smoker following the manufacturer's instructions and preheat to 300°F. Add the wood as specified by the manufacturer.

5. Place the rack in the smoker and smoke the livers until cooked to taste, 30 to 40 minutes for pink in the center. (Make a slit in one of the livers to check for doneness.) Do not overcook.

6. You can serve the livers hot from the smoker. To add a little crunch to the exterior, melt the butter in a large skillet over high heat. Pan-fry the livers until seared and crusty, 1 to 2 minutes per side.

SMOKED LIVER PATE

YIELD: Makes about 1½ cups • **PREP TIME:** 20 minutes •
SMOKING TIME: 30 to 40 minutes

This smoky pâté is a Thanksgiving standby at our house. We make it with the smoked turkey liver augmented with a few chicken livers. For the apotheosis of smoked liver, serve the pâté on slices of Smoked Bread (page 56).

INGREDIENTS

8 ounces turkey livers, chicken livers, or a combination

5 hard-cooked Smoked Eggs (see page 35), peeled

2 tablespoons (¼ stick) butter or olive oil

1 small onion, peeled and minced

¼ cup chicken stock, mayonnaise, or heavy cream

2 teaspoons Scotch whisky or Cognac (optional)

Coarse salt (sea or kosher) and freshly ground black pepper

Crackers or slices of grilled or toasted Smoked Bread (page 56), for serving

1. Smoke the livers as described on the facing page (but without brining them) and the eggs as described on page 35. Transfer to a plate and let cool. Cut the livers and eggs into 1-inch pieces.

2. Melt the butter in a large skillet. Add the onion and cook over medium heat until darkly browned, 5 minutes, stirring often. Transfer the onion to the plate and let cool.

3. Place the livers, eggs, and onion in a food processor and grind as coarsely or finely as you like. Work in enough stock to make a spreadable pâté. If you like the smoky tang of whisky or Cognac, add it. Add salt and pepper; the pâté should be highly seasoned. Refrigerate, covered, until serving. Serve on crackers or grilled or toasted Smoked Bread.

SMOKED NACHOS

YIELD: Serves 6 to 8

METHOD: Hot-smoking

PREP TIME: 20 minutes

SMOKING TIME: 12 to 15 minutes

FUEL: Hickory, or hardwood of your choice—enough for 15 minutes of smoking (see chart on page 6)

GEAR: Perforated grill skillet, 10-inch cast-iron skillet, or 10-inch metal pie plate

SHOP: My personal preference goes to fresh jalapeños, but pickled peppers punch up the flavor with vinegar.

WHAT ELSE: I call for shredded smoked brisket (page 66). Alternatively, use jerk chicken (page, 154), smoked turkey (page 159), pulled pork (page 88), or smoked tofu (page 224) for a vegetarian version.

SMOKED NACHOS ON THE GRILL

Set up the grill for indirect grilling and preheat to medium-high (400°F). Place the nachos pan on the grate away from the heat and toss the wood chips on the coals. Indirect-grill until the cheese is melted and bubbling, 5 minutes.

The year was 1943, and a group of Americans straggled into the Victory Club in Piedras Negras, Mexico, after closing time. The chef had left, but the maitre d', Ignacio "Nacho" Anaya, topped some tostadas with jalapeños and cheese and melted it under the broiler. A classic was born. His legacy lives on, and I bet he'd admire the smoked nachos created by our *Project Smoke* TV fire wrangler and Barbecue University alum Rob Baas. Rob starts with slow-smoked brisket, which he combines with the usual array of tortilla chips, black beans, jalapeños, and grated cheese. A blast of hot wood smoke melts the cheese, taking these nachos over the top.

INGREDIENTS

8 cups tortilla chips

2 cups shredded smoked brisket or chicken

1 can (15 ounces) black beans (preferably organic and low-sodium), drained well in a colander, rinsed, and drained again

12 ounces finely grated mixed cheeses (like cheddar, smoked cheddar, Jack, and/or pepper Jack; about 3 cups)

4 fresh jalapeño peppers, stemmed and thinly sliced crosswise, or ⅓ cup drained pickled jalapeño slices

4 scallions, trimmed, white and green parts thinly sliced crosswise

2 to 4 tablespoons of your favorite hot sauce (I like Cholula) or barbecue sauce

¼ cup coarsely chopped fresh cilantro (optional)

1. Set up your smoker following the manufacturer's instructions and preheat to 275°F. Add the wood as specified by the manufacturer.

2. Loosely arrange one third of the tortilla chips in the grill skillet. Sprinkle one third of the shredded brisket, beans, cheese, jalapeños, and scallions on top. Shake on hot sauce. Add a second layer of these ingredients, followed by a third.

3. Place the skillet with the nachos in your smoker and smoke until the cheese is melted and bubbling, 12 to 15 minutes.

4. Sprinkle the cilantro on top, if using, and dig in. Yes—you eat the nachos right out of the skillet, so be careful not to burn your fingers on the rim.

RED HOT WINGS
WITH PAC-RIM SEASONINGS

My take on the Buffalo wing involves—you guessed it—wood smoke. Crank your smoker up to 375°F. This is hotter than the usual 225°F low and slow, but the heat helps render the fat and crisp the chicken skin. To further pump up the wings, I call for Pac-Rim flavors like sesame oil and sriracha, and use fresh jalapeño peppers to heat up the butter sauce. Napkins and cold beer required.

INGREDIENTS

3 pounds chicken wings
(about 24 pieces)

½ cup finely chopped fresh cilantro

2 teaspoons coarse salt (sea or kosher)

2 teaspoons cracked black peppercorns

2 teaspoons ground coriander
(optional)

2 tablespoons Asian (dark) sesame oil

Vegetable oil, for oiling the rack

6 tablespoons (¾ stick) butter

4 jalapeño peppers, thinly sliced
crosswise (leave the seeds in)

6 tablespoons sriracha (or other
favorite hot sauce)

¼ cup chopped dry-roasted peanuts

1. Place the chicken wings in a large bowl. Sprinkle in ¼ cup of the cilantro, the salt, pepper, and coriander, if using, and stir to mix. Stir in the sesame oil. Cover the bowl and marinate, refrigerated, for 15 to 60 minutes (the longer they marinate, the richer the flavor).

2. Meanwhile, set up your smoker following the manufacturer's instructions and preheat to 375°F. (If your smoker's incapable of reaching that temperature, preheat as hot as the smoker will go.) Add the wood as specified by the manufacturer.

3. Oil the smoker rack and arrange the drumettes on it. Smoke the wings until sizzling, brown with smoke, and cooked through, 30 to 50 minutes. At lower temperatures (for example, at 250°F), you'll need 1½ to 2 hours. In some smokers, the pieces closest to the fire will cook faster; if this is the case, rotate the pieces so all cook evenly. To check for doneness, make a tiny cut in the thickest part of a few of the wings. The meat at the bone should be white, with no traces of red. Do not overcook. Arrange the wings on a heatproof platter.

YIELD: 24 wings, enough for 4 to 6 when served with other food

METHOD: Hot-smoking

PREP TIME: 15 minutes

MARINATING TIME: 15 to 60 minutes

SMOKING TIME: 30 minutes to 2 hours (depending on smoker temperature)

FUEL: Hardwood of your choice (I like alder or cherry)—enough for 50 minutes (or 2 hours, if smoking at a low temperature) of smoking (see chart on page 6)

SHOP: As always, buy organic chicken if you can find it. Sometimes (especially around Super Bowl time), you can buy "drumettes," the meaty first joint of a chicken wing, with the flat and wing tip removed. They make an easy-to-handle alternative to whole wings. Asian (dark) sesame oil is a fragrant oil pressed from roasted sesame seeds. One good brand is Kadoya from Japan.

WHAT ELSE: Once you master the process—meat plus spice plus smoke plus butter plus hot sauce—you can "buffalo" anything: shrimp, sweetbreads, or even pigs' ears or tails (the latter a specialty of Animal restaurant in Los Angeles). For Mexican-style hot wings, substitute cumin for the coriander and Cholula hot sauce for the sriracha. The possibilities are endless.

4. Just before serving, melt the butter in a cast-iron skillet on the stove over high heat. Add the jalapeños and cook until they sizzle and start to brown, 3 minutes. Stir in the sriracha and bring to a boil. Pour over the chicken.

5. Sprinkle the chicken with the peanuts and the remaining ¼ cup cilantro and serve at once with plenty of napkins.

SRIRACHA BEEF JERKY

YIELD: Makes 30 to 36 strips

METHOD: Hot-smoking (but at a very low temperature)

PREP TIME: 10 minutes, plus 1 hour freezing

MARINATING TIME: 4 hours or more

SMOKING TIME: 3½ to 4 hours

FUEL: Hardwood of your choice—enough for 3½ to 4 hours of smoking (see chart on page 6)

GEAR: A wire rack

Jerky is practical: It weighs next to nothing, keeps for weeks without refrigeration, and gives you a quick, beefy shot of energy on a hike, long drive, or camping trip. Jerky is democratic: You find it in trendy restaurants, convenience stores, and everywhere in between. (Of course the quality varies accordingly.) Jerky is elemental: Early versions had no seasonings, but it is capable of gastronomic sophistication. What you may not realize is how easy—and satisfying—it is to make from scratch, especially when you smoke it. (Note: Not all commercial jerky is smoked; much of it is flavored with liquid smoke.) This version delivers the firepower of sriracha (Thai hot sauce) and the soulful umami flavors of fish sauce and wood smoke.

INGREDIENTS

2 pounds lean beef (such as boneless sirloin, top or bottom round, or flank steak)

½ cup sriracha

¼ cup fish sauce or soy sauce

¼ cup Asian (dark) sesame oil

3 cloves garlic, peeled and minced

2 tablespoons chopped fresh cilantro

Vegetable oil, for oiling the rack (optional)

1. Wrap the beef in freezer paper or aluminum foil and freeze until firm but not frozen solid, about 1 hour. (This facilitates slicing.)

2. Meanwhile, make the marinade: Place the sriracha, fish sauce, sesame oil, garlic, and cilantro in a large bowl and whisk to mix.

SHOP: You want a lean cut of boneless beef like sirloin, top or bottom round, or flank steak. Extra points if it's grass-fed. Fish sauce is a fermented anchovy sauce from Southeast Asia; it can be purchased in many supermarkets or online. My favorite brand is Red Boat. Asian (dark) sesame oil is a fragrant oil pressed from roasted sesame seeds.

WHAT ELSE: Tradition calls for cutting the beef into strips along the grain, which gives you jerky strips with plenty of chew. (Jerky is supposed to be chewy.) For softer, more tender strips of jerky, slice the beef against the grain.

3. Using a sharp chef's knife, slice the beef along the grain into ⅛-inch-thick slices, trimming off any visible fat or connective tissue. Add the beef strips to the marinade, stirring to coat well on all sides. Cover with plastic wrap and marinate the beef strips in the refrigerator for at least 4 hours or as long as overnight—the longer they marinate, the spicier the jerky.

4. Cover a rimmed baking sheet with aluminum foil and place a wire rack on the foil. Remove the beef strips from the marinade and arrange them on the rack. Let drain and dry for 30 minutes.

5. Meanwhile, set up your smoker following the manufacturer's instructions and preheat to 160°F. Add the wood as specified by the manufacturer.

6. Remove the rack with the jerky from the baking sheet and place it in the smoker or arrange the beef strips on oiled smoker racks and smoke until dried but still flexible, 3½ to 4 hours.

7. Transfer the still-warm jerky to a large heavy-duty resealable plastic bag. (The resulting steam relaxes the meat.) Let cool to room temperature in the bag. Dig in now or later. Store the jerky in the refrigerator; it will keep at least a week.

JERKY

Smoke-drying was one of the first methods our prehistoric ancestors used to preserve meat and seafood. Native peoples in both North and South America dried thinly sliced strips of meat next to a smoky fire. Our word *jerky* likely comes from *charqui*, the Quecha Incan tribe's term for dried meat.

Today, we Americans consume over two million pounds of jerky annually—most of it commercially produced. Jerky is easy and infinitely superior when made at home; all you need is a smoker and a modicum of patience.

Here's what you need to know.

- Use lean cuts of meat with very little intramuscular fat or connective tissue, such as top or bottom beef round. Fat spoils faster than lean meat.

- Cut the meat into thin slices, ⅛ inch to a maximum of ¼ inch thick. This is easier if you partially freeze the meat first. Alternatively, ask your butcher to cut it for you on the meat slicer.

- Beef is by far the most popular type of jerky in North America, but you can turn many other domesticated and wild meats into jerky. Hunters take note: Venison, moose, mule deer, antelope, elk, rabbit, and bison make great jerky.

- When making turkey or chicken jerky, be sure to cook it to a food-safe 165°F.

- Smoking and drying require low temperatures (typically around 160°F) using hardwood to generate smoke.

- Electric smokers are excellent for jerky—it's easy to achieve a constant low temperature in an electric smoker.

- Store jerky in resealable plastic bags or lidded jars. (Pack it hot—the resulting steam softens and partially rehydrates the meat.) Refrigerate for the longest shelf life.

BACON-CRAB POPPERS

Poppers have been a staple on the barbecue circuit for decades. Does the world really need another recipe? You bet. These poppers riff on a dish from my Baltimore childhood—crab imperial—with salty, smoky bacon to tie them together.

INGREDIENTS

12 large jalapeño peppers

8 ounces cream cheese, at room temperature

Finely grated zest of 1 lemon

1 teaspoon Old Bay seasoning, or to taste

8 ounces crabmeat, drained, picked over, and finely shredded or chopped

Sweet or smoked paprika, for sprinkling

12 strips artisanal bacon, cut crosswise in half

1. Set up your smoker following the manufacturer's instructions and preheat to 350°F. (Yes, I know this is hotter than the conventional low and slow method—it gives you crisper bacon.) Add the wood as specified by the manufacturer.

2. Cut each jalapeño in half lengthwise, cutting through the stem and leaving it in place. Scrape out the seeds and veins; a grapefruit spoon or melon baller works well for this. Arrange the jalapeño halves on a wire rack, cut side up.

3. Place the cream cheese in a mixing bowl. Add the lemon zest and Old Bay seasoning and beat with a wooden spoon until light. Gently fold in the crab. Spoon a heaping tablespoon of crab mixture into each jalapeño half, mounding it toward the center. Sprinkle with paprika.

4. Wrap each jalapeño half with a strip of bacon (you want the filling exposed at each end). Secure the bacon with a toothpick and arrange the poppers in a single layer on the wire rack.

5. Place the wire rack in the smoker. Smoke the poppers until the bacon and filling are browned and the peppers are tender (squeeze them between your thumb and forefinger), 30 to 40 minutes.

6. Transfer the poppers to a platter. Let cool slightly before serving.

YIELD: Makes 24 poppers, enough to serve 6 to 8

METHOD: Hot-smoking

PREP TIME: 20 minutes

SMOKING TIME: 30 to 40 minutes

FUEL: Hardwood of your choice—enough for 40 minutes of smoking (see chart on page 6)

GEAR: A wire rack; toothpicks

SHOP: There are many options for the crab, including blue crab from the Chesapeake Bay or Louisiana, Dungeness crab from the West Coast, or king or snow crab from Alaska.

WHAT ELSE: This recipe uses a different stuffing technique from the one you may be accustomed to: cutting the jalapeños in half lengthwise and stuffing the halves (rather than stuffing them whole). This gives you better browning and a more pervasive smoke flavor.

SMOKED BREAD

YIELD: Makes 1 loaf

METHOD: Hot- or cold-smoking

PREP TIME: 10 minutes

RISING TIME (2 risings): 1½ to 2 hours

SMOKING TIME: 15 to 20 minutes for hot-smoking; 1½ hours for cold-smoking

FUEL: Apple wood or hardwood of your choice—enough for 2 hours of smoking (see chart on page 6)

GEAR: 2 aluminum foil pans; 9-by 5-inch loaf pan; a wire rack

SHOP: Organic flours when possible

WHAT ELSE: Sometimes Villar reinforces the smoky sweetness of the dough with caramelized onions.

At first glance, this looks like a great country loaf—brown crust, inviting honey-wheat aroma, soft crumb. The bread is subtly but unmistakably smoky—not hit-you-over-the-head smoky, like brisket, but infused with a delicate smoke flavor that makes you feel like you're eating it in a French farmhouse that has a wood-burning hearth. The secret: Smoke the flour and water prior to making the dough. Tip 'o the hat to France-born baker Johann Villar, who showed me how to smoke these unexpected ingredients.

INGREDIENTS

2 cups unbleached all-purpose white flour or as needed

1 cup whole wheat flour or 1 additional cup white flour

1 teaspoon coarse salt (sea or kosher), plus extra for sprinkling

1¼ cups water, plus extra as needed

1 envelope (2½ teaspoons) dry yeast

2 tablespoons honey

1 tablespoon extra virgin olive oil, plus oil for the bowl, loaf pan, and top of the bread

1. Set up your smoker following the manufacturer's instructions and preheat it as low as it will go (200°F or below). Spread out the flours and salt in a thin layer (not more than ¼ inch thick) in an aluminum foil pan or on a rimmed baking sheet. Place the water in another foil pan.

2. Place the pans in the smoker and smoke until the white flour is lightly browned on the surface and tastes smoky and the water tastes smoky. Total smoking time is 15 to 20 minutes for hot-smoking or 1 to 1½ hours for cold-smoking.

3. Let the flours cool to room temperature. The water should only cool to warm (105°F).

4. Place the smoked flours, smoked salt, and yeast in a food processor and process to mix. Add the honey, olive oil, and the smoked warm water. Process in short bursts to obtain a soft, pliable dough. If the dough is too stiff, add a little more warm tap water; if too soft, add a little more flour. Alternatively, you can mix and knead the dough by hand or in a stand mixer fitted with a dough hook. Turn the dough onto a lightly floured cutting board and knead by hand into a smooth ball.

5. Place the dough in a large lightly oiled bowl, turning it to oil both sides. Cover with plastic wrap and let the dough rise in a warm spot until doubled in bulk, 1 to 1½ hours.

6. Punch down the dough, knead it into an oblong shape, and place it in an oiled loaf pan. Cover with plastic wrap. Let the dough rise again until doubled in bulk, 30 minutes to 1 hour.

7. Meanwhile, set up a grill for indirect grilling and preheat to 400°F or preheat your oven to 400°F. If your smoker goes up to 400°F, you can bake the bread in it. No need to add wood—you've already smoked the flour.

8. Brush the top of the loaf with a little more olive oil and sprinkle with a little salt. Bake the loaf until the top is browned and firm and the bottom sounds hollow when tapped, 30 to 40 minutes. Transfer the loaf pan to a wire rack and let cool for 10 minutes. Remove the bread from the pan, cool for 10 minutes more, slice crosswise and serve warm. Serve with the smoked butter on page 203 and smoked honey on page 204.

SMOKED GAZPACHO

Gazpacho was one of my first ventures into the realm of nontraditional smoked dishes. I smoked it in a Camerons Stovetop Smoker (see page 275) long before I bought my first outdoor smoker. It remains a family favorite. The smoke sneaks up on you, giving you traditional gazpacho with an element of surprise and depth of flavor you'd never expect from this simple summer soup.

YIELD: Serves 4; can be multiplied as desired

METHOD: Cold-smoking, or using a handheld smoker (see page 276)

PREP TIME: 30 minutes

SMOKING TIME: 1 hour

FUEL: Oak or almond wood in keeping with Spain's grilling tradition—enough for 1 hour of smoking (see chart on page 6)

GEAR: An aluminum foil pan

INGREDIENTS

4 luscious red ripe tomatoes (about 2 pounds), cut in half widthwise

1 medium-size cucumber, peeled, cut in half lengthwise, seeds scraped out

½ green or yellow bell pepper, stemmed, seeded, and cut into 2 pieces

½ red bell pepper, stemmed, seeded, and cut into 2 pieces

1 small sweet onion, peeled and cut lengthwise in quarters

1 clove garlic, peeled

3 tablespoons really good extra virgin olive oil, plus extra for drizzling

About 2 tablespoons red wine or Spanish sherry vinegar

½ cup water, plus extra as needed

Coarse salt (sea or kosher) and freshly ground black pepper

1 tablespoon chopped fresh chives or scallion greens

SHOP: Gazpacho lives or dies by the flavor of the vegetables. Use vine-ripened, garden-grown, farmstand, or heirloom tomatoes—preferably that have never seen the inside of a refrigerator. Anything less results in a pale simulacrum of what this gazpacho can be.

WHAT ELSE: Don't have the gear or patience for cold-smoking? You can hot-smoke the vegetables. Do it at the lowest temperature possible (200° to 225°F)—just long enough to bronze the outside of the tomatoes with smoke, but not so long that you cook them.

GAZPACHO MADE WITH A HANDHELD SMOKER

Puree the tomatoes, cucumber, bell peppers, onion, garlic, oil, and vinegar in a food processor or blender and season the soup as described in Step 4, this page. Pour the gazpacho into a large bowl, cover tightly with plastic wrap, and chill until serving.

Just before serving, lift one edge of the plastic wrap to insert the smoker hose. Fill and light the smoker following the manufacturer's instructions. Insert the tube of the smoker, fill the bowl with smoke, withdraw the tube, and tightly cover the bowl with the plastic wrap. Let infuse for 4 minutes. Stir the gazpacho to incorporate the smoke. Repeat a couple of times or until the gazpacho is smoked to taste.

1. Arrange the tomatoes, cucumber, peppers, and onion, cut side up, in an aluminum foil pan. Add the garlic.

2. Set up your smoker for cold-smoking, following the manufacturer's instructions. Add the wood as specified by the manufacturer.

3. Place the vegetables in the smoker. Smoke until bronzed with smoke (dip your finger in one cut tomato—the juices should taste smoky), 1 hour, or as needed. The vegetables should remain raw.

4. Cut the vegetables into 1-inch pieces, reserving the juices. Place in a food processor and process to a coarse or smooth puree (your choice).

Gradually add the reserved juices, oil, vinegar, and enough water (about ½ cup) to make a pourable soup. Work in salt and pepper to taste, plus a few more drops of vinegar if needed to balance the sweetness of the vegetables. Alternatively, place the vegetables and their juices, oil, vinegar, and water in a blender and blend to your preferred consistency. Season with salt, pepper, and more vinegar. The gazpacho can be made several hours ahead to this stage, covered, and refrigerated, but taste and re-season it before serving.

5. Ladle the gazpacho into serving bowls. Drizzle additional olive oil on top and sprinkle with the chopped chives.

SMOKED FISH CHOWDER

Spend time with this book, and you're going to wind up with a lot of smoked fish—cold-smoked Scandinavian salmon, hot-smoked kippered salmon, smoked arctic char, and so on. All make excellent bases for chowder. The following was inspired by one of the most inspiring fishing spots in North America: the Tutka Bay Lodge, near Homer, Alaska. Like many of the dips, spreads, and soups in this book, consider this recipe your basic marching orders. Deviations encouraged.

YIELD: Serves 8 as a starter, 4 as a light main course

COOKING TIME: 30 minutes

PREP TIME: 30 minutes

SHOP: Wild seafood when possible

INGREDIENTS

- 1 pound smoked salmon and/or other smoked seafood (pages 183 to 198)
- 3 tablespoons butter or extra virgin olive oil
- 2 shallots or 1 small red onion, peeled and finely chopped
- 2 leeks, white part only, trimmed, thoroughly rinsed, shaken dry, and thinly sliced
- 4 red-skinned potatoes (1½ pounds), scrubbed and cut into 1-inch chunks
- 1 bay leaf
- 2 sprigs fresh thyme, plus extra thyme leaves for serving
- Coarse salt (sea or kosher) and freshly ground black pepper
- 4 cups chicken or fish stock (preferably homemade)
- ¾ cup heavy (whipping) cream

1. Remove and discard any skin or bones from the salmon and break the fish into 1-inch flakes (if hot-smoked) or cut into ½-inch squares (if cold-smoked). Set aside.

2. Melt the butter in a large heavy saucepan over medium heat. Add the shallots and leeks and cook until soft, 3 minutes, stirring often.

3. Add the potatoes, bay leaf, and thyme sprigs. Continue cooking until the shallots, leeks, and potatoes are lightly browned, about 5 minutes, stirring often. Season well with salt and pepper.

4. Stir in the stock and simmer over medium heat until the potatoes are tender, about 10 minutes. Stir in the smoked fish and cream and simmer until the soup is richly flavored, 5 minutes more. Correct the seasoning, adding salt and pepper if needed. Remove and discard the bay leaf and thyme stems.

5. Ladle the chowder into serving bowls. Sprinkle thyme leaves on top and dig in.

BEEF

Somewhere between Red Hook in Brooklyn and Studio City in Los Angeles, smoky beef went viral. Notice I didn't mention Texas. For if the Lone Star State gave the world barbecued brisket and beef ribs, a new generation of pit masters now smokes everything from strip steak (using an ingenious technique called reverse searing) to beef tenderloin (accompanied by horseradish whipped cream). From home-smoked pastrami to big bad beef ribs. From reverse-seared tri-tip to smoked prime rib served with—you guessed it—smoked *jus*. This chapter celebrates beef in all its smoky awesomeness.

BIG BAD BEEF RIBS
SMOKED SALT-AND-PEPPER BEEF PLATE RIBS

YIELD: Makes 3 ribs, enough to serve 3 really hungry people

METHOD: Hot-smoking

PREP TIME: 10 minutes

SMOKING TIME: 8 to 10 hours

RESTING TIME: 1 hour

FUEL: Tradition calls for oak, hickory, or mesquite, or a combination of the three—enough for 10 hours of smoking (see chart on page 6).

GEAR: An aluminum foil drip pan; instant-read thermometer; an insulated cooler (optional)

SHOP: You'll need to order beef plate ribs from a butcher. Tell him or her you want full plate short ribs, cut into individual bones. (Or cut them yourself.) They come three to a plate.

WHAT ELSE: This salt, pepper, red pepper, and smoke treatment works great for ribs of all sorts, including pork and lamb.

The new sparerib? That's one way to describe the beef plate rib, aka the biggest, baddest rib on Planet Barbecue. (Brisket on a bone is another.) Billy Durney serves it at Hometown Bar-B-Que in Brooklyn. So do Hugh Mangum at Mighty Quinn's Barbeque in New York and New Jersey and the folks at Butcher and the Boar in Minneapolis. And you're about to dish up these bigger-than-life bones hot from the smoker at your home. Big? Each meaty bone tips the scale at 2 to 2½ pounds. Seasonings? Keep them simple: salt, pepper, and hot red pepper flakes. Focus on the meat and smoke.

INGREDIENTS

3 full beef plate short ribs (rack is 6 to 7½ pounds)

3 tablespoons coarse salt (sea or kosher), plus extra for serving

3 tablespoons cracked black peppercorns

2 tablespoons hot red pepper flakes

Beer (optional)

1 cup beef stock (preferably homemade)

1. Cut the rack lengthwise into individual bones and place them on a rimmed baking sheet.

2. Place the salt, pepper, and hot red pepper flakes in a small bowl and mix well. Generously sprinkle the rub on the ribs on all sides, including the ends, rubbing it into the meat with your fingertips.

3. Set up your smoker following the manufacturer's instructions and preheat to 225° to 250°F. If your smoker has a water pan, fill it with water or beer to a depth of 3 inches.

If it doesn't have a water pan, fill a disposable aluminum foil pan with water or beer to a depth of 3 inches and place it below the rack on which you'll be smoking the ribs. (Note: You don't need to do this on a ceramic cooker.) Add wood as specified by the manufacturer.

4. Place the ribs in the smoker fat side up, with at least 2 inches between ribs. Smoke the ribs until darkly browned on the outside and very tender inside, 8 to 10 hours. If working on a smoker with the firebox at one end, shuffle the ribs a couple

times so they cook evenly. To test for doneness, insert a metal skewer in the largest rib (through one end and parallel to the bone); it should pierce the meat easily. Another test for doneness is to insert an instant-read thermometer parallel to but not touching the bone; it should read 200°F. (Check the ribs to make sure all are done.) When done, the meat will have shrunk back from the ends of the bones by 1 to 2 inches.

5. Transfer the ribs to a large foil pan with the beef stock. Loosely cover the pan with aluminum foil and place it in an insulated cooler. Let the ribs rest for 1 hour before serving.

6. Just before serving, season each rib with a light sprinkling of salt.

BEEF SMOKING CHART

FOOD	AMOUNT	SMOKER TEMP	TIME	INTERNAL TEMP/ DONENESS
Brisket (packer)	14-18 pounds	225°-250°F	12-18 hours	200°F
Brisket (flat)	6-8 pounds	225°-250°F	8-10 hours	200°F
Pastrami (beef navel)	6-8 pounds	225°-250°F	8-10 hours	200°F
Beef tenderloin	4 pounds (trimmed)	225°-250°F + high heat for searing	45-60 minutes for smoking + 6-10 minutes for grilling	120°-125°F (rare) 130°-135°F (medium-rare)
Prime rib	6 pounds (3 ribs)	250°F	2-3 hours	120°-125°F (rare) 130-135°F (medium-rare)
Top round	6 pounds	225°-250°F	4-6 hours	120°-125°F (rare) 130°-135°F (medium-rare); 145°F (medium)
Beef plate ribs	2-2½ pounds (each rib)	225°-250°F	8-10 hours	200°F; meat shrinks back 1-2 inches from ends of bones
Tri-tip	2-2½ pounds (each)	225°-250°F + high heat for searing	1 hour for smoking + 4-6 minutes for grilling	120°-125°F (rare) 130°-135°F (medium-rare)
Strip steak	1½-1¾ pounds (each)	225°-250°F + high heat for searing	45-60 minutes for smoking + 4-6 minutes for grilling	120°-125°F (rare) 130°-135°F (medium-rare)
Beef jerky (page 54)	2 pounds	160°F	3½-4 hours	Browned and dried, but still flexible

OAK-SMOKED TOP ROUND

You love the intense beefy flavor of prime rib. You admire the carnivorous awesomeness of smoked whole beef tenderloin. But you don't want to break the bank on a roast. I hear your pain. Matthew Keeler has the answer: a smoked top round. Keeler runs a barbecue joint in the heart of Virginia pork country. But ask him—the third-generation pit master of King's Famous Barbecue in Petersburg—to name his favorite meat, and he'll point to a basketball-size Angus top round that he smokes as dark and shiny as Appalachian coal. Make that ten beef rounds every morning, some medium-rare, some medium, and a few well done. "We don't go in for a lot of spices," says Keeler, who seasons the beef solely with salt and pepper. "And we don't like our meats overly smoked." That's why he prefers the mild smoke of white oak to the more pungent hickory used at most Virginia barbecue joints.

YIELD: Serves 12

METHOD: Hot-smoking

PREP TIME: 5 minutes (plus 10 minutes to make the sauce)

SMOKING TIME: 4 to 6 hours

FUEL: White oak—enough for 7 hours of smoking (see chart on page 6)

GEAR: Remote or instant-read thermometer; a wire rack

SHOP: You'll want a top round weighing around 6 pounds. Alternatively, you could use a top sirloin. Try to buy one covered with a generous sheath of fat.

WHAT ELSE: Cooking times depend on how done you like your beef:

- About 4 hours for rare (120° to 125°F on an instant-read thermometer)
- About 5½ hours for medium-rare (130° to 135°F on an instant-read thermometer)
- About 6 hours for medium (145°F on an instant-read thermometer)

1 beef top round (about 6 pounds; buy one that has plenty of fat on it)

Coarse salt (sea or kosher) and cracked black peppercorns

12 hamburger buns (optional)

3 tablespoons salted or unsalted butter, melted (optional)

Three Hots Horseradish Sauce (page 78), for serving

1. Set up your smoker following the manufacturer's instructions and preheat to 225° to 250°F. Add the wood as specified by the manufacturer.

2. Very generously season the meat on all sides with salt and pepper. Place it in your smoker directly on the rack, fat side up. Smoke until crusty and darkly browned on the outside and cooked to taste (see "What Else").

3. When the beef is close to the desired temperature (remember— it will continue cooking out of the smoker), transfer it to a wire rack over a rimmed baking sheet. *Loosely* tent with aluminum foil (do not bunch the foil around the meat) and let rest for 15 minutes.

4. If using buns, brush the cut sides with melted butter and lightly toast on a grill or griddle.

5. Trim off and discard any big lumps of fat from the top round; leave a little in place for flavor. Thinly slice or chop the beef and serve it on the buns, if using. Try to include some crusty end slices and pink center slices. Slather with the horseradish sauce and serve.

SLAM-DUNK BRISKET

YIELD: Serves 8 to 10, with leftovers

METHOD: Hot-smoking

PREP TIME: 20 minutes

SMOKING TIME: 8 to 10 hours

RESTING TIME: 1 to 2 hours

FUEL: Oak, apple, mesquite, and hickory are traditionally associated with brisket—enough for at least 8 hours of smoking (see chart on page 6).

GEAR: An aluminum foil pan; instant-read thermometer; unlined butcher paper; an insulated cooler

SHOP: Buy a brisket flat (the flat bottom muscle—see page 68) with a generous layer of fat on top.

WHAT ELSE: As you smoke a brisket, the temperature will steadily rise, then plateau around 160°F (and in some instances, actually drop a few degrees) for an hour or so—sometimes more. This is called the *stall* and it results from the evaporation of the moisture from the surface of the brisket. (You may even see a puddle of liquid gather on the top.) This evaporation cools the meat much the way sweat helps cool you off in hot weather. Be patient—the stall will stop and the temperature will start climbing again.

If there's one dish that epitomizes barbecue, that every aspiring smoke master hopes to perfect, it's brisket. If there's one dish that intimidates—even if you've long since reached your comfort zone with smoking pork shoulders and ribs—it's brisket. The challenge is the tough connective tissue, not to mention a muscle structure in a whole brisket that has the grain going in two separate directions. I'm going to tell you how to smoke a perfect brisket every time—and that's whether you start with the whole 18-pound packer brisket; with the 6- to 8-pound brisket flat you find at your local butcher shop; or the trimmed (make that scalped) 3- to 5-pound center-cut brisket often sold at the supermarket. Up first: the brisket flat.

INGREDIENTS

1 first-cut (flat) brisket (6 to 8 pounds)

¼ cup Dijon mustard (optional)

¼ cup dill pickle juice (optional)

Coarse salt (sea or kosher) and cracked black peppercorns

6 strips artisanal bacon (optional)

Beer (optional)

Favorite barbecue sauce, for serving (optional)

1. Trim the brisket, leaving a fat cap on top at least ¼ inch thick. Place the brisket on a rimmed baking sheet. If using the mustard and pickle juice, mix them together in a small bowl, then brush on both sides of the brisket. Very generously season all over, including the ends, with salt and pepper. If your brisket lacks a sufficient fat cap, drape the top with bacon.

2. Set up your smoker following the manufacturer's instructions and preheat to 225° to 250°F. If your smoker has a water pan, fill it with water or beer to a depth of 3 inches. If it doesn't have a water pan, fill an aluminum foil pan with water or beer to a depth of 3 inches and place it below the rack on which you'll be smoking the ribs. (Note: You don't need to do this on a ceramic cooker.) Add the wood as specified by the manufacturer.

3. Place the brisket fat side up in your smoker. Cook until the outside is darkly browned and the internal temperature registers 175°F on an instant-read thermometer, 8 to 10 hours. (Don't panic if the temperature seems to stall around 165°F: this is normal.) Replenish the charcoal and wood as needed.

4. Remove the brisket from the smoker and tightly wrap it in butcher paper. Return it to the smoker.

HOW TO SLICE A PACKER BRISKET

Because of its unique anatomical structure, with the grain of the deckle running at roughly a 60 degree angle to the grain of the flat (and separated by a layer of fat), brisket requires a special slicing technique.

1. Holding the blade of a slicing knife parallel to the cutting board, cut the deckle off the flat.

2. Scrape off the excess fat from the bottom of the deckle and the top of the flat.

3. Trim any dry or burnt edges off the sides of the deckle and flat. Chop or dice these with a little of the fat to serve as burnt ends or to add to baked beans.

4. Place the deckle on the trimmed flat, rotating it about 60 degrees so the meat fibers in both cuts run in the same direction, front to back.

5. Slice the deckle and flat crosswise across the grain. This way you get both lean and fatty meat. Make your slices about ¼ inch thick.

Continue cooking until the internal temperature is 200°F and the meat is tender enough to pierce with a gloved finger or wooden spoon handle, an additional 1 to 2 hours, or as needed. (You'll need to unwrap the brisket to check it.)

5. Transfer the wrapped brisket to an insulated cooler and let rest for 1 to 2 hours. Unwrap the brisket and transfer to a cutting board. (Discard the bacon slices if using.) Pour any juices that accumulated in the butcher paper into a bowl.

6. To serve, trim off any large lumps of fat and slice the brisket across the grain into ¼-inch-thick slices (or as desired). Spoon the juices over the slices. Barbecue sauce? Not necessary, but serve on the side if you want it.

Variations

Smoking a full packer brisket:
A whole brisket—sometimes called a packer brisket—weighs 14 to 18 pounds and includes the lean **flat** (also referred to as first-cut brisket) that terminates in a triangular point, and a fatty muscle on top called the **point** or the **deckle**.

Trim the brisket leaving a ½-inch-thick cap of fat on top. There's a hard ball of fat between the deckle and the flat on one side of the brisket: Cut out as much as possible without separating the two. Brush the brisket with equal parts mustard and pickle juice, if desired, then season with salt and pepper as described on page 67.

Smoke the brisket until the internal temperature reaches 175°F, 10 to 14 hours. Tightly wrap the brisket in butcher paper and continue smoking until the internal temperature reaches 200°F and the meat is tender enough to pierce with a gloved finger or wooden spoon handle—another 2 to 4 hours, a total of 12 to 18 hours, depending on the size of the brisket. Let the wrapped brisket rest in the cooler for 1½ to 2 hours before slicing (see sidebar).

Smoking a small, lean center-cut brisket flat: Perhaps the only brisket your supermarket sells is a center-cut section of the flat weighing 3 to 5 pounds, from which some misguided butcher has trimmed off all the fat. (It happens.) Don't despair: You can turn it into a respectable smoked brisket, too. Season it as described on page 66 and place it in a disposable aluminum foil pan, covering the top with strips of bacon. Smoke as described on page 66. After 4½ hours, cover the pan with aluminum foil, crimping it to the edges, poke small holes in the top to release the steam, and return it to the smoker. The total cooking time will be 6 to 7 hours. There is no need to wrap the brisket in butcher paper, but you should rest it in a cooler for 1 hour before carving and serving. (There won't be much flavor left in the bacon—discard it.)

THE TEN STEPS TO BRISKET NIRVANA

Aaron Franklin (Franklin Barbecue, Austin, Texas), Hugh Mangum (Mighty Quinn's Barbeque, New York and New Jersey), and Billy Durney (Hometown Bar-B-Que, Brooklyn, New York) run three of the best barbecue joints in North America. When they talk brisket, it's worth listening.

1. The quality of the meat matters and so does the source. When I interviewed pit masters for my book *BBQ USA* in the early 2000s, everyone spoke of the pit, wood, and seasonings. No one mentioned the actual meat. Modern masters insist on natural or organic beef, ideally from farms in their region. The new brisket bragging rights include terms like *humanely raised*, *hormone-free*, and *grass-fed*. In other words, where your meat comes from and how it's raised matter as much as how you smoke it.

2. Keep the seasonings simple. Forget arcane rubs. Aaron Franklin seasons with only two ingredients: salt and cracked black pepper. Hugh Mangum uses three: salt, pepper, and paprika.

3. Burn wood only, but go easy on the smoke. The ultimate fuel for brisket is wood. But make sure your brisket tastes like meat, not like smoke. "I like to say our meat is 'kissed' by smoke," Mangum says, "not overwhelmed by it."

4. Keep the air flowing. "Keep plenty of air flowing through the pit at all times," says Franklin. "That's the secret to a good, clean fire." For even heat circulation, leave at least 3 inches between briskets. This is especially important when using a home smoker.

5. Keep it moist. A succulent brisket demands a moist pit. Mangum keeps 10 gallons of meat drippings from a previous smoke session in the drip pan during the entire length of the cooking process. At home, place a water pan in the smoker.

6. Slow it down. Here's one point on which the upstarts and old masters agree: Cook your brisket low and slow. It takes a low temperature (225° to 250°F) and long cooking time to melt the collagen, fat, and other tough connective tissue.

7. Don't cook to temperature. Tradition holds that the best way to cook a brisket to the proper doneness is to use an instant-read thermometer to reach a target temperature of 200° to 205°F. But Billy Durney works more by look and touch. "A properly cooked brisket will jiggle when you shake it. Think Jell-O comprised of animal protein and beef fat." With practice, you'll learn the right feel, but it's always good to double check with a thermometer.

8. Wrap it up. For the last couple of hours of cooking, Franklin wraps his briskets in butcher paper. "The paper is porous enough to let the meat 'breathe,' unlike aluminum foil, which produces a 'pot-roasty' consistency," he says. Once the paper becomes soaked through with brisket fat, it seals in the juices. A side benefit: It also makes it easier to move the briskets around from pit to warming box to cutting board. At Mighty Quinn's, the moment the briskets come off the pit, Mangum and crew swaddle them in plastic wrap. And at both establishments, the brisket is rewrapped after each slicing to keep the meat moist.

9. Give it a rest. Durney smokes his brisket for 18 hours, but the meat isn't ready to serve until it rests in an Alto-Shaam (a professional warming oven) for 4 hours. "This allows the juices to be reabsorbed into the meat," he says. Don't have an Alto-Shaam? An insulated cooler works great—and once you've rested the brisket, use the cooler to chill the beer.

10. It's not about the sauce. All three men serve their brisket unsauced. They hope you'll try it by itself before you reach for barbecue sauce. Amen.

TO WRAP OR NOT TO WRAP

Much ink and ire have been spilled on whether, when, and how to wrap meats—especially brisket—during smoking. Partisans argue that wrapping seals in moisture and steam that helps break down tough meat fibers. Opponents counter that wrapping (particularly in aluminum foil) gives meats a stewed, pot roast-like consistency that's unworthy of being called great barbecue.

Who's right?

Wrapping has some pretty powerful proponents:

- Wayne Mueller at the celebrated Louie Mueller Barbecue in Taylor, Texas, double-wraps briskets, first in plastic, then in paper.

- At Snow's BBQ in Lexington, Texas, pit master Tootsie Tomanetz wraps briskets in aluminum foil two-thirds of the way through the smoking process and finishes cooking them in the foil.

Critics of this technique deprecatingly call it the Texas crutch, and yet Snow's ranks consistently among the top-rated barbecue joints in the Lone Star State. For many years I used the Texas crutch, wrapping my briskets halfway through smoking. My briskets—always moist and tender—drew raves. And yet, in retrospect, they *did* have a pot-roasty texture and taste that fell short of the very best Texas pit-roasted briskets.

Which brings me to another aluminum-foil wrapping technique used for ribs: the **3-2-1 method**, in which you smoke ribs 3 hours unwrapped, then 2 hours wrapped in foil, then finished for 1 hour unwrapped. Yes, it produces ribs that are exceedingly moist and tender. But they, too, have a stewed quality that deters me, at least, from wrapping in foil.

Since then, I've come to use what I call the **butcher paper method**: wrapping the brisket in unlined butcher paper for the last 2 hours of cooking, then resting the meat for 1 to 2 hours (still wrapped) in an insulated cooler. Butcher paper has two advantages over foil: Being porous, it "breathes," releasing steam that would otherwise make the bark (crust) soggy. And being absorbent, it pulls out and absorbs excess fat. Indeed, the more it becomes saturated with fat, the more it seals in moisture.

RAICHLEN'S BOTTOM LINE:

- Seal brisket in unlined butcher paper the last 2 hours of cooking and while resting.

- Seal ribs in unlined butcher paper if you are resting them. (I usually serve them hot off the smoker, so I skip this step.)

- If you've always wrapped your meat in foil or plastic wrap and you're pleased with the results, carry on. You, too, are doing it right.

NOTE: The butcher paper must be unlined. Do not use the plastic-lined butcher paper used in a growing number of supermarket meat departments. It will not breathe or absorb fat.

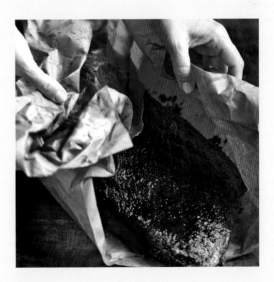

HOME-SMOKED PASTRAMI

YIELD: Serves 8 to 10, with leftovers

METHOD: Hot-smoking

PREP TIME: 30 minutes

BRINING TIME: 12 days

SMOKING TIME: 8 to 10 hours

RESTING TIME: 1 to 2 hours

FUEL: Fette Sau uses a mixture of apple, cherry, and oak, but any hardwood will do. You'll need enough wood for 10 hours of smoking (see chart on page 6).

GEAR: Two jumbo resealable plastic bags; an aluminum foil pan (optional); instant-read thermometer; unlined butcher paper (without a plastic coating); an insulated cooler

SHOP: Organic, grass-fed, or locally raised beef brisket. Pink curing salt contains salt and sodium nitrite (page 17); buy it at a good meat market or order it online from Amazon. The traditional cut of beef for pastrami is navel—a belly cut with clearly visible striations of meat and fat. If you wish to try it, special-order beef navel from your butcher, then cure, rub, and smoke it as you would brisket. I call for leaner, tenderer brisket here.

The best pastrami I ever tasted? It wasn't at a landmark New York deli. It wasn't even in Manhattan—it was at Fette Sau, a barbecue joint in Williamsburg, Brooklyn. Imagine the perfect ratio of beef to spice to wood smoke—meaty enough to sink your teeth into yet fatty enough to melt on your tongue. Spicy, as all good pastrami is spicy, yet focused on the two classic seasonings: coriander seed and black peppercorns. Tender? You could cut it with the side of a fork.

These virtues do not come easily. You need to start with superior beef—in this case, hormone- and antibiotic-free Black Angus, raised on a small farm in New Jersey. You brine it with onions and garlic for almost two weeks, then smoke it for 14 hours. Here's the *Project Smoke* version. Rye bread optional.

INGREDIENTS

FOR THE BRISKET AND BRINE

1 beef brisket flat with plenty of fat intact (6 to 8 pounds)

2 quarts hot water and 2 quarts ice water

⅔ cup coarse salt (sea or kosher)

2 teaspoons pink curing salt (Prague Powder No. 1 or Insta Cure No. 1)

1 small onion, peeled and cut in half widthwise

8 cloves garlic, peeled and cut in half widthwise

FOR THE SPICE RUB

½ cup cracked black peppercorns

½ cup coriander seeds

2 tablespoons mustard seeds

1 tablespoon light or dark brown sugar

1 teaspoon ground ginger

Beer (optional)

1. Trim the brisket, leaving a fat cap on top at least ¼ inch thick.

2. Make the brine: Place the hot water, coarse salt, and pink salt in a large bowl or plastic tub and whisk until the salt crystals are dissolved. Stir in the ice water, onion, and garlic. Place the brisket in a jumbo heavy-duty resealable plastic bag. Add the brine and seal the top, squeezing out the air as you go. Place in a second bag and seal, then place in an aluminum foil pan or roasting pan to contain any leaks. Brine the brisket in the refrigerator for 12 days, turning it over once a day.

FROM BASTURMA TO PASTRAMI

America is experiencing a pastrami renaissance with soulfully cured, assertively spiced smoked meat turning up at top barbecue joints across the country, darkly crusted with crushed coriander seed and fiery with black pepper. Meat so moist it squirts when you cut into it and so flavorful, you don't *really* need mustard, pickles, or rye bread.

And if you think the pastrami sun rises and sets on beef belly, well, check out the "porkstrami" at Tails & Trotters, a pork-centric butcher and deli in Portland, Oregon, or the lamb pastrami at The Restaurant at Wente Vineyards in Livermore, California. And while you're at it, dig your fork into New York chef David Burke's pastrami salmon or the electrifying kung pao pastrami stir-fry at Mission Chinese Food in San Francisco and New York.

The truth is, pastrami is less a single dish than a process. I wouldn't be surprised if someone, somewhere, is about to apply it to tofu. But I get ahead of myself, because I really wanted to begin this story not in New York or even the United States, but at the Spice Bazaar in Istanbul. It was here, on my *Barbecue! Bible* research tour, that I came across arm-long strips of meat caked with orange-colored aromatic spices hanging unrefrigerated from the shop rafters. I had eaten versions of this cured meat—usually beef, once camel—throughout the Middle and Near East, where it goes by the name of *basturma* (sometimes written *pasturma*). It was cured and dried, not smoked, and the spicing differed dramatically from the pepper-coriander rub on American pastrami. But the two—etymologically and gastronomically—shared a common ancestor.

It has been hypothesized that basturma originated with an Anatolian air-dried beef made since Byzantine times. Today, that beef would be salted, dried, pressed, then salved with a pungent paste of garlic, cumin, fenugreek, and hot paprika. This makes it food safe for extended periods at room temperature and salty and spicy enough to enjoy sliced to accompany raki (a Turkish anise-flavored aperitif), scrambled with eggs, or crisped over a charcoal grill. Beef is the preferred meat today, but you also find basturma made with lamb, goat, water buffalo, or the aforementioned camel.

So how did Ottoman basturma become Jewish pastrami, and how did it migrate from Istanbul to New York's Lower East Side? And why has a new generation of American pit masters embraced this classic deli meat with such gusto? The most likely transfer agents were Jewish immigrants from Romania who brought pastrami to New York in the late 1800s. In the old country they made it with the budget meat of that time—goose. Even cheaper in the New World was beef navel (a fatty cut from the steer's underbelly), which became the meat of choice. Somewhere along the line, the name acquired an *i* at the end—perhaps to rhyme with other popular immigrant foods like salami or spaghetti.

Traditional deli pastrami involves a four-step process that includes brining (like corned beef), a rub (like Texas barbecue), and smoking (but less heavily than Southern or Texas barbecue). The fourth step is steaming, which further softens the meat and keeps it warm and moist throughout the day for serving. Modern barbecue joints achieve a similar texture by wrapping the pastrami in butcher paper or aluminum foil after smoking and resting it in an insulated cooler.

3. Make the rub: Place the peppercorns, coriander seeds, mustard seeds, brown sugar, and ginger in a spice mill and grind to a coarse powder, running the machine in short bursts, working in batches as needed. The final rub should feel gritty like coarse sand.

4. Drain the brisket, rinse well under cold running water, and blot dry with paper towels. Place it on a rimmed baking sheet or in a roasting pan and thickly crust it on all sides with the rub.

5. Set up your smoker following the manufacturer's instructions and preheat to 225° to 250°F. If your smoker has a water pan, fill it with water or beer to a depth of 3 inches. If it doesn't have a water pan, fill an aluminum foil pan with water or beer to a depth of 3 inches and place it below the rack on which you'll be smoking the ribs. (Note: You don't need to do this on a ceramic cooker.) Add the wood as specified by the manufacturer.

6. Place the pastrami fat side up in the smoker, directly on the rack. Smoke the pastrami until crusty and black on the outside and cooked to 175°F on an instant-read thermometer, 7 to 8 hours.

7. Wrap the pastrami in butcher paper. Return it to the smoker. Continue cooking until the internal temperature is 200°F and the meat is tender enough to pierce with a gloved finger or wooden spoon handle, an additional 1 to 2 hours, or as needed. (You'll need to unwrap it to check it.)

8. Transfer the wrapped pastrami to an insulated cooler and let rest for 1 to 2 hours. Unwrap and slice crosswise (across the grain) for serving.

WHAT ELSE: When serving the pastrami hot, cut it into ¼-inch-thick slices. When serving cold, slice it paper-thin—preferably on a meat slicer. You don't really need a sauce or condiment, but I wouldn't say no to horseradish mustard.

SMOKED BEEF TENDERLOIN

Need a wow dish in a hurry? Smoke a whole beef tenderloin. Yes, it's expensive, but it's quick and easy to prepare, and it brings most beef addicts to immediate intoxication.

But you can't smoke beef tenderloin the way you would brisket or other tough, fatty cuts. Tenderloin demands a sizzling crust with a blood-rare or medium-rare center. Enter the so-called reverse-sear method (see box, page 83), where you partially cook the beef by slow-smoking at a low temperature, then finish it over a screaming hot fire. Ideally you'll have a dual function smoker (that both smokes and grills), but I've included workarounds if you don't.

YIELD: Serves 8

METHOD: Reverse sear (smoking, then grilling)

PREP TIME: 5 minutes

SMOKING TIME: 45 to 60 minutes

GRILLING TIME: 6 to 10 minutes

INGREDIENTS

1 whole beef tenderloin, trimmed
(about 4 pounds)

Smoked salt (see page 204) or
coarse salt (sea or kosher)

Cracked or freshly ground black pepper

1 to 2 tablespoons extra virgin olive oil,
plus extra for basting

Vegetable oli, for oiling the rack

Three Hots Horseradish Sauce
(recipe follows), for serving

1. Set up your smoker following the manufacturer's instructions and preheat to 225° to 250°F. Add the wood as specified by the manufacturer.

2. Place the tenderloin on a rimmed baking sheet and season very generously on all sides with salt and pepper. Drizzle the tenderloin on all sides with olive oil, rubbing it into the meat.

3. Place the tenderloin in the smoker and insert the probe of your remote thermometer (if using) through the thick end of the tenderloin into the center. (Alternatively, check for doneness toward the end of cooking, using an instant-read thermometer.) Smoke the tenderloin until the internal temperature is about 110°F, 45 to 60 minutes. Transfer it to a platter and let it rest for 10 minutes.

4. Meanwhile, set up your grill for direct grilling and preheat to high. Brush and oil the grill grate. If you happen to be smoking on a charcoal grill, rake the coals into a mound, after the smoking is completed, adding fresh coals as needed, to build a hot fire.

5. Transfer the tenderloin to the grill, with the thermometer probe still attached. Direct grill, rotating it like a log, until all sides are crusty, dark, and sizzling and the internal temperature in the thickest part of the tenderloin reaches 120° to 125°F (for rare beef) or 130° to 135°F (for medium-rare), 6 to 10 minutes. Brush the tenderloin with additional olive oil as it grills, and if you like, give it a quarter turn on each side halfway through grilling to lay on a crosshatch of grill marks.

6. Place the tenderloin on a cutting board and remove the strings. Cut the meat crosswise into ¼- to ½-inch-thick slices. It just may be the best beef tenderloin you'll ever taste.

NOTE: Upright barrel smokers like the Pit Barrel cooker (see page 263) work great for smoking beef tenderloin. Hang the tenderloin head end up from the meat hook. You can smoke and cook it simultaneously—there's no need for separate smoking and grilling. (The PBC runs at just shy of 300°F.) Cooking time will be 45 minutes to 1 hour. Use a kamado-style cooker the same way.

FUEL: I like cherry, but any hardwood will do. You'll need enough for 1 hour of smoking (see chart on page 6).

GEAR: A remote digital thermometer or instant-read thermometer (see page 14) so you can monitor the internal temperature during smoking and grilling

SHOP: As always, use grass-fed or organic beef when possible. Ask your butcher to trim it for you. (And tell him you want to keep the "chain"—a slender ropey muscle that runs the length of the tenderloin—for separate use. It makes great shish kebab.) A beef tenderloin is comprised of three parts: head, center, and tail. Tie the head into a compact cylinder with butcher's string. The slender tail cooks faster than the rest of the tenderloin, so unless you like that section well done, fold under the last 5 inches and tie this section to the center.

WHAT ELSE: Here's how to choreograph the smoking and cooking of the tenderloin. If working on a charcoal kettle grill, set it up for indirect grilling (use a half chimney of coals plus wood chunks or chips) to smoke it. If working on an offset smoker, smoke the tenderloin in the smoke chamber, then finish it on a grate over the firebox (if your smoker has one) or on a hot charcoal or gas grill.

THREE HOTS HORSERADISH SAUCE

YIELD: Makes 2½ cups

This cream sauce owes its firepower to horseradish, mustard, and hot sauce. The whipped cream gives the sauce an airy consistency—you'll love the way it melts into the hot meat.

INGREDIENTS

½ cup mayonnaise, preferably Hellmann's or Best Foods

½ cup prepared undrained horseradish or finely and freshly grated horseradish root

1 tablespoon Dijon mustard

1 teaspoon hot sauce (use your favorite; optional)

1 cup heavy (whipping) cream

Coarse salt (sea or kosher) and freshly ground black pepper

1. Place the mayonnaise, horseradish, mustard, and hot sauce, if using, in a large bowl and whisk to mix.

2. Beat the cream to soft peaks in a chilled metal bowl using a stand or handheld mixer. Fold the whipped cream into the mayonnaise mixture. Gently stir in salt and pepper to taste. You can make and refrigerate the sauce up to an hour before serving.

SMOKED PRIME RIB

YIELD: Serves 6 very hungry people, with leftovers, or 8 people with normal appetites

METHOD: Hot-smoking

PREP TIME: 10 minutes

SMOKING TIME: 2 hours for rare; 2¼ to 3 hours for medium-rare

Prime rib may be the most expensive hunk of meat you'll ever buy. The sight awes: smoke-bronzed bones rising from a pepper-flecked crust, with the meat inside sufficiently sanguine to thrill any carnivore. Prime rib is highfalutin enough to impress the Downton Abbey crowd (untold generations of Englishmen have called it roast beef), but primitive enough to give you a caveman rush from gnawing the meat off the rib bones. (One of life's injustices: The meat on a prime rib serves twice as many people as there are bones.) So you may be surprised to learn that preparing a prime rib is monastically simple—especially when you cook it in a smoker. The low, steady heat—and use of a remote thermometer—virtually eliminate the risk of overcooking.

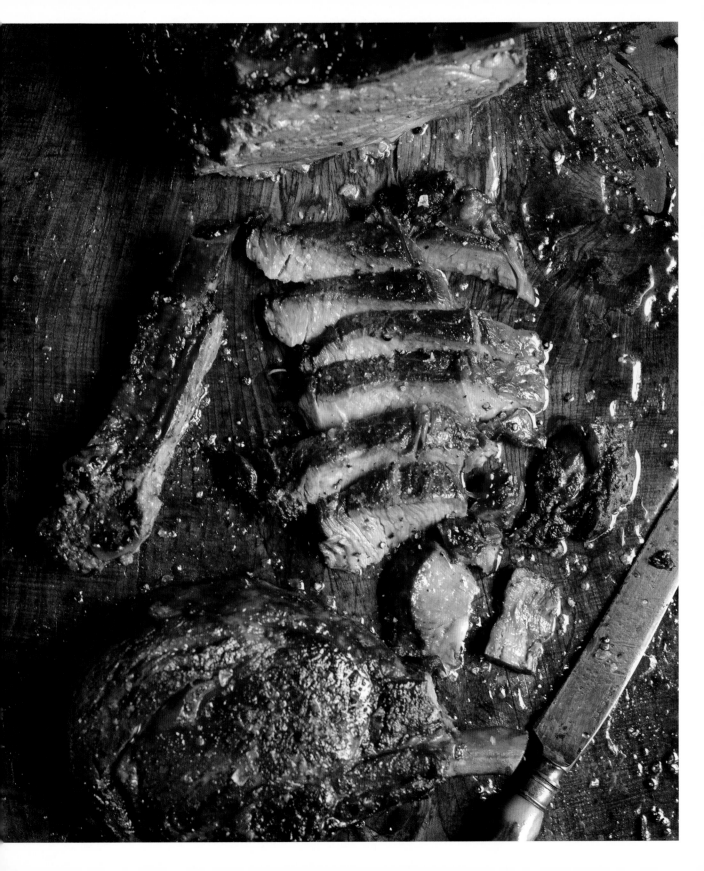

FUEL: I like a blend of oak and apple, but any hardwood will do. You'll need enough for 3 hours of smoking (see chart on page 6).

GEAR: A remote digital thermometer so you can monitor the internal temperature during smoking; a cutting board with a groove and well to catch the juices

SHOP: Prime rib (the cut) comes in two grades: prime and choice beef. (Confused yet?) Choice beef gives you a delectable roast. True prime beef (it comes from an exceptionally well-marbled steer) will probably leave you speechless. This recipe calls for a three-bone roast weighing about 6 pounds—enough to serve 6 to 8. (A whole prime rib has seven bones and tips the scale at around 20 pounds).

WHAT ELSE: Ask your butcher to cut your section of prime rib from the loin end; this gives you more meat, less sinew and fat. Also ask him or her to french the ribs—that is, scrape the meat and fat from the last 2 inches of the bones. Make sure the butcher saves the fat—rendered, it comes in handy for making Yorkshire pudding. Also—and this is *very* important—ask your butcher to leave at least a ¼-inch-thick cap of fat on the meaty part of the roast. This keeps the meat moist and gives you a spectacular crust. With smoked prime rib, I like to serve Smoked Jus and/or Three Hots Horseradish Sauce (page 78).

INGREDIENTS

1 loin end 3-bone prime rib (about 6 pounds)

Coarse salt (sea or kosher; even better if it's smoked salt—see page 204)

Cracked or coarsely and freshly ground black pepper

Onion powder and/or garlic powder (optional)

2 tablespoons extra virgin olive oil, plus extra as needed

Smoked Jus (recipe follows; optional)

Three Hots Horseradish Sauce (page 78)

1. Generously—and I mean *generously*—season the roast on all sides with salt and pepper, and with onion and/or garlic powder, if using. Rub the seasonings into the meat. Drizzle the olive oil over the roast and rub it into the meat as well.

2. Set up your smoker following the manufacturer's instructions and preheat to 250°F. You want to be on the low and slow scale. Add the wood as specified by the manufacturer.

3. Place the roast in the smoker directly on the rack, bone and fat side up, inserting the probe of your thermometer through the wider portion of the meat.

4. Smoke the roast until the exterior is sizzling and darkly browned and the internal temperature of the meat is about 120° to 125°F for rare (about 2 hours), 130° to 135°F for medium-rare (2¼ to 3 hours). Remember, the roast will continue to cook as it rests.

5. Transfer the roast to a cutting board with a groove and a well to catch the juices (or place the cutting board on a rimmed baking sheet) and *loosely* drape a sheet of aluminum foil over the meat. (Do not bunch the foil around the roast or you'll steam it and make the crust soggy.) Let rest for 10 to 15 minutes. This "relaxes" the meat, making it juicier.

6. To carve the prime rib, slide a long sharp knife down the inside of the rib bones to loosen the cylindrical meat part of the roast. Lift away the bones and cut the meat crosswise into ¼-inch-thick slices, or however thick you like. Then slice the ribs into individual bones. (Return them to the hot grill if a crustier texture is desired.) Good luck on figuring out who gets them.

SMOKED JUS

YIELD: Makes about 3 cups

Jus is the French word for meat juices. Start with high-quality low-sodium stock, preferably homemade.

INGREDIENTS

3 cups beef or chicken stock

Meat juices accumulated on the cutting board

Place the stock in an aluminum foil drip pan next to the prime rib in the smoker. Smoke the stock while you smoke the prime rib. (Added advantage—the steaming stock keeps the prime rib moist.) Strain the stock into a serving bowl and keep warm until serving. Pour any meat juices that accumulate on the cutting board into the stock and serve in a bowl for ladling over the meat.

SMOKED TRI-TIP

If you live in Southern California, you've probably grilled tri-tip. If you live east of the Mississippi, you may never have seen this cut in your local supermarket. An elongated triangle-shaped muscle, tri-tip comes from the bottom end of the sirloin primal and weighs 1½ to 2½ pounds. Tradition calls for direct grilling tri-tip over an oak log fire, but I like to use the reverse searing method (see box, page 83). You slow-smoke the tri-tip to an internal temperature of about 110°F, then let it rest. Just before serving, you sear it over a hot fire to an internal temperature of about 125°F. This gives you rare smoky beef that slices like brisket but retains the sanguine succulence of steak. It also gives you great flexibility in the cooking time. Tri-tip belongs in your repertoire—even if you live on the East Coast.

YIELD: Serves 4 to 6

METHOD: Reverse searing

PREP TIME: 10 minutes

SMOKING TIME: 1 hour

GRILLING TIME: 4 to 6 minutes

FUEL: The traditional wood in tri-tip's birthplace, Santa Maria, California, is red oak. You can buy California red oak smoking chips online from Susie Q's (susieqbrand.com). Any hardwood will work—you'll need enough for 1 hour of smoking (see chart on page 6).

GEAR: A remote digital thermometer or instant-read thermometer (see page 14) so you can monitor the internal temperature during smoking and grilling

SHOP: Tri-tip is widely available in West Coast supermarkets; here in Miami, I've begun to see it at Fresh Market. One good mail order source is Snake River Farms (snakeriverfarms.com).

WHAT ELSE: If you have a smoker with grilling capabilities, such as a charcoal grill, ceramic cooker, pellet grill, or offset barrel smoker with a grate over the firebox, you can cook this recipe on a single device. Otherwise, you'll need to smoke the tri-tip low and slow, then finish it on a charcoal or gas grill. Tradition calls for serving tri-tip with grilled garlic bread, salsa, and pinquito beans.

INGREDIENTS

2 teaspoons coarse salt (sea or kosher)

2 teaspoons freshly ground black pepper

2 teaspoons garlic powder

2 teaspoons dried rosemary, crumbled between your fingers

1 teaspoon dried oregano

1 large beef tri-tip (2 to 2½ pounds)

Vegetable, for oiling the grate

Extra virgin olive oil

1. Set up your smoker following the manufacturer's instructions and preheat to 225° to 250°F. Add the wood as specified by the manufacturer.

2. Place the salt, pepper, garlic powder, rosemary, and oregano in a small bowl and stir to mix. Place the tri-tip in a baking dish and sprinkle the rub on all sides, rubbing it into the meat with your fingertips. Insert the thermometer probe through one end of the tri-tip, deep into the center.

3. Remove the tri-tip from the baking dish and place it in the smoker as far away from the fire as possible. Smoke the tri-tip until the internal temperature reaches 110°F, 45 minutes to 1 hour, or as needed.

4. Transfer the tri-tip to a wire rack set over a rimmed baking sheet and let rest, loosely tented with aluminum foil, for at least 10 minutes or up to a half hour.

5. Meanwhile, set up your smoker or grill for direct grilling and heat to high. Brush and oil the grill grate.

6. Lightly brush or drizzle the tri-tip on both sides with olive oil. Place it on the grate over the fire and direct grill until the top and bottom are sizzling and darkly crusted and the internal temperature on an instant-read thermometer inserted into one of the ends deep into the middle reaches 120° to 125°F for rare to 130° to 135°F for medium-rare (2 to 3 minutes per side, 4 to 6 minutes in all), turning with tongs. If you like, give the tri-tip a quarter turn on each side halfway through searing to lay on a crosshatch of grill marks.

7. Serve the tri-tip hot off the grill, very thinly sliced across the grain. (There's no need to let it rest—you did so after smoking.)

REVERSE SEARING

When I started smoking meat twenty-five years ago, no one had heard of reverse searing. Today, you can hardly browse a barbecue website without being urged to try it. The process turns the traditional method of cooking a steak or roast—a hot sear followed by a slow roast—on its head. You start by smoking the meat low and slow to an internal temperature of 100° to 110°F, *then* you char it over a hot fire to raise it to the desired doneness, applying the smoky caramelized crust at the end.

Reverse searing has several advantages: Better heat control, as you can cook the steak to a consistent degree of doneness. The meat cooks more evenly, with no more "bull's-eye" effect—the dark crust with a gray-brown ring of meat just beneath it, fading to pink, and finally the reddish-blue core characteristic of a really thick steak grilled over a really hot fire. And because you rest the meat between the low-heat smoking and high-heat searing, you can serve it hot off the grill. Best of all, it enables you to smoke the one cut of beef most people would never dare cook in a smoker: steak.

So why not use it for all steaks all the time? The truth is that most steaks (especially if they're thinner than 1½ inches) taste better and have better texture cooked over a hot fire. There's an energy—dare I even say violence?—in exposing raw red meat to blazing embers, and that energy comes through in the taste. Perhaps that's why all the great steak cultures on Planet Barbecue—Italy, Spain, and Argentina, for example—grill over fires of hot wood embers.

In this book you'll find recipes for reverse-seared strip steak, tri-tip, and beef tenderloin. The dark crust, the uniformly and perfectly cooked center, and the unexpected smoke flavor will make any carnivore's heart beat faster.

CHERRY-SMOKED STRIP STEAK

Steak is one cut of beef you don't normally smoke. It requires a hot fire to sear the exterior while keeping the inside sanguine and juicy. But there is a way to smoke a steak low and slow, and if you're fortunate enough to start with a monster-thick strip or rib eye, this is one of the best methods I know for bringing its interior to a luscious 135°F medium-rare while achieving a sizzling dark crust. You guessed it—reverse searing (you slow-smoke the steak first to cook it through, then rest it, then finally sizzle it over a hot fire to sear the crust—see box, above).

YIELD: Makes 1 really thick steak, enough to serve 2 or 3

METHOD: Reverse searing

PREP TIME: 5 minutes

SMOKING TIME: 45 minutes to 1 hour

GRILLING TIME: 4 to 6 minutes

INGREDIENTS

1 thick (2- to 3-inch) boneless strip steak, rib steak, or sirloin (1½ to 1¾ pounds)

Coarse salt (sea or kosher) and cracked or freshly ground black pepper

Extra virgin olive oil

1. If using a charcoal kettle grill, light 10 to 12 pieces of charcoal (preferably natural lump charcoal) in a chimney starter. When ready, place the charcoal in one side basket or on one side of the bottom grate. Adjust the top and bottom vents to heat your grill to 225° to 250°F.

2. Meanwhile, very generously season the steak on the top, bottom, and sides with salt and pepper. Insert the thermometer probe through the side of the steak, deep into the center.

3. Add the wood to the coals. Place the steak on the grate as far away from the fire as possible. Cover the grill and smoke the steak until the internal temperature reaches 110°F. This will take 45 minutes to 1 hour.

4. Remove the steak from the grill and let rest for 10 minutes.

5. Meanwhile, add 10 to 15 fresh coals to the bed of embers and build a hot fire in your grill, readjusting the vents as needed.

6. Lightly brush or drizzle the steak on both sides with olive oil. Place it on the grate over the fire and direct grill until the top and bottom are sizzling and darkly crusted and the internal temperature on an instant-read thermometer reaches 120° to 125°F for rare to 130° to 135°F for medium-rare (2 to 3 minutes per side, 4 to 6 minutes in all), turning with tongs. If you like, give the steak a quarter turn on each side halfway through searing to lay on a crosshatch of grill marks. For really thick steaks, grill the edges, too.

7. Serve hot off the grill. I like to cut the steak on the diagonal into ¼-inch-thick slices. I wouldn't say no to an additional drizzle of extra virgin olive oil.

FUEL: I like cherry for smoking this steak, but any hardwood will do. You'll need enough hardwood chunks or chips (soaked and drained if using the latter) for 1 hour of smoking (see chart on page 6).

GEAR: A remote digital thermometer or instant-read thermometer (see page 14) so you can monitor the internal temperature during smoking and grilling

SHOP: Reverse searing works best with really thick steaks: 2- to 3-inch-thick strip steak, porterhouse, rib steak, and sirloin steak

WHAT ELSE: This steak works best on a charcoal-burning grill or smoker, like a kettle grill or offset barrel smoker with a grill grate over the firebox. That enables you to smoke low and slow, then sear over a hot fire. Otherwise, you'll need to start the steak in a smoker and finish it on a grill (follow the instructions for the Smoked Tri-Tip on page 81).

PORK

Think of your favorite smoked foods: ham, bacon (belly and Canadian), pork shoulder, ribs (spares and baby backs), pork belly, chops, and tenderloin. All come from the pig. Wood smoke transforms pork's abundant fat and sweet, rich meat in ways nothing short of wondrous—and that's whether you smoke an upper cut like chops or loins or a lower cut like bacon or ham hocks. In this chapter, you'll learn how to rub and smoke pork shoulders and ribs; how to cure and smoke bacon and ham; and how to smoke cuts you normally grill like monster-thick rib chops. Hog plus spice plus smoke equals happiness. Eat high—and low—off the hog. Do it now.

PORK SHOULDER
SMOKED, PULLED, AND VINEGAR-SAUCED IN THE STYLE OF NORTH CAROLINA

YIELD: Serves 8 to 10

METHOD: Hot-smoking

PREP TIME: 20 minutes, plus 1 to 4 hours (or more) if soaking the wood

SMOKING TIME: 6 to 8 hours

RESTING TIME: 20 minutes

FUEL: Oak and hickory logs or equal parts oak and hickory chunks or chips—enough for 8 hours of smoking (see chart on page 6)

GEAR: Instant-read thermometer or remote digital thermometer; a meat cleaver or claws, or insulated rubber gloves, for pulling and shredding the pork

SHOP: Buy a cut from the upper shoulder, aka Boston butt, preferably from a heritage breed like Berkshire or Duroc.

New to the craft of smoking? Start with pork shoulder. Sheathed in and veined with fat, it stays moist—even with prolonged smoking. And unlike a tough muscle like beef brisket (page 66), pork shoulder remains tender no matter how you cook it. It's mercifully hard to mess up. To the moist, tender meat add crusty, smoky bark and you'll understand how pulled pork went from a regional speciality (of the Carolinas and Tennessee) to an American—and dare I say global—icon. You don't even need to worry about its appearance (although a whole one is gorgeous), as most pork shoulder winds up served chopped, shredded, or thinly sliced. Pulled pork is as close to set-it-and-forget-it barbecue as anything you'll find in this book, and it's infinitely customizable. (For example, try marinating it in the Jamaican Jerk Seasoning on page 157). Don't be intimidated by the length of this recipe; it's really just a series of simple steps.

INGREDIENTS

FOR SOAKING THE WOOD (OPTIONAL)

1 onion, cut in quarters

2 cloves garlic, smashed with the side of a chef's knife or cleaver

1 or 2 cups cider vinegar

Water

FOR THE RUB

4 teaspoons coarse salt (sea or kosher)

4 teaspoons freshly ground black pepper

2 teaspoons garlic powder

2 teaspoons onion powder

1 teaspoon cayenne pepper or hot paprika

1 Boston butt (upper section of the pork shoulder—5 to 7 pounds)

Carolina Vinegar Sauce (recipe follows)

FOR SERVING

3 tablespoons butter, melted

12 sesame seed buns, split

Smoked Slaw (page 202), Smoked Potato Salad Slaw (page 206), or Creamed Smoked Corn (page 213), optional

1. If using logs, place them in a watertight container just large enough to hold them. Add the onion, garlic, 2 cups of vinegar, and water to cover.

WHAT ELSE: If you start with good pork, season it like you mean it, and smoke it with hardwoods. You don't really need more flavor. But, some people—especially on the competition barbecue circuit—like to inject shoulders with melted butter, stock, and/or cider or bourbon. Note that soaking the wood in vinegar is optional, but definitely separates you from the crowd.

Soak the wood for at least 4 hours or as long as overnight. If using wood chunks or chips, place in a large bowl or bucket with the onion, garlic, and 1 cup of vinegar. Add water to cover and soak for at least 1 hour.

2. Make the rub: Place the salt, black pepper, garlic powder, onion powder, and cayenne in a small bowl and mix well. Sprinkle the rub on the pork shoulder on all sides, rubbing it into the meat with your fingers.

3. Set up your smoker following the manufacturer's instructions and preheat to 225° to 250°F. Drain the wood if you soaked it. Add the wood as specified by the manufacturer.

4. Place the pork shoulder in the smoker, fat side up. Smoke the pork shoulder until darkly browned and crusty on the outside and the meat reaches an internal temperature of 200°F. (Check it with an instant-read thermometer or remote digital thermometer.) Another test for doneness is to pull on the ends of any protruding bones—they should come out easily. The total smoking time will be 6 to 8 hours. Replenish the wood as needed.

ANATOMY OF A RIB (AND OTHER SMOKED FOODS)

Great smoked foods are built on layers of flavor. Each layer has its own texture, aroma, and taste. Consider that archetype of great barbecue, the baby back rib.

Bark: The dark brown crust consisting of smoke, spice, fat, and caramelized (browned) meat. This is the first thing you taste when you bite into a rib, brisket, or pork shoulder. Good bark will be smoky, salty, spicy, and firmer than the rest of the meat (ideally, somewhat crisp).

Smoke ring: The subcutaneous layer of pinkish-red found just below the crust—the result of a naturally occurring chemical reaction between the carbon monoxide and nitrogen dioxide in the smoke and myoglobin in the muscle tissue of the meats. The smoke ring is a visual sign that that the smoke flavor has penetrated into the meat.

Meat: The meat below the smoke ring will be grayish in color for uncured meats (like brisket and pork shoulder) and crimson-pink in color (for meats cured with sodium nitrate, like ham and pastrami). The meat should be tender, but not soft or mushy—it should have just a little chew to it. Think al dente for ribs.

Fat: Many smoked and barbecued foods start with abundantly marbled meats with visible striations of fat, like brisket or pork belly. Some of this fat will melt out during cooking, but a portion of it will remain, becoming cooked and gelatinized. This is in part responsible for the lusciousness you associate with great barbecue.

Bone: No, you can't eat it, but you sure can gnaw on it. With a properly cooked rib, the meat will just barely stick to the bone. If you can pull the bone out without resistance, the rib is overcooked.

5. When the pork is cooked, transfer it to a large cutting board or chopping block. *Loosely* tent with aluminum foil and let rest for 20 minutes. (Don't bunch the foil around the pork or you'll make the crust soggy.)

6. If your pork shoulder came with skin (not all will), pull it off and scrape off any excess fat (for crisping the skin, see "Don't forget the skin," page 93).

7. Pull out and discard any bones from the meat. Pull the meat into fist-size pieces, discarding any internal bones and large lumps of fat. (But remember, you need some fat to keep the pork moist.) Using a cleaver or a heavy chef's knife, coarsely chop the pork into pieces. Alternatively, pull the pork into shreds using meat claws, two large forks, or your hands. Note: You need to pull the pork when it's uncomfortably hot to the touch (wear insulated food gloves).

8. Transfer the pork to a large bowl and stir in enough sauce to give the pork a terrific flavor and keep it moist but not soupy. You'll need 1 to 2 cups.

9. To serve, butter then grill or toast the buns. Place ¾ cup pork (about ¼ pound) on each bun. Serve any leftover sauce on the side. Top the meat with slaw, if using, and dig in.

CAROLINA VINEGAR SAUCE

YIELD: Makes 2 cups

Think of this as the alter-ego of the thick, sugary sauces served too often with American barbecue. It's thin. Sharp. Salty and fiery, with only a faint whisper of sweetness. But when it comes to saucing pulled or chopped pork, nothing else comes close to counterpointing the rich fatty meat.

INGREDIENTS

1½ cups cider vinegar

¾ cup water

2 tablespoons sugar, or to taste

1½ tablespoons coarse salt (sea or kosher)

2 teaspoons freshly ground black pepper

2 teaspoons hot red pepper flakes (optional)

Place the vinegar and water in a nonreactive bowl. Add the sugar, salt, black pepper, and hot red pepper flakes, if using. Whisk until the sugar and salt are dissolved. Alternatively, place the ingredients in a large jar with a tight-fitting lid and shake to mix.

HOW TO SMOKE A WHOLE HOG

A whole hog is the apex of barbecue. As you climb the ladder of smoking enlightenment, at some point you'll want to try one. There are too many variables (hog size, smoker design, weather, wood, and so on) to cover in a single recipe. Here are the basic guidelines.

The hog: Hogs range in size from 20-pound suckling pigs to 225-pound monsters. The first time you smoke a hog, I recommend a 50-pounder (that's gutted weight, by the way, but with the head on). It's small enough to handle by yourself, and it'll cook in half a day—yet, it's large enough to establish your smoking bona fides. You'll need to order your hog ahead of time. As always, look for organic or heritage breeds from small farms. Ideally, you'll pick it up the morning you plan to smoke it. (The butcher's refrigerator is bigger than yours.) In a pinch, you can keep your hog chilled in a large insulated cooler or in a bathtub filled with ice. (When using the latter, do warn your spouse.)

The cut: Hogs smoked whole with legs tucked under the body are what you often see at barbecue competitions. But I prefer a butterflied hog—split through the belly to the backbone and opened up like a book. Why? When you smoke a whole hog, in effect you stew the meat in the skin. Yes, it comes out juicy and tender— but sometimes with a stewed quality. I like my pork with some crust and chew to it. When you smoke a butterflied hog, you expose more of the meat to the smoke and fire.

The smoker: You'll need a serious smoker—especially for jumbo hogs. That puts you in competition rig territory: respected brands include Horizon, Yoder, Klose, Lang, Pitmaker, Pitt's & Spitt's, Backwoods, and Cookshack. One interesting alternative for pig roasting is the "Cajun microwave" or its Cuban analogue, the *caja china* (Chinese box). Picture a wooden or steel box with an indented metal top.

You pile lit charcoal on this metal lid, turning the box into an outdoor oven. The result: amazingly moist tender pork, but without a pronounced smoke flavor. Attach a smoke generator (page 14) and you fix that, and get competition-quality barbecue, to boot. Note: You can also smoke a 50-pounder on a Weber Ranch grill or Big Green Egg XXXL.

The fuel: You can burn charcoal and pimp the smoke with wood chunks or chips. But for meat this big, I like a straight log fire. Follow the instructions for building a wood fire on page 26. You'll need at least an hour to get a good bed of embers. Add two or three logs an hour to maintain the heat and generate smoke. Texans use oak; southerners use hickory; midwesterners burn apple. Any seasoned hardwood will give you great results. Make sure you have good airflow so the smoke passes over the meat, instead of smothering it.

The temperature: There are many schools of thought here: low and slow in the style of traditional Southern barbecue or hot and fast in the style of Texas. The larger your hog, the lower the heat you need to cook it through without burning the exterior. I recommend a target temperature of 225° to 250°F. For a suckling pig, you could go as high as 325°F.

Timing: The time it takes to cook your hog depends on many factors: the size of the hog, the type and temperature of the pit, the weather, and even how much beer you and your crew have drunk. Your goal is an internal temperature of about 195°F in the shoulders and about 175°F in the deepest part of the hams (the upper hind leg). Another test for doneness is that the bones should pop loosely out of the meat. As a *very* rough guide, figure on 1 to 1½ hours for every 10 pounds of hog. Thus a 50-pound hog will take 5 to 7 hours; a 180-pounder needs more like 18 hours. (Note: For a really small pig, you need to bump up the time—a 20-pound hog still needs 3½ to 4 hours.)

Serving your hog: One of the ironies of going whole hog is that for all the effort you expend roasting and showing it off whole, serving it involves shredding or chopping it into tiny bits, then dousing it with vinegar sauce and piling it on a bun. Wearing insulated rubber gloves, pull large chunks of meat away from the bones, discarding the bones and any large lumps of fat. Set the skin aside for crisping (see below). Transfer the meat to a cutting board and chop it with heavy cleavers or shred it with meat claws (page 16).

Don't forget the skin: During the smoking process, the skin will become tough and leathery (and richly infused with wood smoke). Pull it off with your (gloved) hands. Using a knife, scrape away and discard the excess fat, then tear or cut the skin into 5- or 6-inch squares. Direct grill it over a hot fire (starting fat side down) until crisp, or deep-fry it in hot oil or lard. Chop or break the crisp skin into bits and sprinkle them over the meat.

How many will it serve? Figure on 1½ pounds raw meat or 6 to 8 ounces cooked meat per person (4 to 6 ounces if that pork is destined for sandwiches). **Note:** The larger the hog, the higher the overall yield. Thus, a 50-pound hog will serve about 30 people; a 225-pound hog will serve 150 people.

CUTS OF PORK

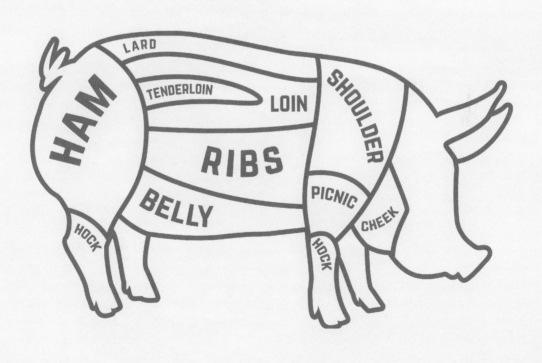

OAK-SMOKED CHERRY-GLAZED BABY BACK RIBS

Cut from high on the hog (adjacent to the backbone), baby back ribs, aka top loin ribs, offer the perfect ratio of tender meat to moisturizing flavorful fat. Smoke baby backs low and slow and you get a softer texture and richer smoke flavor. Smoke-roasting at a higher temperature crisps the meat fibers, so you get a crustier, chewier rib than with slow-smoking, and you cut the cooking time to less than 90 minutes. (Do not try this with spareribs.) Detailed instructions for both methods follow.

One doesn't normally associate baby backs with Texas, but Jason and Jake Dady have made them an object of cultlike adoration at their Two Bros. BBQ Market in San Antonio. They do so by applying a smoked paprika-coriander-brown sugar rub to the ribs prior to a four-hour smoke with Texas oak in brick pits blackened with age and creosote. But wait: What's that sweet-sour fruity note caressing your palate? And why do you find yourself thinking of the cherry in a Manhattan? This brings us to the Dady secret, for the brothers glaze their baby backs with cherry syrup during the smoking process and again just before serving, a combination that's as beguiling as it is unexpected. Normally, I recommend a half rack of baby backs per serving, but with these cherry-glazed bones, you may want to commandeer a whole rack for yourself.

YIELD: Makes 4 racks, enough to serve 4 really hungry people, or 6 to 8 as part of a larger meal

METHOD: Hot-smoking

PREP TIME: 20 minutes

SMOKING TIME: 3½ to 4 hours

FUEL: Oak logs, chunks, or chips—enough for 4 hours of smoking (see chart on page 6)

GEAR: A rib rack (optional)

SHOP: For the pork, ideally ribs from a heritage breed like Berkshire or Duroc.

For the cherry syrup, you want an imported brand like Torani from Italy. Look for it at your local coffeehouse or gourmet shop, or online from Amazon.

WHAT ELSE: I offer two methods here: traditional low-and-slow smoking and, as a variation, higher heat smoke-roasting. The first gives you meltingly tender ribs. The second produces meat you gnaw off the bone.

INGREDIENTS

4 racks baby back ribs
(2 to 2½ pounds each)

5 tablespoons sweet paprika

¼ cup brown sugar
(light or dark—your choice)

3 tablespoons Spanish smoked paprika
(pimentón)

2 tablespoons ground coriander

2 tablespoons fennel seeds

2 tablespoons coarse salt (sea or kosher)

1 tablespoon cayenne pepper

2 teaspoons ground cumin

1½ cups cherry syrup, plus extra as needed

1. Arrange the ribs on a rimmed baking sheet. Remove the thin, papery membrane from the back of each rack of ribs following the instructions on page 97 (number 3).

2. Make the rub: Place the sweet paprika, brown sugar, smoked paprika, coriander, fennel seeds, salt, cayenne, and cumin in a small bowl and stir to mix, breaking up any lumps in the brown sugar with your fingers.

3. Sprinkle 1 to 1½ tablespoons of the rub on both sides of the ribs, rubbing it into the meat with your fingertips. (This makes more rub than you'll need for this recipe; store the excess in a sealed jar away from heat and light. It will keep for several weeks.)

4. Set up your smoker following the manufacturer's instructions and preheat to 225° to 250°F. Add the wood as specified by the manufacturer.

5. Place the ribs directly on the rack in the smoker, bone side down. If space is limited, use a rib rack to smoke them vertically. Smoke the ribs until browned and almost tender, 3 hours.

6. Brush the racks of ribs on both sides with cherry syrup. Continue smoking until very tender, ½ to 1 hour more. Baste the ribs twice during the last hour—the cherry syrup should cook to a sticky glaze.

7. There are three ways to check for doneness: The meat will have shrunk back from the end of the bones by ¼ to ½ inch. When you lift a whole rack with tongs, it will bend like a bow and start to break. And you should be able to pull the individual ribs apart with your fingers.

8. Transfer the ribs to a cutting board. Brush the racks on both sides with cherry syrup one final time. You can serve the racks whole, cut in half, or cut into individual bones. Serve any remaining syrup on the side.

Variation
SMOKE-ROASTED CHERRY-GLAZED BABY BACKS

1. Prepare and rub the ribs as described in Steps 1 and 2 in the previous recipe. Set up your grill for smoke-roasting (indirect grilling—see page 262) and preheat to 325°F. Place the ribs in a rib rack over the drip pan between the mounds of coals.

2. Smoke-roast (indirect-grill) the ribs until browned and almost tender, 1 hour. Brush with cherry syrup. Continue smoke-roasting the ribs until cooked (follow the doneness tests in Step 7), another 15 to 30 minutes. Glaze once or twice more during cooking. Give the ribs a final glaze, then carve and serve them as described previously.

SIX THINGS YOU NEED TO KNOW ABOUT PORK RIBS

Pork ribs have it all: rich-tasting meat with plenty of luscious fat, as well as bones to provide structure and flavor, at a price that remains relatively affordable—especially when compared to beef. Ribs are capable of culinary sophistication, yet primal—even joyful—enough to devour with your bare hands.

1. Pork ribs come in many cuts, shapes, and sizes.

Baby back ribs: Cut from "high off the hog" (next to the backbone), these are tender, well-marbled, and quick and easy to cook. A full slab has 11 to 13 bones. Typical American baby backs tip the scales at 2 to 2½ pounds; figure on 1 to 2 servings per rack. Racks of Danish baby back ribs weigh about 1 pound each; figure on 1 serving per rack.

Spareribs: Cut from lower down on the ribcage, spareribs are meatier, fattier, and tougher than baby backs. Their big porky flavor makes the extended cooking time worth it. A typical rack weighs 3 to 4 pounds and serves 2 or 3.

St. Louis ribs: A trimmed section of spareribs that looks and cooks like baby backs. The cartilaginous tips and a flap of meat have been removed to "square" the rack. A favorite cut of competition barbecuers, the St. Louis rack weighs in at 2 to 2½ pounds.

Country-style ribs: The "ribs" that look and cook like pork chops. Cut from the front of the hog at the top of the shoulder. May or may not have bones. A typical country-style rib weighs 4 to 6 ounces; figure on 2 per person.

Rib tips: The cartilaginous ends of spareribs. The sort of cut smoke masters tend to keep for themselves while serving spares and baby backs to their guests.

2. When buying ribs, look for heavy racks with lots of meat. Avoid "shiners"—racks with so much meat trimmed off, the tops of the bones are exposed. Figure on 1 pound per person.

3. Ribs have a papery membrane on the inside (concave side). Do you absolutely need to remove it? No, but many believe it impedes the absorption of the spice and smoke flavors. To remove it, loosen it from a middle bone with an instant-read thermometer (wiggle the end of the probe under the membrane at the bone). Grab the membrane with a paper towel or dishcloth (it's slippery) and gently pull it off. If the membrane isn't obvious, it was probably removed by the butcher.

4. Tight on space? To cook four racks of ribs in a water smoker, kettle grill, kamado-style smoker, or other smoker with limited space, use a rib rack, which enables you to cook the bones standing upright. Added advantage: This helps drain off the fat.

5. Never boil ribs. I repeat: Never boil ribs. You can achieve the requisite tenderness by smoking. Smoke spareribs and St. Louis-cut ribs low and slow (at 225° to 250°F) to soften the tough connective tissue. You can smoke baby backs low or at a higher temperature (325°F). The latter gives you a crustier, meatier rib.

6. If using barbecue sauce, don't apply it too early. The sugars will burn before the meat is fully cooked. I brush it on the last 5 minutes and move the ribs directly over the fire, searing the sauce into the meat. Better yet, serve the sauce on the side.

CHINATOWN SPARERIBS
WITH BEIJING BARBECUE SAUCE

YIELD: Makes 2 racks, enough to serve 4

METHOD: Hot-smoking

PREP TIME: 15 minutes

SMOKING TIME: 4½ to 5 hours

FUEL: Cherry or apple wood—enough for 5 hours of smoking (see chart on page 6)

GEAR: A rib rack (optional); spray bottle

SHOP: You'll need to know about a few Asian ingredients, most available at larger supermarkets or online. Five-spice powder is a traditional Chinese blend with a smoky anise flavor, made from fennel, cinnamon, star anise, Szechuan peppercorns, and cloves. Rice wine is an alcoholic beverage made from fermented rice; if you can't find Chinese *shaoxing*, substitute sake or sherry. Hoisin sauce is a thick sweet-salty condiment made with soybeans. Asian (dark) sesame oil is an aromatic oil pressed from roasted sesame seeds.

WHAT ELSE: I call for spareribs here, but you can certainly use baby backs or St. Louis-cut ribs. Figure on 4 hours or so for smoking baby backs or St. Louis-cut ribs.

U nlike most of the people I met while researching this and my other books, I did not grow up with barbecue. No ancestral line of pit masters passed me the torch; no smoker burned away in our backyard. The closest I got to ribs growing up was weekly Chinese carryout, and I never thought to question whether those "barbecued" spareribs ever saw the inside of a pit. (Oven and fryer, yes, but not a smoker.) Well, if you think the sweet-salty-umami flavors of Chinese ribs are good, wait until you try them enhanced with old-fashioned American wood smoke. These ribs get a quadruple blast of flavor: first from an anise-scented 5-4-3-2-1 Rub (the derivation of the name will be obvious); then from a rice wine-cider spray to keep them moist; then from fragrant cherry wood smoke. The last step is lacquering and grilling with a sweet-spicy Beijing Barbecue Sauce.

INGREDIENTS

2 racks spareribs (3 to 4 pounds each)

5-4-3-2-1 Rub (recipe follows)

½ cup Chinese rice wine (*shaoxing*), sake, or dry or cream sherry

½ cup apple cider

Beijing Barbecue Sauce (page 101)

1. Arrange the ribs on a rimmed baking sheet. Remove the thin papery membrane from the back of each rack of ribs following the instructions on page 97 (number 3).

2. Sprinkle the rub on both sides of the ribs, rubbing it into the meat with your fingertips. You'll need 3 to 4 tablespoons of rub for each rack of ribs.

3. Set up your smoker following the manufacturer's instructions and preheat to 225° to 250°F. Add the wood as specified by the manufacturer.

4. Place the ribs directly on the rack in the smoker, bone side down. If space is limited, use a rib rack to smoke them vertically. Smoke the ribs for 1 hour.

5. Place the rice wine and apple cider in a spray bottle and shake to mix. Start spraying the ribs with this

mixture on both sides after 1 hour of smoking. Repeat every hour.

6. Brush the ribs on both sides with the sauce after 4 hours of smoking. Brush again in 30 minutes. The ribs are cooked when the meat has shrunk back from the ends of the bones by about ½ inch and you can pull the individual ribs apart with your fingers. (See doneness tests on page 96, Step 7.) Total cooking time will be 4½ to 5 hours.

7. You can serve the ribs hot out of the smoker with any remaining barbecue sauce on the side, cut into individual bones. But for even more flavor, set up a grill for direct grilling and preheat to high. Brush and oil the grill grate. Brush the ribs on both sides with more barbecue sauce and direct grill until sizzling and browned, 1 to 2 minutes per side. Serve at once with any extra sauce on the side.

5-4-3-2-1 RUB
(ASIAN BARBECUE RUB)
YIELD: Makes about 1 cup

This easy-to-remember rub packs a one-two punch of licoricy Chinese five-spice powder and spicy pepper. Great with all meats—especially pork and duck.

INGREDIENTS

5 tablespoons turbinado sugar or dark brown sugar

4 tablespoons coarse salt (sea or kosher)

3 tablespoons freshly ground black pepper

2 tablespoons Chinese five-spice powder

1 tablespoon onion powder

Place the sugar, salt, pepper, five-spice powder, and onion powder in a bowl and mix, breaking up any lumps in the brown sugar with your fingers. This recipe will give you more rub than you need for two racks of spareribs (or four racks of baby backs). Store any excess in a sealed jar away from heat and light; it will keep for several weeks.

BEIJING BARBECUE SAUCE

YIELD: Makes about 1½ cups

Here's how barbecue sauce would taste if it came from Asia: sweet with hoisin sauce and honey, nutty with sesame oil, and spicy with Thai sriracha. You'll want to eat it straight off the spoon.

INGREDIENTS

1 cup hoisin sauce

3 tablespoons Asian (dark) sesame oil

3 tablespoons honey

3 tablespoons sriracha

Place the hoisin sauce, sesame oil, honey, and sriracha in a saucepan over medium heat and whisk to mix.

Gently simmer the sauce for 5 to 8 minutes to blend the flavors.

ST. LOUIS RIBS
WITH VANILLA-BROWN SUGAR GLAZE

The St. Louis rib offers the best of two ribs: the lush marbling of baby backs and the meaty richness of spareribs. Picture a center-cut section of a rack of spareribs trimmed down to the approximate shape and size of a rack of baby backs. It's easy to cook, tender to the tooth, with flavor that just doesn't quit. That's why the St. Louis cut is our go-to rib at Barbecue University. And few prepare it better than Chris Conger of the Smoke Shack in San Antonio, Texas. He cures the ribs overnight with a rub rich in garlic powder—lots of garlic powder—and brown sugar. He smokes the ribs low and slow, and just before serving, swabs on an irresistible glaze brewed from brown sugar and butter. Said glaze contains a mystery ingredient that tastes familiar, but that you rarely associate with barbecued ribs. Chris would challenge you to guess its identity, but I've revealed the mystery in the glaze's name.

YIELD: Make 4 racks, enough to serve 4 really hungry people, or 6 to 8 with another main dish

METHOD: Hot-smoking

PREP TIME: 20 minutes, plus 12 hours or overnight for curing the ribs

SMOKING TIME: 3½ to 4 hours

FUEL: Hickory and/or pecan wood— enough for 4 hours of smoking (see chart on page 6)

GEAR: A rib rack (optional); instant-read thermometer

SHOP: St. Louis ribs are available at a growing number of supermarkets—or you can preorder them from your local butcher. Extra points for Berkshire or another heritage breed. Note the use of granulated brown sugar (available at the supermarket) for the rub—it's less likely to clump than conventional brown sugar (although the latter will work if that's what you have).

WHAT ELSE: For maximum flavor, rub the ribs the night before so they have time to cure in the refrigerator before smoking. Pressed for time? You'll still get good flavor if you smoke the ribs immediately after applying the rub. Note the unusual membrane technique here: Conger slits the membrane but leaves it on to keep in moisture. He removes it just before glazing and serving.

INGREDIENTS

FOR THE RIBS AND RUB

4 racks of St. Louis-cut ribs (each 2½ to 3 pounds)

½ cup granulated brown sugar or regular light brown sugar

½ cup sweet paprika

¼ cup granulated garlic powder (Conger really likes garlic)

¼ cup coarse salt (sea or kosher)

3 tablespoons cracked or coarsely ground black pepper

2 tablespoons granulated onion powder

2 tablespoons pure chile powder (such as ancho)

1 tablespoon ground cumin

FOR THE VANILLA-BROWN SUGAR GLAZE

8 tablespoons (1 stick) unsalted butter

½ cup granulated brown sugar or regular light brown sugar

2 tablespoons honey

1 teaspoon pure vanilla extract

3 to 4 tablespoons water

1. To cook the ribs the way Chris does, use the tip of a paring knife to make a lengthwise slit in the membrane on the back (hollow, or concave, side) of each rack midway between the top and bottom of the ribs.

2. Make the rub: Combine the brown sugar, paprika, garlic powder, salt, pepper, onion powder, chile powder, and cumin in a mixing bowl and mix well. If using conventional brown sugar, break up any lumps with your fingers.

3. Place the ribs on a rimmed baking sheet and sprinkle both sides of them with the rub, rubbing it into the meat. Use enough rub to coat the ribs (1½ to 2 tablespoons on each side of each rack); store any excess in a sealed jar away from heat or light. It will keep for several weeks.

4. Cover the ribs with plastic wrap and cure overnight in the refrigerator. The overnight cure is optional, but it gives you a richer flavor.

5. Set up your smoker following the manufacturer's instructions and preheat to 225° to 250°F. Add the wood as specified by the manufacturer.

6. Place the ribs directly on the rack in the smoker, rounded (convex) side up. Smoke the ribs until they're very tender and the meat has shrunk back from the end of the bones by ¼ to ½ inch. When you lift a whole rack with tongs, it will bend like a bow and start to break. And you should be able to pull the individual ribs apart with your fingers. (See doneness tests on page 96, Step 7.) Total cooking time will be 3½ to 4 hours.

7. Meanwhile, make the glaze: Melt the butter in a saucepan over medium heat. Stir in the brown sugar, honey, vanilla, and 3 tablespoons water. Bring to a boil, stirring well, until the sugar has melted and the ingredients are well combined, 5 minutes. The glaze should be thick but pourable; add additional water if needed. Brush the ribs all over with the glaze 5 minutes before the end of cooking.

8. Transfer the ribs to a cutting board. Pry up the membrane on the back of each rack with the probe of an instant-read thermometer and pull it off, grabbing it with a dish cloth or paper towel. Brush the racks on both sides with the glaze a second time. You can serve the racks whole, cut in half, or as individual bones. Serve any remaining glaze on the side.

THE 3-2-1 METHOD FOR COOKING RIBS

In a field as disorderly as barbecue, numbers bring a certain comfort. Perhaps that explains the popularity of the 3-2-1 method for cooking ribs.

Not familiar with it? It arose on the competition barbecue circuit where it's sometimes referred to as the Texas crutch. In a nutshell, you break cooking ribs into three time blocks.

- 3 hours of smoking unwrapped at 225°F, followed by

- 2 hours of cooking wrapped in aluminum foil, with a little liquid, such as apple cider, followed by

- 1 hour of cooking unwrapped at a higher temperature with a generous basting of barbecue sauce

I've tried the method several times and understand its appeal. The process gives you meat so tender it virtually slides off the bone, with the flavor most of us associate with great barbecue. And within a predictable six-hour time frame, too.

It's relatively fail-proof, meaning that if you follow the directions, you are almost guaranteed to avoid the dual pitfalls of ribs that are tough or dry. And if you serve ribs cooked by the 3-2-1 method, 95 percent of the people who taste them will react with delight and declare you a barbecue genius. My guests sure did, and I did not deflect their praise.

And yet . . . and yet . . . I felt a certain unease accepting their compliments. These were good ribs—very good ribs. These were easy ribs. Safe ribs. These were ribs almost anyone could love on account of their moistness and tenderness. But they weren't Hall of Fame ribs—ribs with character, with soul, ribs that test a smoke master's mettle. They suffered from a transgression I have consistently condemned in all my books: boiling. For when you wrap and cook ribs in foil, you are, in effect, boiling them in their own juices. Hence the almost supernatural tenderness coupled with what I would call a washed-out flavor.

True connoisseurs—and Kansas City Barbecue Society-trained judges—prefer their rib meat with a bit of chew, a perceptible bit of resistance.

Of course, three hours of smoking spice-crusted ribs puts in plenty of flavor, and the last hour spent cooking the ribs at a higher temperature—unwrapped and sauced—is designed to apply a sweet-savory glaze to the surface. (In some versions of the method, you finish the ribs by direct grilling over a hot fire.)

Raichlen's bottom line: Most people will love ribs cooked by the 3-2-1 method. Purists like me remain skeptical. Form your own conclusions by doing a side-by-side comparison. Please post your results and photos on the Barbecue Board at barbecuebible.com and on my Facebook and Twitter pages (@stevenraichlen).

HONEY-CURED HAM RIBS

Combine the briny, smoky, umami flavors of country ham with the crusty, gnaw-off-the-bone pleasure of barbecued baby backs and you wind up with ham ribs. I wish I could say I thought of it, but I got the idea from a man utterly obsessed with pork, smoke, and fire: Chris Shepherd of Underbelly in Houston, Texas. Curing the ribs in ham brine prior to smoking produces a gorgeous color, uncommon succulence (in the way most brine-cured meats are succulent), and an astonishing honey-ham flavor.

INGREDIENTS

1 rack spareribs (3 to 4 pounds)

¾ cup coarse salt (sea or kosher)

¾ cup honey

1½ teaspoons pink curing salt
    (Prague Powder No. 1 or
    Insta Cure No. 1)

1½ cups hot water

1½ cups cold water

8 whole cloves

3 bay leaves

Mustard Seed Caviar (page 106),
    for serving (optional)

1. Arrange the ribs on a rimmed baking sheet or cutting board. Remove the thin papery membrane from the back of each rack of ribs following the instructions on page 97 (number 3). Cut the rack in half widthwise between the middle bones. Place the ribs in a jumbo heavy-duty resealable plastic bag or nonreactive baking dish just large enough to hold them.

2. Make the brine: Place the coarse salt, honey, pink curing salt, and hot water in a large bowl and whisk until the honey and salts are dissolved. Whisk in the cold water and add the cloves and bay leaves. Let cool to room temperature.

3. Pour the brine over the ribs, squeeze out the air, seal the bag, and place in an aluminum foil pan or roasting pan (to contain any leaks), or cover the baking dish with plastic wrap. Brine the ribs in the refrigerator for 3 days (for half racks) or 4 days (for whole racks), turning them over twice daily so they cure evenly.

4. Drain the ribs well, discarding the brine, and blot dry with paper towels. Arrange the ribs on a wire rack over a rimmed baking sheet and let dry in the refrigerator for 2 hours.

5. Set up your smoker following the manufacturer's instructions and preheat to 225° to 250°F. Add the wood as specified by the manufacturer.

YIELD: Serves 2 or 3; can be multiplied as desired

METHOD: Hot-smoking

PREP TIME: 15 minutes, plus 2 hours drying

BRINING TIME: 3 to 4 days

SMOKING TIME: 4 to 5 hours

FUEL: Oak and pecan wood—enough for 5 hours of smoking (see chart on page 6)

GEAR: A jumbo heavy-duty resealable plastic bag (optional); a large aluminum foil pan

SHOP: You'll need one ingredient that may be out of your comfort zone: pink curing salt, also known as Prague Powder No. 1 or Insta Cure No. 1. (It contains 93.75 percent salt and 6.25 percent sodium nitrite.) Buy it at a good meat market or order it online from Amazon.

WHAT ELSE: "If you're expecting ribs that fall off the bone, you've come to the wrong place," Shepherd says, a gentle reminder that ribs—even after smoking for 5 hours—should have a little chew to them. That's why God gave you teeth. Pork chops and pork collar (cut from the neck) are also delicious cured and smoked in this fashion.

6. Place the ribs directly on the rack in the smoker, bone side down. Smoke 4 to 5 hours, adding wood as needed. When done, the ribs will be tender enough to pull apart with your fingers and the meat will have shrunk back from the ends of the bones by about ½ inch. (See doneness test on page 96, Step 7.)

7. You can serve the ribs hot off the smoker, cut into individual ribs. Serve with Mustard Seed Caviar, if desired. That's how I serve them, because patience is not part of my genetic makeup. (Chris Shepherd likes to add an additional step: He chills the ribs, cuts them into individual bones, then grills them over a hot wood fire to crisp the exterior.)

MUSTARD SEED CAVIAR

YIELD: Makes 1¼ cups; enough to serve 4 to 6

Think of this "caviar" as deconstructed mustard, and don't think about serving smoked ham or other pork without it. The slow simmer in vinegar softens the mustard seeds to the crunchy-gooey texture of sturgeon caviar. Serve with Honey-Cured Ham Ribs (page 105) or the Smokehouse Shoulder Ham on page 120.

INGREDIENTS

½ cup yellow mustard seeds

½ cup cider vinegar

½ cup sorghum syrup (such as Golden Barrel) or dark corn syrup

½ cup water, plus extra as needed

1 tablespoon Dijon mustard

1 teaspoon hot sauce (use your favorite), or to taste

About 1 teaspoon coarse salt (sea or kosher), or to taste

About ½ teaspoon freshly ground black pepper, or to taste

1. Place the mustard seeds, vinegar, syrup, and ½ cup water in a heavy saucepan and stir to mix. Bring to a boil over high heat, then gently simmer, covered, over low heat until the mustard seeds are semisoft, like caviar, 30 to 45 minutes. Stir often and add water as needed to keep the mustard seeds from drying out.

2. Stir in the prepared mustard, hot sauce, and salt and pepper to taste. The caviar should be highly seasoned. Simmer for 3 minutes. Serve hot or let cool to room temperature. In the unlikely event that you have any left, it will keep for several weeks in your refrigerator.

SMOKEHOUSE CHAR SIU
CHINESE BARBECUED PORK

China is one of the few countries in Asia with specialties in the world canon of great smoked dishes. Think Tea-Smoked Duck (page 168). And don't forget the barbecued pork strips known as *char siu*. The name literally means "fork-roast"—a reference to an ancient Cantonese practice of roasting pork on fork-shaped skewers over charcoal. Today char siu is almost always oven roasted, but the irresistible interplay of sweet (from sugar and honey), salty (from soy sauce and oyster sauce), and fat (traditionally, the meat strips are cut from fatty pork shoulder) plays to the same palate as great barbecue in the West. That set me wondering what would happen if you cooked char siu in a smoker. Simply some of the best pork you'll taste in *Project Smoke*.

YIELD: Serves 6 to 8 as a starter, 4 as a main course

METHOD: Hot-smoking

PREP TIME: 20 minutes

MARINATING TIME: 6 to 8 hours

SMOKING TIME: 1¼ to 1½ hours

FUEL: Cherry or apple wood—enough for 1 hour of smoking (see chart on page 6)

GEAR: An instant-read thermometer

SHOP: If your meat market sells boneless pork shoulder, you're ahead of the game. If not, buy a small bone-in pork shoulder and cut out the shoulder blade yourself.

You'll need to know about a few Chinese ingredients. Oyster sauce is a thick brown sauce with the briny tang of oysters. See page 98 for five-spice powder, hoisin sauce, rice wine, and Asian (dark) sesame oil.

INGREDIENTS

FOR THE PORK AND RUB

2 pounds boneless pork shoulder (preferably well-marbled)

3 tablespoons turbinado sugar or dark brown sugar

1 tablespoon Chinese five-spice powder

1 tablespoon freshly ground white pepper

FOR THE MARINADE

3 tablespoons honey

3 tablespoons soy sauce

2 tablespoons oyster sauce

2 tablespoons rice wine (shaoxing), sake, or dry sherry

1 tablespoon Asian (dark) sesame oil

1 tablespoon hoisin sauce (optional)

Vegetable oil, for oiling the smoker rack

FOR SERVING (OPTIONAL)

2 scallions, trimmed, white and green parts thinly sliced crosswise

1 tablespoon toasted sesame seeds

½ cup prepared Chinese mustard

1. Cut the pork with the grain into strips about 8 inches long and 1½ inches wide and thick. Place them in a large bowl.

2. Make the rub: Place the sugar, five-spice powder, and pepper in a small bowl and mix with your fingers.

Sprinkle over the pork and rub it in with your fingers to season the strips well on all sides.

3. Make the marinade: Place the honey, soy sauce, oyster sauce, rice wine, sesame oil, and hoisin sauce, if using, in a small bowl and mix well.

WHAT ELSE: Want a leaner version of this dish? Use pork loin, tenderloin, or boneless country-style ribs. Want a fattier version? The rub and marinade are excellent on spareribs and baby backs (follow the smoking temperatures and times in the chart below). Note that the char siu you order in Chinese restaurants often has a reddish hue, achieved with a few drops of red food coloring in the marinade. I don't bother, but you can if you like.

Pour over the pork, turning the strips to coat. Cover the pork with plastic wrap and marinate for 6 to 8 hours in the refrigerator.

4. Set up your smoker following the manufacturer's instructions and preheat to 225° to 250°F. Add the wood as specified by the manufacturer.

5. Oil the smoker rack. Drain the pork well, reserving the marinade in a small saucepan. Place the pork directly on the rack and smoke for 1 hour. Meanwhile, bring the marinade to a boil over medium-high heat and boil for 3 minutes. Now you can safely use it as a baste. Let cool slightly.

6. Brush the pork on all sides with the marinade and continue smoking until the internal temperature reaches 160°F, 15 to 30 minutes more. (Use an instant-read thermometer inserted through the end of the strips to check the temperature.) Transfer the pork to a platter and drizzle with any remaining marinade.

7. To serve, sprinkle with the scallions and sesame seeds, if using. For an appetizer, impale the pork strips on toothpicks. Many people (including me) like to accompany char siu with Chinese mustard.

PORK SMOKING CHART

FOOD	AMOUNT	SMOKER TEMP	TIME	INTERNAL TEMP/ DONENESS
Pork shoulder (Boston butt)	5-7 pounds	225°-250°F	6-8 hours	200°F
Pork belly (bacon)	3-3½ pounds	160°-175°F	3½-4 hours	155°F
Pork belly (barbecued)	3 pounds	225°-250°F	3-3½ hours	160°F
Pork loin (Irish or Canadian bacon)	2½-3 pounds	225°-250°F	3-4 hours	160°F
Pork chops (thick)	1-1½ pounds (each)	225°-250°F + direct high heat for searing	1½-2 hours + 4-6 minutes	150-160°F
Baby back ribs	2-2½-pound racks	225°-250°F or 325°-350°F	3½-4 hours or 1¼-1½ hours	Tender; meat shrinks back by ¼-½ inch from ends of bones
St. Louis ribs	2½-3-pound racks	225°-250°F	3½-4 hours	Tender; meat shrinks back ¼-½ inch from ends of bones
Spareribs	3-4-pound racks	225°-250°F	4½-5 hours	Tender; meat shrinks back ½ inch from ends of bones
Shoulder ham	9-10 pounds	100°F or less 225°-250°F	12 hours for cold-smoking + 12 hours for hot-smoking	160°F
Whole ham (leg)	18-20 pounds	100°F or less 225°-250°F	24 hours for cold-smoking + 18 hours for hot-smoking	160°F

MONSTER PORK CHOPS
SMOKED AND GRILLED IN THE STYLE OF BUTCHER AND THE BOAR

Good things come in small packages? Maybe when it comes to jewelry, but not from the smoker or grill. If you want to know how awesome big can be, order the brined, smoked, chile-grilled double-thick pork chop at Butcher and the Boar in Minneapolis. The recipe deploys three strategies to keep the pork chops moist. Start with double-thick chops (each tips the scale at over 1 pound), which increases the ratio of interior meat to surface area. (The surface is where the chop dries out.) Cure the chops in a brine of salt, sugar, and pink curing salt. This loosens the strands of proteins, allowing the chops to retain more liquid (see Brining on page 163). After smoking, coat the chops with olive oil and a chile powder rub and sear over a hot wood fire. This seals in moisture, sets the crust, and intensifies the flavor. Don't be deterred by the seemingly long preparation time. You're looking at less than 30 minutes of actual work.

YIELD: Serves 4

METHOD: Hot-smoking

PREP TIME: 20 minutes

BRINING TIME: 12 hours

SMOKING TIME: 1½ to 2 hours

GRILLING TIME: 4 to 6 minutes (optional)

FUEL: Butcher and the Boar uses a blend of apple, cherry, and oak—enough for 2 hours of smoking (see chart on page 6)

GEAR: A jumbo heavy-duty resealable plastic bag (optional); an instant-read thermometer

SHOP: The easiest way to obtain double-thick pork chops is to buy an 8-rib center-cut rack of pork and cut it crosswise into two-bone sections. Alternatively, special-order double-thick chops, preferably from a heritage breed, from your butcher. Pink curing salt contains salt and nitrites (see page 105 for percentages); buy it at a good meat market or order it online from Amazon.

INGREDIENTS

FOR THE PORK AND BRINE

4 double-thick bone-in pork chops (1¼ to 1½ inches thick and 1 to 1½ pounds each)

1 cup coarse salt (sea or kosher)

⅓ cup sugar

4 teaspoons pink curing salt (Prague Powder No. 1 or Insta Cure No. 1)

1 quart hot water

1 quart cold water

Vegetable oil, for oiling the smoker rack

FOR THE RUB (OPTIONAL)

¼ cup pure chile powder (such as ancho)

¼ cup dark or light brown sugar

3 tablespoons coarse salt (sea or kosher)

¼ cup extra virgin olive oil, plus extra as needed

1. Place the pork chops in a nonreactive baking dish just large enough to hold them, or a heavy-duty resealable plastic bag.

2. Make the brine: Place the coarse salt, sugar, and curing salt in a large bowl. Add the hot water and whisk until the salts and sugar dissolve. Whisk in the cold water and let the brine cool to room temperature. Pour

WHAT ELSE: You can certainly serve the pork chops hot out of the smoker without the extra steps of rubbing and grilling. Imagine a pork chop channeling a hot-smoked ham. But you'll get even more fire and spice if you sizzle the chops on the grill just before serving. There's an added advantage here: You can smoke the chops several days ahead, then heat them on the grill just before serving. (Cool to room temperature after smoking, then cover and refrigerate until you're ready to grill.) The Mustard Seed Caviar on page 106 makes a great accompaniment.

the brine over the pork chops. Cover the baking dish with plastic wrap, or squeeze out the air and seal the bag and place it in an aluminum foil pan or roasting pan to contain any leaks. Brine the chops in the refrigerator for 12 hours, turning them over once or twice.

3. Meanwhile, if you intend to grill the chops after smoking, make the rub: Place the chile powder, brown sugar, and salt in a mixing bowl and mix well, breaking up any lumps in the brown sugar with your fingers.

4. Drain the pork chops, discarding the brine. Rinse under cold water and blot dry with paper towels.

5. Set up your smoker following the manufacturer's instructions and preheat to 225° to 250°F. Add the wood as specified by the manufacturer.

6. Oil the smoker rack. Place the pork chops directly on the rack and smoke them until lightly browned and the internal temperature reads 145°F. (Insert your instant-read thermometer through the *side* of the chop.) This will take 1½ to 2 hours. You can serve the chops at this stage; if you do, cook the chops until the internal temperature is 150°F.

7. But you'll get more flavor and crust if you rub and grill the chops as described in these next steps. Set up your grill for direct grilling and preheat to medium-high. Brush and oil the grill grate.

8. Rub or brush the chops all over with olive oil. Sprinkle the rub on all sides of the chops, rubbing it into the meat with your fingertips.

9. Direct grill the chops until sizzling and browned on both sides, 2 to 3 minutes per side. Give each a quarter turn halfway through grilling to lay on a crosshatch of grill marks. Be sure to grill the edges of the chops, too.

MADE-FROM-SCRATCH BACON

When it comes to the cool factor—not to mention bragging rights—few home-smoked foods can beat bacon. And by smoking your own, you get to control the quality of the pork belly, the seasonings in the cure, the flavor profile of the wood smoke, and even the thickness of the slice. When you pull your first homemade bacon off the smoker—and this is a common sentiment—your heart will swell with pride. Below are your general marching orders, with suggestions for how to customize the bacon to suit your taste.

INGREDIENTS

⅓ cup coarse salt (sea or kosher)

3 tablespoons freshly ground black pepper or cracked black peppercorns

2 teaspoons pink curing salt (Prague Powder No. 1 or Insta Cure No. 1)

⅓ cup packed dark brown sugar, granulated sugar, unrefined cane sugar (like Sucanat), maple sugar, or a combination of these sweeteners

1 piece (3 to 3½ pounds) pork belly (preferably from a heritage hog like a Berkshire or Duroc—page 18), skin removed (see Note)

YIELD: Makes 3 to 3½ pounds

METHOD: Hot-smoking (but at a relatively low temperature)

PREP TIME: 10 minutes

CURING TIME: 6 days

DRYING TIME: 4 hours or up to overnight

SMOKING TIME: 3½ to 4 hours

CHILLING TIME: 4 hours or up to overnight

FUEL: Hickory or maple and apple or cherry (in roughly equal proportions)—enough for 4 hours of smoking (see chart on page 6). Note: Electric smokers work great for bacon. It's easier to maintain consistent low temperatures in an electric smoker than in a wood- or charcoal-burning smoker.

GEAR: A wire rack; unlined butcher paper (optional); an instant-read thermometer

1. Place the coarse salt, pepper, and curing salt in a mixing bowl and mix well with your fingers. Mix in the sugar, breaking up any lumps in the brown sugar.

2. Place the pork belly on a rimmed baking sheet. Sprinkle half of the cure on top and rub it into the meat. Turn the belly over, sprinkle with the remaining cure, and rub it in. Place the belly plus any excess cure in a large heavy-duty resealable plastic bag. (Tip: Roll the top of the bag down an inch to the outside before inserting the meat to keep the gritty cure out of the bag's closure tracks.) Squeeze out

the air and seal the bag. Place in an aluminum foil pan or roasting pan to contain any leaks.

3. Cure the belly for 6 days, turning it over each day to redistribute the liquid that will accumulate. As the cure dehydrates the bacon, liquid will gather in the bag. It's supposed to. Think of it as brine.

4. Drain the pork belly and rinse well with cold water. Blot dry with paper towels. Place the belly on a wire rack over a rimmed baking sheet in the refrigerator or in a cool place in front of a fan (the goal is to create

SHOP: Pork belly used to require a special order from your local butcher shop. Now you can buy it at Whole Foods. A full pork belly weighs 10 to 12 pounds. This recipe calls for a 3- to 3½-pound slab, which will be easier to handle at home. Make your life easy and ask the butcher to remove the skin. Pink curing salt contains salt and nitrites (see page 16); buy it at a good meat market or order it from Amazon.

WHAT ELSE: Bacon makers divide pretty evenly into those who cure with a dry seasoning and those who use brine. I belong to the former—I find that a dry cure gives you a richer, tangier taste. If you want to try the latter, use one of the brine recipes on pages 109 and 120. You have multiple options for sweeteners. I like the earthy flavor of dark brown sugar. For a spicier finish, replace up to 1 tablespoon of black pepper with an equal amount of hot red pepper flakes.

good airflow) and let it dry for at least 4 hours or as long as overnight. This helps form the pellicle—an exterior skin that feels papery and dry and just a touch tacky—for the smoke to adhere to.

5. Set up your smoker following the manufacturer's instructions and preheat it to around 170°F. Add wood as specified by the manufacturer.

6. Place the pork belly directly on the grate in the smoker. Smoke until bronzed with wood smoke and the internal temperature reaches 155°F. (Insert the instant-read thermometer through the *side* of the bacon.) This will take 3½ to 4 hours depending on the size of the pork belly and your smoker.

7. Transfer the bacon to a wire rack over a rimmed baking sheet and let it cool to room temperature. Tightly wrap it in butcher's paper or plastic wrap and refrigerate for at least 4 hours, ideally overnight. This sets the flavor and texture. Refrigerated, the bacon will keep for at least 5 days; frozen for several months.

8. To serve, cut the bacon into ⅛- to ¼-inch-thick slices. Crisp in a cast-iron skillet (start with a cold skillet to minimize shrinkage). Or cook the bacon on the grill (direct grilling over medium-high heat). Leave plenty of open grate space so you can move the bacon as needed to dodge flare-ups. You can also bake or indirect-grill the bacon (the oven or grill should be 375°F) on a wire rack—a great way to prepare it for a crowd.

NOTE: Remove the skin from a pork belly using a long sharp knife. Starting at one corner, place the knife between the skin and the meat and saw back and forth with it. Once you've released 2 inches of skin, make a ½-inch slit in the released corner about 1 inch from the edges. Insert your finger and lift the skin with one hand. Continue cutting the skin away from the belly, lifting with your finger as you cut. With a little practice, you'll be doing it like a pro.

IRISH BACON OR CANADIAN BACON

You'd hardly call bacon health food (although for many members of our barbecue community, it's a dietary essential). But there is a type of bacon made from lean pork loin, as opposed to fatty pork belly. Actually, there are two: Irish bacon and Canadian bacon. Both start with meat cut from high on the hog: Irish bacon (known on its home turf as "rashers") comes with a perimeter of fat, which gives it some of the lusciousness you associate with belly bacon; Canadian bacon has most of the fat trimmed off. Here's how Kansas City, Missouri, butcher and smoke master Alex Pope makes it at his must-visit butcher and sandwich shop, Local Pig.

YIELD: Serves 6 to 8

METHOD: Hot-smoking

PREP TIME: 20 minutes, plus 2 hours to let the cure cool to room temperature

BRINING TIME: 4 to 5 days

SMOKING TIME: 2½ hours or as needed

FUEL: Apple wood—enough for 2½ hours of smoking (see chart on page 6)

GEAR: An instant-read thermometer; wire rack; jumbo heavy-duty resealable plastic bag

SHOP: Buy pork loin, preferably a heritage breed, with some surrounding fat intact. Pink curing salt contains salt and nitrites (see Shop, page 105 for percentages); buy it at a good meat market or order it online from Amazon. Star anise is harvested from a tree in the pine family native to China and Vietnam. It has a smoky licoricy flavor; you'll find it at most supermarkets.

WHAT ELSE: Unlike the Made-from-Scratch Bacon on page 113, Irish and Canadian bacons are cured in brine, not with dry flavorings. (Because pork loin is so lean, the brine helps keep it moist during smoking.) If you're curious to try brine-curing belly bacon, use the brine in this recipe.

INGREDIENTS

6 whole star anise

1½ teaspoons fennel seeds

1½ teaspoons black peppercorns

2 quarts water

1 cup coarse salt (sea or kosher)

⅔ cup sugar

2 teaspoons pink curing salt (Prague Powder No. 1 or Insta Cure No. 1)

1 cup coarsely chopped fresh fennel (bulb and fronds)

2 sprigs fresh thyme or 1 teaspoon dried

1 bay leaf

1 clove garlic, peeled and smashed with the side of a chef's knife or cleaver

2½- to 3-pound center-cut pork loin

1. Make the brine: In a dry heavy-bottomed stockpot, roast the star anise, fennel seeds, and peppercorns over medium-high heat until toasted and aromatic, 2 to 3 minutes, stirring frequently. Add the water, the coarse salt, sugar, curing salt, fennel, thyme, bay leaf, and garlic. Bring to a boil, stirring occasionally, and boil until the salts and sugar dissolve, 3 minutes. Remove from the heat and let cool completely to room temperature.

2. Place the pork loin in a jumbo heavy-duty resealable plastic bag. Add the brine, squeeze out the air, seal the bag, and place it in an aluminum foil pan or roasting pan. (The pan catches any potential leaks from the bag.) Brine the pork in the refrigerator for 4 to 5 days, turning it over once a day. Note: You can speed up the process by 1 day by injecting the pork loin with some of the brine (see page 164) on day 1 and injecting again after 2 days.

3. Drain the pork loin well, discarding the brine. Rinse the loin and blot dry with paper towels. Set the loin on a wire rack over a rimmed baking sheet and let it air-dry at room temperature for 30 minutes.

4. Meanwhile, set up your smoker following the manufacturer's instructions and preheat to 225° to 250°F. Add the wood as specified by the manufacturer.

5. Place the pork loin directly on the rack in the smoker. Smoke until bronzed with wood smoke and the internal temperature reaches 160°F, about 2½ hours. (Insert an instant-read thermometer through one of the ends into the center of the pork loin.)

6. Transfer the pork loin to a wire rack over a rimmed baking sheet and cool to room temperature. Wrap tightly in plastic wrap and refrigerate.

7. To serve the bacon, slice thinly across the grain. Heat by grilling or pan-frying.

BARBECUED PORK BELLY

YIELD: Serves 6 to 8

METHOD: Hot-smoking

PREP TIME: 10 minutes

SMOKING TIME: 3 to 3½ hours

FUEL: Magee uses equal parts hickory and cherry. You'll need enough wood for 3½ hours of smoking (see chart on page 6).

GEAR: An instant-read thermometer

SHOP: Pork belly used to require a special order from your local butcher shop. Now you can buy it at Whole Foods.

Bacon is about smoke and salt. Barbecue is about smoke and spice. They join forces in this barbecued pork belly—inspired by a new-school barbecue restaurant in Kansas City, Missouri, called Q39, run by an old-school chef and pit master named Rob Magee. What is most remarkable about this sizzling, spice-crusted barbecued belly is how it retains the sweet, meaty taste of fresh pork. You'd never mistake it for bacon. Serve the tangy Mustard Vinegar Sauce alongside.

INGREDIENTS

1 piece (3 to 3½ pounds) pork belly

2 tablespoons coarse salt (sea or kosher), plus extra for seasoning

2 tablespoons sugar

2 tablespoons sweet paprika

1 tablespoon granulated garlic

1 tablespoon pure chile powder

1 tablespoon ground cumin

1½ teaspoons freshly ground black pepper, plus extra for seasoning

1½ teaspoons dry mustard powder (preferably Colman's)

½ teaspoon freshly ground white pepper, or more black pepper

½ teaspoon cayenne pepper

Mustard Vinegar Sauce (optional; recipe follows)

1. Remove the skin from the pork belly (see Note on page 114). Score both sides, cutting a 1-inch crosshatch pattern with cuts ¼ inch deep.

There are
many ways to serve this pork
belly. For example, cut it
into ¼-inch-thick slices and
use it in place of bacon on a
BLT. Or atop a hamburger or
cheeseburger (page 136). Or
over the Smoked Vegetable
Cassoulet on page 220. The
best just might be cut into
bite-size pieces and devoured
off the ends of toothpicks.

2. Make the rub: Place the salt,
sugar, paprika, garlic, chile powder,
cumin, black pepper, mustard powder,
white pepper, if using, and cayenne
in a bowl. Mix well with your fingers.
Sprinkle the rub over the top, bottom,
and sides of the pork belly, rubbing it
into the meat with your fingertips.

3. Set up your smoker following the
manufacturer's instructions and
preheat to 225° to 250°F. Add the
wood as specified by the manufacturer.

4. Place the pork belly on the rack in
the smoker, fat side up. Smoke until
bronzed with wood smoke and the
internal temperature reaches 160°F.
This will take 3 to 3½ hours.

5. Serve the pork belly as is, cut into
dice or crosswise (against the grain)
into ½-inch-thick slices. Pass the
sauce, if using.

6. To serve the slices browned, lightly
season them with salt and pepper.
Preheat a grill to hot. Arrange the
slices on the grate on a diagonal and
grill until sizzling and browned on
both sides, about 2 minutes per side.
(Give each slice a quarter turn after
1 minute to lay on a crosshatch of
grill marks.) The melting fat may
cause flare-ups, so you'll want to leave
yourself plenty of maneuvering room
to dodge the flames. Alternatively,
brown in a skillet.

MUSTARD VINEGAR SAUCE

YIELD: Makes about 4 cups

To go with your pork belly, here's a tangy mustard vinegar sauce with the hopsy malt finish of dark beer.

INGREDIENTS

2 cups ketchup

¾ cup cider vinegar, or to taste

½ cup Dijon mustard

½ cup dark beer

1½ teaspoons hot red pepper flakes

1 teaspoon freshly ground black pepper

1 teaspoon sugar

1 teaspoon onion powder

½ teaspoon coarse salt (sea or kosher),
  or to taste

Place all the ingredients in a heavy
saucepan and whisk to mix. Simmer
until thick and richly flavored, 6 to 10
minutes, whisking often. Correct the
seasoning, adding vinegar or salt to
taste: The sauce should be tangy and
sharp.

GREAT HAMS OF THE WORLD

Ham is a hog's leap to immortality. At its simplest, ham consists of a hog's hind leg dry-cured with salt or wet-cured in brine, then dried, smoked, and sometimes baked. Not all the world's great hams are smoked—think Italian prosciutto or Spanish Serrano. But smoking adds a depth of flavor prized by ham fanatics all over the world.

Hams come in two broad categories: **cooked hams** and **cured hams**.

Cooked hams start with a **brine** or **wet cure** (page 163), infused into the fresh pork by immersion, injection, or tumbling.

The rosy color comes from curing agents like sodium nitrite (page 163), without which ham would look and taste like pork roast. These hams come precooked and lightly smoked, so they're ready to eat the moment you carve them. The best owe their smoke flavor to real wood smoke. Inexpensive mass-market cooked ham never sees the inside of a smokehouse; the "smoke" flavor comes from liquid smoke in the brine. Great cooked hams include:

Harrington ham: A cooked ham from Vermont cured with salt, granulated sugar, maple sugar, nitrites, and Vermont spring water and smoked with maple wood and corncobs.

Jambon de Paris (Paris ham): The quintessential French cooked ham. Moist, meaty, and mildly smoky, it's used in the French grilled ham and cheese sandwich, *croque monsieur*.

Cured hams start with a dry cure of salt, sodium nitrite, often sugar, and other seasonings, such as cloves or juniper berries. The cure dehydrates the ham, retards spoilage, and simultaneously imparts rich umami flavors characteristic of the world's great hams. After curing, the hams are rinsed, air-dried, smoked, and aged for anywhere from three months to two years. European cured hams like Italian speck are ready to eat after aging. American hams, such as Virginia or Tennessee hams, undergo heavier salting,

which requires them to be soaked in several changes of fresh water before cooking and serving. Great cured hams include:

Speck: A juniper- and coriander-cured ham from the Italian Alps. Smoked over juniper wood, speck owes its unique Alpine flavor to the mountain winds funneled through the smokehouse and a minimum of twenty-two weeks' aging. One of my favorite brands is Valdovan. Serve sliced paper thin with caraway crackers.

Schwarzwälder Schinken and **Westphalian Schinken:** German dry-cured heavily smoked hams respectively from the Black Forest region in western Germany and the oak forests of Westphalia in northwest Germany. The former is salted and seasoned with garlic, coriander, juniper berries, and other spices, before being cold-smoked over juniper for several weeks. The latter is made from pigs fattened on acorns; it is smoked over beech wood and juniper.

Smithfield ham/Virginia ham: Heavily salted, hickory-smoked ham from the Smithfield region in southern Virginia. Unlike European smoked cured hams, Virginia hams are meant to be soaked in water to remove excess salt, then cooked before slicing and serving.

Surreyano: An incredibly sweet, smoky, slow ham from S. Wallace Edwards & Sons in Surrey, Virginia. No soaking required: tastes best sliced paper-thin.

Tennessee ham: Sweet smoky ham from the mountains of Tennessee. One excellent brand is Benton's in Madisonville. The hams are cured with salt, brown sugar, pepper, and sodium nitrite and aged for at least ten months prior to smoking over hickory wood.

York ham: a dry-cured, lightly smoked cooked ham from York, England, recognizable by its rosy-colored flesh, firm texture, and meaty porky taste.

SMOKEHOUSE SHOULDER HAM

YIELD: Makes 1 shoulder ham, enough to serve 12 to 16 as a starter, 8 to 10 as a main course

METHOD: Cold-smoking followed by hot-smoking

PREP TIME: 30 minutes

BRINING TIME: 7 days

COLD-SMOKING TIME: 12 hours. I normally cold-smoke in a smokehouse, water smoker, or electric smoker.

HOT-SMOKING TIME: 10 to 12 hours. I like to hot-smoke the ham in a kamado-style cooker fitted with a temperature controller, but you can use a water smoker, electric or propane smoker, or a kettle grill set up for smoking.

FUEL: Hickory and/or apple wood—enough for 24 hours of smoking (see chart on page 6)

GEAR: A meat injector; jumbo heavy-duty resealable plastic bag; wire rack; large food-safe plastic bucket or stockpot; sturdy butcher's string (optional); instant-read or remote digital thermometer

This is it, the Big Kahuna: a whole ham you cure and smoke yourself. The process involves four classic techniques: curing in brine, injecting with brine, cold-smoking, then hot-smoking. Each adds a distinctive layer of flavor. The brine gives the pork a characteristic sweet, salty, hammy, umami flavor, while injecting accelerates the curing process. Cold-smoking drives the wood smoke flavor deep into the meat. The hot-smoking cooks the ham.

But why bother—can't you buy great ham ready-made and ready to slice? Sure, but when you pull this monster off your smoker—the exterior darkly bronzed with smoke, the meat pink as a cherub, with smoke and salt flavors that won't quit—you'll feel a sense of pride money just can't buy. Not only that, but you control the quality of the pork and make sure your ham is all meat, without industrial fillers. True, the process is a bit time consuming (1 week from start to finish), but there's little actual labor. Tip o' the hat to Dallas smoke master Tim Byres, who turned me on to the dual cold-smoke/hot-smoke method.

INGREDIENTS

FOR THE BRINE

1 pound (3¼ cups) coarse salt (sea or kosher)

8 ounces (1 cup) packed dark brown sugar

2 tablespoons pickling spice

1 tablespoon pink curing salt (Prague Powder No. 1 or Insta Cure No. 1)

3 quarts hot water plus 2 quarts ice water

ADDITIONAL FLAVORINGS (OPTIONAL)

10 whole cloves

5 juniper berries, smashed with the side of a chef's knife or cleaver

4 bay leaves

4 strips orange zest (½ inch by 2 inches)

4 cloves garlic, peeled and lightly crushed with the side of a cleaver

1 tablespoon whole black peppercorns

FOR THE HAM

1 fresh shoulder ham (aka picnic ham; 9 to 10 pounds)

1. Make the brine: Place the coarse salt, sugar, pickling spice, curing salt, and 3 quarts hot water in a large nonreactive pot. Stir in additional flavorings, if using. Bring to a boil over high heat and continue boiling until the salts and sugar are completely dissolved, stirring from time to time, 3 minutes. Remove from the heat and add the ice water. Let cool completely, then refrigerate until cold.

2. Strain 2 cups brine into a measuring cup. Using a meat injector, inject this portion of the brine deep into the ham at 1½-inch intervals along the bone. Continue injecting until all the measured brine is used.

3. Place the ham in a jumbo heavy-duty resealable plastic bag. Place it in a roasting pan or a large, deep nonreactive container, such as a clean food-grade plastic bucket or a deep stockpot. Add the brine to the bag (the ham should be completely submerged), then squeeze the air out and seal the bag. Cure in the refrigerator for 7 days. Turn the ham over daily so it cures evenly. Halfway through the curing time (3½ days), measure out 2 more cups of brine, strain it, and reinject the ham with it. A properly cured ham will look pink (like commercially cured ham).

4. After 7 days, drain the ham well, rinse thoroughly with cold water, and dry with paper towels. If you plan to hang the ham in your smoker, securely tie the shank (narrow) end with butcher's string; make sure the string is substantial enough to support the weight of the ham. You can also smoke the ham on a rack in your smoker. No string needed.

5. Set up your smoker for cold-smoking following the manufacturer's instructions; the temperature should be below 100°F (see page 108). Add the wood as specified by the manufacturer. Hang the ham in the smoker or place it on one of the racks. Cold smoke the ham at no more than 100°F for 12 hours. (Cold-smoking infuses the meat with smoke flavor without cooking the meat.)

6. Set up your smoker for hot-smoking following the manufacturer's instructions and preheat to 225° to 250°F. Add the wood as specified by the manufacturer.

7. Hot-smoke the ham until cooked through (the internal temperature should reach about 160°F), 10 to 12 hours. I use a remote digital thermometer (page 14), but you can also check for doneness with an instant-read thermometer. In either case, insert the probe deep into the meat but not touching the bone.

8. You can serve the ham hot out of the smoker, or let it cool on a wire rack to room temperature, then cover and refrigerate it until you're ready to serve. Refrigerated, it will keep for at least a week. Glaze and reheat it as you would a commercial ham.

NOTE: A true ham would be made with the hind leg of a hog. However, you'll be facing an 18- to 20-pound hunk of meat. Double the amount of brine and brining time. You'll need 24 hours for cold-smoking and 16 hours for hot-smoking.

SHOP: To speed up the process, I call for a shoulder ham, the lower half of the pork shoulder that is sometimes called a picnic ham. As always, when possible, buy local pork or a heritage breed, like Berkshire or Duroc. Pickling spice contains coriander and mustard seeds, peppercorns, bay leaf, and more. Use a good commercial brand like McCormick. Pink curing salt contains salt and nitrites (see page 16); buy it at a good meat market or order it from Amazon.

WHAT ELSE: I like the look of a ham with the skin intact, so I leave it on. However, you can't really eat the skin (it does, however, add a soulful smoke flavor to soups, stews, beans, and collard greens); alternatively, you can grill or deep-fry it to make awesome cracklings. Feel free to remove it if you prefer, but keep the subcutaneous fat layer intact.

LAMB

According to the USDA, the average American eats less than one pound of lamb per year. You could have fooled me. Hometown Bar-B-Que in Brooklyn can't smoke it fast enough to satisfy the demand for its popular lamb belly *banh mi*. Then there's Owensboro, Kentucky, the self-proclaimed barbecued mutton capital of the world, where local pit masters (many descended from Dutch sheep farmers) smoke more than ten *tons* of mutton each May to serve the 80,000 people who—excuse the metaphor—flock to the annual International Bar-B-Que Festival. Perhaps you smoke lamb already, in which case you know how wood smoke transforms the rich meaty flavor of lamb into gustatory nirvana. Perhaps you don't, in which case the following Almost Barbecued Mutton with Black Dip, Smoke-Braised Lamb Shanks, Denver-cut ribs, and Barbecued Lamb Belly will make you a believer.

ALMOST BARBECUED MUTTON
WITH BLACK DIP

YIELD: Serves 6 to 8

METHOD: Hot-smoking

PREP TIME: 15 minutes

SMOKING TIME: 6 to 8 hours

FUEL: Hickory—enough for 8 hours of smoking (see chart on page 6).

GEAR: A remote digital thermometer or instant-read thermometer; insulated rubber gloves; a cleaver or meat claws for pulling and shredding the lamb

SHOP: You have two options for lamb: shoulder, which has more fat, or leg, which is more readily available. Given the choice, I'd use shoulder, but both make superlative sandwiches.

WHAT ELSE: If you're used to cooking lamb to a fashionable medium-rare, the 195°F target temperature may surprise you, but you need to fully cook—even overcook—the lamb to achieve the requisite tenderness.

Spread out a map of Kentucky and plant a pin in the city of Owensboro on the Ohio River. Now draw an imaginary half circle around it large enough to include the counties to the south, west, and east. Outside that circle lies the barbecue comfort zone: a familiar realm of brisket, ribs, pulled pork, and smoked chicken with red (or occasionally white) barbecue sauce. But inside, people eat hickory-smoked mutton with what may be the world's only black barbecue sauce (in local parlance called "dip," not "sauce"). If the prospect of mutton fails to make you salivate, you're not alone. Until you taste it smoked the better part of a day in brick pits fired with smoldering hickory, assertively sauced with lemon and Worcestershire sauce, then piled on a butter-toasted bun.

Mutton is virtually impossible to find outside this part of Kentucky, so I've adapted the traditional recipe to more readily available lamb—hence the name "Almost Mutton."

INGREDIENTS

Black Dip (page 126)

1 bone-in lamb shoulder or leg (5 to 6 pounds)

Coarse salt (sea or kosher) and freshly ground black pepper

6 to 8 hamburger buns (preferably with sesame seeds) or crusty rolls, for serving (optional)

2 tablespoons (¼ stick) butter, melted, for serving (optional)

Dill pickle slices (optional)

1. Set up your smoker following the manufacturer's instructions and preheat to 225° to 250°F. Add the wood as specified by the manufacturer.

2. While the smoker is heating, make the Black Dip. Set aside 1 cup for mopping and 1 cup for mixing with the cooked lamb; reserve the remaining cup for serving.

3. Very generously season the lamb on all sides with salt and pepper. Place the lamb directly on the rack in the smoker, fat side up. Insert the probe of the thermometer, if using, through the side of the shoulder or end of the leg deep into the center. Otherwise, check the internal temperature with an instant-read thermometer once the meat is smoked.

4. Starting after 2 hours and then every hour, mop or baste the outside of the lamb with dip. Replenish the charcoal and wood chunks or chips as needed. Smoke the lamb until crusty and brown on the outside and very tender: The internal temperature should be 195°F. When cooked, the meat will be so tender you can pull out the bones with a tug. Total cooking time will be 6 to 8 hours.

5. Transfer the lamb to a cutting board. *Loosely* drape a sheet of aluminum foil over the lamb and let it rest for 15 minutes. (Don't bunch the foil around the lamb or you'll steam it and make the crust soggy.) Wearing insulated gloves, pull out and discard the bones. Pull off and discard any large lumps of fat. Coarsely chop the lamb with a cleaver or pull it into large meaty shreds with meat claws. Stir in 1 cup of the remaining dip, or to taste.

6. If serving as sandwiches, butter the buns or rolls and toast on the grill or in a skillet, then pile the lamb and pickle slices, if desired, on the buns. Serve with the remaining dip on the side.

BLACK DIP

YIELD: Makes about 3 cups

A jolting amalgam of Worcestershire sauce, lemon juice, and tomato sauce with minimal brown sugar for sweetness and hot pepper flakes to crank up the heat—use it as both a basting mixture and barbecue sauce.

INGREDIENTS

1 cup Worcestershire sauce

1 cup tomato sauce

1 cup water

3 tablespoons fresh lemon juice

⅓ cup packed dark brown sugar, or to taste

2 tablespoons (¼ stick) butter

1 to 2 teaspoons hot red pepper flakes

Coarse salt (sea or kosher) and freshly ground black pepper

Place the Worcestershire sauce, tomato sauce, water, lemon juice, brown sugar, butter, and hot red pepper flakes in a heavy saucepan and whisk to mix. Bring to a boil over medium heat, whisking often. Reduce the heat and gently simmer the sauce until richly flavored, 5 minutes, whisking from time to time. Correct the seasoning, adding salt and pepper to taste and a little more brown sugar if you like your sauce sweeter. Remove the sauce from the heat and let cool to room temperature.

LAMB SMOKING CHART

FOOD	AMOUNT	SMOKER TEMP	TIME	INTERNAL TEMP/DONENESS
Shoulder (bone-in)	5-6 pounds	225°-250°F	6-8 hours	195°F
Shanks (hocks)	1¼-1½ pounds (each)	225°-250°F	4-6 hours	195°F
Ribs	1½-pound racks	225°-250°F	2-3 hours	Meat shrinks back ½ inch from ends of bones
Belly	2½-3 pounds	225°-250°F	3-4 hours	195°F

WHAT IS A SMOKE RING AND HOW DOES IT FORM?

Call it the red badge of honor of great barbecue. The smoke ring is a pinkish-red band found just below the surface of barbecued meats. So what causes it and how can *you* achieve a handsome smoke ring every time?

Meat owes its bright red color to a protein called myoglobin. This color darkens and changes when subjected to air or heat. Burning wood releases many compounds, including a gas called nitrogen dioxide. As the gas dissolves into the meat, it converts to nitrous acid, then nitric oxide, which binds with the myoglobin to form a stable pink molecule that resists heat. Thus, the wood smoke locks in that prized pinkish-red color.

Because the nitrogen dioxide gas is absorbed from the outside in, the smoke ring occurs only at the outside edge of the meat. Typical smoke rings will be ⅛ to ½ inch deep. Want to maximize the smoke ring? The secret is moisture.

- Swabbing your brisket with mop sauce or spraying it with, say, apple cider creates a wetter surface. This helps drive more nitrogen dioxide deeper into the meat.

- Another way to achieve a better smoke ring is to soak your wood chips before adding them to the coals. Water-soaked wood produces more nitrogen dioxide when burned than dry wood.

- A third way to is to place a pan of water or other liquid in the smoke chamber.

If natural wood smoke isn't delivering the smoke ring you want, there's a hack people use to fake it: Lightly rub the meat with sodium nitrite-based curing salt prior to smoking and you'll get a smoke ring the bright color of cured ham. Just don't count on it to help you win competitions. The Kansas City Barbecue Society (KCBS) has ceased making a smoke ring one of the criteria for professional judges. Warning: Sodium nitrite is toxic in large doses.

SMOKE-BRAISED LAMB SHANKS
WITH ASIAN SEASONINGS

YIELD: Makes 2 shanks, enough to serve 2; can be multiplied as desired

METHOD: Hot-smoking

PREP TIME: 20 minutes

SMOKING TIME: 4 to 6 hours

FUEL: Any hardwood—with Asian seasonings, I especially like cherry or apple. You'll need enough for 10 hours of smoking (see chart on page 6).

GEAR: A large aluminum foil drip pan; an instant-read thermometer

SHOP: Most supermarkets sell lamb shanks; otherwise, order from your local butcher. Rice wine is an alcoholic beverage made from fermented rice; if you can't find Chinese *shaoxing*, substitute sake or sherry. Asian (dark) sesame oil is a fragrant oil pressed from roasted sesame seeds.

WHAT ELSE: Star anise is a star-shaped spice with a smoky licorice flavor. Look for it in Asian markets and natural foods stores, or substitute Chinese five-spice powder.

Like most braised meats, the shanks reheat well. Killer today and even better tomorrow.

Lamb shanks pack big flavors, but like all extremity cuts, the tough connective tissue requires a low heat and long cooking time to make them tender. You also need a moist environment to keep the meat from drying out. Enter a technique I call smoke-braising. Traditional braising means cooking meat with a little liquid in a sealed Dutch oven with embers below and on top of it. In smoke-braising, you smoke the meat in an open pan with an inch of liquid so it benefits from the moisturizing environment of braising and the smoke flavor of true barbecue. This recipe takes its inspiration from Chinese red cooking—the soy sauce and seasonings give the meat a reddish hue. Sweet, salty, spice-scented, and rich in umami flavors—it's Asian barbecue at its most awesome.

INGREDIENTS

2 lamb shanks (1¼ to 1½ pounds each)

1 to 2 cups water

½ cup soy sauce

½ cup rice wine (shaoxing), sake, or sherry (cream or dry)

½ cup packed dark or light brown sugar

3 tablespoons Asian (dark) sesame oil

4 strips orange or tangerine zest (½ inch by 1½ inches each)

3 whole star anise, or 1½ teaspoons Chinese five-spice powder

2 cinnamon sticks (each about 3 inches long)

1. Using a sharp, slender implement like the probe of an instant-read thermometer, pierce each lamb shank all over, about 20 times. (This encourages the absorption of the flavorings.) Place the shanks in a large aluminum foil pan.

2. Place the water, soy sauce, rice wine, brown sugar, and sesame oil in a bowl and whisk until the sugar dissolves. Add the orange zest, star

anise, and cinnamon sticks. Pour over the lamb.

3. Meanwhile, set up your smoker following the manufacturer's instructions and preheat to 225° to 250°F. Add the wood as specified by the manufacturer.

4. Place the lamb with its braising liquid in the foil pan, in the smoker. Smoke until the lamb is dark brown

and very tender, 8 to 10 hours. Turn the shanks with tongs every 30 minutes so they brown evenly. Add water as needed (1 to 2 cups) to keep the liquid level over ½ inch. (Try not to add any the last 30 minutes so as not to dilute the sauce.) Add fuel and wood as needed. When ready, the lamb will have shrunk back from the end of the bone and will be tender enough to pull apart with your fingers. The internal temperature on an instant-read thermometer inserted in the thickest part of the shank not touching the bone will be 195°F.

5. Transfer the lamb to a platter or plates. Skim any visible fat off the braising liquid and strain it over the shanks by way of a sauce.

BARBECUED LAMB BELLY

YIELD: Serves 4

METHOD: Hot-smoking

PREP TIME: 10 minutes

SMOKING TIME: 3 to 4 hours

RESTING TIME: 30 minutes

FUEL: Durney burns oak, but any hardwood will do. You'll need enough for 4 hours of smoking (see chart on page 6).

GEAR: Instant-read thermometer; unlined butcher paper; an insulated cooler

SHOP: Lamb breast is a fatty cut from the underbelly, characterized by thin bones and striated layers of meat and fat.

WHAT ELSE: Can't find lamb breast? Barbecued pork belly makes equally awesome banh mi.

Beef belly ("navel" as it's known in butcher-speak) gives us pastrami, and pork belly offers so much human happiness, it used to trade on the Chicago Mercantile Exchange. The next cut from the undercarriage to add to your must-try list is lamb belly (aka lamb breast). Just ask Billy Durney. The bodyguard-turned-pit master can't cook enough of it at his booming Hometown Bar-B-Que in Red Hook, Brooklyn. "We smoke the lamb breast longer than you'd expect. Actually, we overcook it to the point where the bones just pop out. The idea is to render all the fat." Here's how Durney does it, complete with a delivery system from Vietnam: Lamb Belly Banh Mi (page 132).

INGREDIENTS

1 lamb breast (aka lamb belly; 2½ to 3 pounds)

3 tablespoons coarsely ground black pepper

1 tablespoon coarse salt (sea or kosher)

1 tablespoon turbinado sugar

Sriracha-Lime Hot Sauce (recipe follows), for serving

1. Set up your smoker following the manufacturer's instructions and preheat to 225° to 250°F. Add the wood as specified by the manufacturer.

2. Trim any papery membrane or bloody spots off the lamb breast and place on a rimmed baking sheet.

3. Make the rub: Combine the pepper, salt, and sugar in a small bowl and mix with your fingers. Sprinkle the lamb breast on all sides with the mixture, rubbing it into the meat with your fingertips. Store any leftover rub in a sealed jar. It will keep for several weeks.

4. Place the lamb breast fat side up (the rounded side of the ribs should face up) on the rack in your smoker. Smoke the lamb until meltingly tender, 3 to 4 hours. (Depending on the size and cut of the lamb, you may need an additional 1 to 2 hours.) The internal temperature on an instant-read thermometer inserted in the meat but not touching the bone should be 195°F, and the meat should be so tender that the bones pull out without any resistance.

5. Wrap the lamb in double sheets of unlined butcher paper and place in an insulated cooler. Let rest for 30 minutes. To serve, cut the lamb belly into individual ribs. Or pull out and discard the bones and coarsely chop the lamb. Serve with the hot sauce.

SRIRACHA-LIME HOT SAUCE

YIELD: Makes about 1 cup; you'll have leftovers, which you'll definitely appreciate later.

Think of this sauce as ketchup for pyromaniacs—and don't think of serving barbecued lamb belly without it.

INGREDIENTS

¾ cup sriracha

1 teaspoon freshly grated lime zest

2 tablespoons fresh lime juice

2 tablespoons soy sauce

2 tablespoons honey

3 tablespoons minced fresh cilantro

Place the sriracha, lime zest and juice, soy sauce, honey, and cilantro in a small bowl and whisk to mix. It will keep in the refrigerator for several weeks.

LAMB BELLY BANH MI

YIELD: Serves 4

Here's the *real* reason you want to smoke Hometown Bar-B-Que's lamb belly: to make Vietnamese-style sandwiches. You'll love the way the crisp, mildly acidic slaw cuts the fattiness of the lamb belly. For the best results, prepare the slaw a couple of hours before you make the sandwiches.

INGREDIENTS

FOR THE VINEGAR SLAW

2 carrots, peeled

1 medium-size (about 8 ounces) daikon radish, peeled

1 pickling (Kirby) cucumber or small cucumber

1 teaspoon coarse salt (sea or kosher)

¼ cup sugar

¾ cup rice vinegar

2 whole cloves

2 black peppercorns

FOR THE SANDWICHES

1 large or 2 small crusty baguettes

2 tablespoons (¼ stick) butter, at room temperature (optional)

1 Barbecued Lamb Belly, boned and chopped (page 130)

Sriracha-Lime Hot Sauce (page 131) or straight sriracha

1 bunch fresh cilantro, washed, shaken dry, and torn into sprigs

1. Make the slaw: Cut or shred the carrots, daikon, and cucumber lengthwise into matchstick slivers. Place in a medium-size bowl and stir in the salt and sugar. Let marinate for 5 minutes. Add the rice vinegar, cloves, and peppercorns and stir until the sugar dissolves. Let the slaw marinate for at least 1 hour or as long as overnight, covered, in the refrigerator. Before serving, discard the cloves and peppercorns.

2. Cut the baguette crosswise into 7-inch lengths. Cut each section almost in half through the side. If you're feeling ambitious, slather the cut face of each bread with butter and toast on a grill or in a skillet. (This is optional, but it gives the bread extra flavor and crunch.) Place chopped lamb belly, slaw (add it with a slotted spoon to drain off the excess vinegar), and sauce on the bottom half of each piece of baguette. Pile on the cilantro, close the sandwich, and dig in.

BARBECUED LAMB RIBS
WITH FRESH HERB WET RUB

More tender than beef and more flavorful than pork, lamb ribs can stand up to any spice or smoke you throw at them. By way of a seasoning, I use a fresh herb wet rub from my *Barbecue University* TV show days. Pungent. Spicy. Smoky. They're everything barbecued ribs should be.

INGREDIENTS

4 racks Denver-cut lamb ribs (the equivalent of a pork sparerib; about 1½ pounds each)

2 cups tightly packed chopped mixed fresh herbs, including parsley, sage, rosemary, and/or thyme

5 cloves garlic, roughly chopped

1 tablespoon coarse salt (sea or kosher)

1 tablespoon sweet paprika

2 teaspoons freshly ground black pepper

2 teaspoons sugar

1 teaspoon hot red pepper flakes, or to taste

½ teaspoon ground mace

⅓ to ½ cup vegetable oil, plus extra as needed

1. Prepare the ribs: Place a rack of ribs meat side down on a rimmed baking sheet. Remove the thin, papery membrane from the back of the rack. Turn the ribs over and, using a knife, score a crosshatch pattern on the meat. Make cuts about ½ inch apart and ¼ inch deep. Repeat with the remaining racks. Arrange the racks in a single layer in a baking dish.

2. Place the herbs, garlic, salt, paprika, pepper, sugar, hot red pepper flakes, and mace in a food processor and finely chop. Work in enough oil to obtain a thick paste.

3. Spread the wet rub over the lamb on both sides using a rubber spatula. Smoke the ribs now, or to get more flavor, let them marinate in the refrigerator for 3 hours or overnight.

4. Set up your smoker following the manufacturer's instructions and preheat to 225° to 250°F. Add wood as specified by the manufacturer.

5. Place the ribs directly on the rack in the smoker and smoke until tender and the meat shrinks back from the ends of the bones about ½ inch, 2 to 3 hours.

6. Transfer to a cutting board and cut into individual ribs and serve.

YIELD: Makes 4 racks, enough to serve 4

METHOD: Hot-smoking

PREP TIME: 30 minutes

MARINATING TIME: 3 hours

SMOKING TIME : 2 to 3 hours

FUEL: Hardwood of your choice—enough for 3 hours of smoking (see chart on page 6)

GEAR: A food processor

SHOP: You'll probably need to preorder lamb ribs from your supermarket meat department or local butcher shop. Or look for them at a Greek, Middle Eastern, or halal meat market. You can also order them online from jamisonfarm.com.

WHAT ELSE: Can't find lamb ribs? The wet rub makes great smoked baby back pork ribs.

BURGERS, SAUSAGES, AND MORE

People have been smoking ground meats such as sausages for millennia. It's time to broaden your reach. In this chapter, you'll cold-smoke hamburgers with fragrant blasts of hay smoke. You'll discover *boulettes* (French-Canadian meatballs) smoked with maple and served with maple-mustard barbecue sauce. You'll learn to smoke bratwurst for big flavor and no flare-ups—it's a *lot* easier than the customary direct grilling. If you're looking for excess, the Tulsa Torpedo (aka the Fatty) rolls breakfast sausage, kielbasa, and hot links in one spectacular smoky bacon weave. Grind it up and smoke it. Here's how.

HAY-SMOKED HAMBURGERS

YIELD: Makes 4 burgers

METHOD: Hay-smoking

PREP TIME: 15 minutes

SMOKING TIME: 3 minutes

COOKING TIME: 8 minutes

FUEL: Charcoal and about 2 quarts hay—enough for 3 minutes of smoking

GEAR: A large (9 by 13 inches) aluminum foil drip pan and a wire rack that fits on top of it; an instant-read thermometer

SHOP: Buy organic or grass-fed beef when possible (I like 18 percent fat content). The 2 pounds called for will give you four 8-ounce burgers. For a smaller burger, use 1½ pounds ground beef. Look for hay at garden centers or tack shops. It's also available online from Amazon.

WHAT ELSE: Good food safety calls for cooking the burgers to at least 160°F. One way to keep them moist at this temperature is to fold coarsely grated cheese, such as smoked provolone or Cheddar, into the ground beef. The cheese melts as the burger grills, producing a rich, juicy mouthfeel. I call these inside-out cheeseburgers.

Smoking a hamburger is harder than it seems. Forget prolonged smoking in a conventional smoker—low and slow works great on tough muscles like brisket, but hamburgers become rubbery and dry without a hot fire to sear the exterior. The secret lies in a technique used to smoke cheese in central Italy: hay-smoking (see page 42). Lit hay produces a dense cloud of intensely flavored smoke that lasts a few minutes—long enough to smoke the burgers, but brief enough to leave the meat raw so you can sear it on a conventional grill. An added advantage: Hay-smoking works great on a gas grill.

INGREDIENTS

2 pounds ground chuck or ground sirloin or a mixture of the two

8 ounces smoked provolone or smoked cheddar cheese, coarsely grated (2 cups; optional)

Vegetable oil, for oiling the grate

Coarse salt (sea or kosher) and freshly ground black pepper

4 hamburger buns

2 tablespoons (¼ stick) butter, melted

SUGGESTED TOPPINGS AND CONDIMENTS

Lettuce leaves

Sliced ripe tomatoes

Sliced avocados

Sliced dill pickles or sweet pickles

Grilled bacon

Sliced or caramelized onions

Ketchup

Mustard

Mayonnaise

1. Place the ground beef in a large bowl. Stir in the grated cheese, if using, with a wooden spoon. Lightly moisten your hands with cold water. Working quickly and with a light touch, pat the meat into 4 patties 4 inches in diameter and 1 inch thick.

2. Arrange the burgers, well spaced, on a wire rack. Refrigerate until time to smoke.

3. Just before putting the burgers in the smoker or on the grill, fill a large aluminum foil pan with ice cubes (about two thirds of the way) and place the rack with the burgers on the top lip of the pan. The meat should not touch the ice.

4. On a charcoal smoker or grill: Place a small mound of charcoal in the smoker firebox (or to one side of a kettle grill) and light it. When the

coals glow red, toss the hay on the coals. If using a kettle grill, place the hay on the coals, then put the grate in place. Place the burgers on their rack over ice in the smoke chamber, as far away as possible from the fire. Close the smoker or grill. Smoke the burgers until lightly filmed with smoke; this will take about 3 minutes. You can smoke the burgers several hours ahead, but keep them covered with plastic wrap and refrigerated after smoking.

On a gas grill: Light one side of the grill on high. Place the burgers on their rack over ice on the opposite side of the grill. Place the hay over the lit burner and close the grill lid. Smoke the burgers until lightly filmed with smoke; this will take about 3 minutes. You can smoke the burgers several hours ahead, but keep them covered with plastic wrap and refrigerated after smoking.

5. Set up your grill for direct grilling and preheat to high. (On your charcoal grill, you'd rake the coals into a mound in the center.) Brush and oil the grill grate. Generously season the burgers with salt and pepper on both sides and direct grill until sizzling and browned on the outside and cooked to at least 160°F, about 4 minutes per side. (To check the doneness, insert an instant-read thermometer through the side of the burger.) Transfer the burgers to a platter and let rest while you grill the buns.

6. Brush the buns with butter and toast them on the grill, cut side down, about 1 minute.

7. Place the burgers on the buns, adding your favorite toppings and condiments. Tip: A lettuce leaf under the burger prevents the bun from getting soggy.

GROUND MEAT SMOKING CHART

FOOD	AMOUNT	SMOKER TEMP	TIME	INTERNAL TEMP/ DONENESS
Burgers (hay-smoked)	½ pound (each)	225°-250°F + high heat for searing	3 minutes + 4 minutes per side on the grill	160°F
Meatballs	1½-inch (1 ounce each)	225°-250°F	1-1½ hours	160°F
Fatty (bacon-wrapped sausage roll)	3 pounds	225°-250°F	2½-3 hours	160°F
Bratwurst	2 pounds	300°F	30-45 minutes	160°F

SMOKER AND FOOD SAFETY

The main reason we smoke food these days is for flavor, but in earlier times (make that most of human history) smoke was equally prized for its ability to prevent foods from spoiling. Which brings us to some commonsense—but worth highlighting—principles to prevent *your* food from spoiling and keep everyone safe when you smoke.

SETTING UP YOUR SMOKING AREA

- Position your smoker downwind of your prep and eating areas, out in the open, away from your house and overhanging trees or eaves, and certainly not in a garage, carport, or covered patio.

- If you smoke on a wooden deck, place a heatproof grill pad (such as a DiversiTech) under the firebox.

- Have a fire extinguisher and a bucket of sand on hand for extinguishing any unexpected fires.

HANDLING THE FOOD

- Keep perishable foods, from meats to seafood to mayonnaise, cold until they go into the smoker. That means refrigerator-cold or nested in a pan of ice. They should be kept at a temperature of 41°F or lower.

- Avoid cross contamination: Use separate cutting boards for trimming raw meats you plan to smoke and for cutting salads, vegetables, and fruits. Use different cutting boards for raw meats and cooked meats. (Commercial kitchens often use color-coded cutting boards to prevent mistakes.) Never let cooked meat touch a surface that's come in contact with raw meat, such as a platter, pan, spatula, and so on.

- Always wash your hands with hot soapy water before handling food and between food tasks, especially after coming in contact with raw meat. (Follow hand washing with a squirt of hand sanitizer.) Many people also use disposable latex or plastic gloves.

- When tailgating or working outdoors, make a sanitizing solution for plastic and wooden cutting boards by adding 1 tablespoon of household bleach to every 1 gallon of water. Use this mixture for wiping down cutting boards, knives, utensils, and countertops. Rinse with water after sanitizing to lose the bleach smell.

- Never brush the marinade from raw meat on cooked or smoked meat unless you've boiled the marinade for at least 3 minutes before brushing. Never brush basting or barbecue sauces onto raw meat—always wait until the exterior is cooked.

- Use an instant-read thermometer to test for doneness—especially when cooking poultry and ground meats. Cook poultry to at least 165°F and ground meats to at least 160°F.

- Hold hot foods at 140°F or higher. Hold cold foods at 41°F or lower.

- When smoking foods you intend to serve cold (kippered salmon, ham, and so on), let them cool at room temperature for no more than 2 hours, then refrigerate immediately.

MONTREAL MEATBALLS
WITH MAPLE-MUSTARD BARBECUE SAUCE

Perhaps you never thought of smoking meatballs. You haven't met Jonathan Nguyen, co-owner of Montreal's lively Le Boucan Smokehouse restaurant. (The name comes from the Franco-Caribbean word for smoke, which, incidentally, gave us the pirate term *buccaneer*.) Nguyen takes his inspiration from Kansas City and Memphis, but adds plenty of Quebec touches. "Our grandmothers cooked with apples and sweet spices like cinnamon and nutmeg, which we incorporate into our sauces and rubs," Nguyen says. The restaurant piles pulled pork and apple barbecue sauce onto its poutine. Even Quebec's homey meatballs (here enriched with buttermilk and energized with chipotle chiles) come smoked. Le Boucan serves them with maple syrup-inflected mustard barbecue sauce.

YIELD: Makes 24 meatballs (1½-inch meatballs), enough to serve 6 to 8 as a starter, 3 or 4 as a main course

METHOD: Hot-smoking

PREP TIME: 30 minutes

CHILLING TIME: 30 minutes

SMOKING TIME: 1 to 1½ hours

FUEL: Like all good Quebec barbecue buffs, the crew at Le Boucan smokes with local maple and apple wood. You'll need enough wood for 1½ hours of smoking (see chart on page 6).

GEAR: A wire rack or meatball basket for smoking the meatballs

SHOP: Le Boucan grinds sparerib trimmings for its meatballs, but any ground pork with a 20- to 30-percent fat content will do. Extra points for a heritage breed. Be sure to use pure maple syrup for the sauce; dark amber is usually less expensive and, in my opinion, more flavorful.

WHAT ELSE: For extra smoke flavor, Le Boucan cooks their barbecue sauce in the smoker. You can smoke the sauce alongside the meatballs (conveniently, it also takes 1 to 1½ hours) or at a separate smoke session.

1 hamburger bun or 2 slices white bread, torn into ½-inch pieces

⅓ cup buttermilk or milk

1 tablespoon butter or olive oil

1 slice artisanal bacon, minced

1 small onion, peeled and finely chopped (about ¾ cup)

1 clove garlic, peeled and minced

1 to 2 canned chipotle chiles, minced

3 tablespoons minced fresh cilantro or flat-leaf parsley

2 pounds ground pork

Coarse salt (sea or kosher) and freshly ground black pepper

Maple-Mustard Barbecue Sauce (recipe follows)

1. Place the torn bun or bread in a large bowl. Stir in the buttermilk and let soak until soft, 5 minutes.

2. Meanwhile, melt the butter in a medium-size skillet. Over medium heat, add the bacon, onion, and garlic and cook 1 to 2 minutes, stirring often. Stir in the chipotles and cilantro and cook until the onion is golden brown, 2 minutes more. Let the mixture cool to room temperature.

3. Add the bacon mixture, pork, 2 teaspoons salt, and 1 teaspoon pepper to the soaked bun or bread and mix well by hand or with a wooden spoon. To taste for seasoning, fry a small ball of the pork mixture in the skillet or cook it on a hot grill. Add salt and/or pepper as needed.

4. Line a rimmed baking sheet with aluminum foil or parchment paper (for easier cleanup). Divide the meatball mixture into four portions and roll each into a cylinder. Cut each cylinder into 6 equal portions and roll into 1½-inch meatballs for a total of 24. Periodically wet your hands with cold water to make rolling the meat easier. Place the meatballs on the baking sheet and chill in the refrigerator for at least 30 minutes.

5. Meanwhile, set up your smoker following the manufacturer's instructions and preheat to 225° to 250°F. Add the wood as specified by the manufacturer.

6. Arrange the meatballs in a meatball basket or on a wire rack and place in the smoke chamber. Smoke the meatballs until bronzed with smoke and cooked through (they'll be firm), 1 to 1½ hours. In some smokers, the meatballs closest to the fire will cook faster; if this is the case, rotate as needed so all cook evenly.

7. To serve, arrange the meatballs on a platter and spoon the sauce over them. Or impale on toothpicks and arrange on a platter, with the sauce in a bowl for dipping.

MAPLE-MUSTARD BARBECUE SAUCE

YIELD: Makes about 1½ cups

Le Boucan's take on a Carolina-style mustard sauce—enriched with maple syrup and Canadian dark beer.

INGREDIENTS

½ cup Dijon mustard

½ cup cider vinegar

½ cup dark beer (preferably Canadian)

¼ cup pure maple syrup (preferably dark amber)

¼ cup packed brown sugar, or to taste

Coarse salt (sea or kosher) and freshly ground black pepper

Place the mustard, vinegar, beer, maple syrup, and brown sugar in a small heavy saucepan and bring to a boil over medium-high heat. Reduce the heat to medium-low and gently simmer the sauce, uncovered, until thick and richly flavored, about 10 minutes, stirring often. Add salt, pepper, and additional brown sugar, if needed, to taste. Let the sauce cool to room temperature before serving. The sauce will keep in a covered container in the refrigerator for several weeks.

NOTE: For even *more* flavor, cook the sauce in the smoker, uncovered, with the meatballs. Smoke until thick and richly flavored, 1 to 1½ hours.

TULSA TORPEDO
BACON AND SAUSAGE FATTY

Sometimes less is more. Sometimes more is more. When it comes to excess, it's hard to imagine a more unrepentantly rich dish than the Fatty, served at Burn Co. in Tulsa, Oklahoma. Think meatloaf made with three kinds of pork sausage (breakfast, Polish, and hot links), swaddled in woven bacon, and slow-smoked in Oklahoma's distinctive charcoal cooker, the Hasty-Bake. Think flavor bomb as bold tastes of pork, spice, and wood smoke fight for dominance on your taste buds. Just don't think of going through life without trying this amazing creation in your smoker.

YIELD: Serves 8

METHOD: Hot-smoking

PREP TIME: 30 minutes, plus chilling

SMOKING TIME: 2½ to 3 hours

FUEL: Burn Co. uses hickory and oak. You'll need enough wood for 3 hours of smoking (see chart on page 6).

GEAR: A jumbo heavy-duty resealable plastic bag; an instant-read thermometer

SHOP: Nothing out of the ordinary here, but Burn Co. uses Oklahoma-based J.C. Potter hot links.

INGREDIENTS

16 strips thick-sliced artisanal bacon (about 1 pound), uniformly sized, well chilled

2½ pounds bulk breakfast sausage, well chilled

6 ounces pepper Jack cheese, coarsely grated (about 1½ cups)

1 kielbasa or 2 cooked Polish garlic sausages (12 to 16 ounces in all)

8 ounces cooked hot links, thinly sliced

1. Moisten a kitchen towel and lay it on your countertop. (This keeps the aluminum foil from slipping.) Lay a sheet of foil (at least 18 by 24 inches) on top of the towel, narrow end parallel to the edge of the countertop.

2. Make the bacon weave: Lay 8 strips of bacon horizontally on the foil, positioning them so they touch. Use the remaining 8 strips to make a weave pattern: Start weaving the first strip vertically by going over and under the 8 horizontal strips in an alternating pattern. The second strip would then go under and over the 8 strips. Alternate the 8 weaving strips

to create a tight woven square, about 12 by 12 inches.

3. Lay a large sheet of plastic wrap over the weave (you may need two sheets) and gently flatten the weave with a rolling pin to tighten and enlarge it. Note its dimensions to determine the approximate size of the breakfast sausage layer: You're looking for a 12-inch square. Without removing the foil or plastic wrap, carefully slide the weave off the towel onto a baking sheet and refrigerate for 1 hour to firm up the bacon.

4. In the meantime, place the breakfast sausage in a jumbo resealable plastic bag. Using a rolling pin or your hands, roll or press the meat into a rectangle slightly smaller than the finished bacon weave. For easier handling, seal the bag and refrigerate for at least 30 minutes.

5. When you're ready to assemble the torpedo, place the bacon weave on your countertop and remove the plastic wrap. Slit the sides of the bag containing the breakfast sausage and fold one side down to expose the meat. Position the bag, meat side down, over the bacon weave. Release the meat by peeling off the remaining side of the bag.

6. Sprinkle the top of the breakfast sausage evenly with the cheese.

7. Cut the ends off the Polish sausages on a 45-degree angle and arrange the sausages end to end on the sausage meat rectangle about 2 inches up from the edge closest to you, parallel to the narrow end, to form one long sausage. If using kielbasa, cut it into 4-inch lengths, again with diagonal ends, so you can butt them together to form a continuous line. Distribute the hot link slices over the remainder of the rectangle, leaving a 1-inch border at the edges.

8. Lifting the edge of the foil closest to you and pushing the edge away from you, start rolling the bacon and sausage rectangle around the Polish sausage. (The motion is similar to rolling sushi with a bamboo mat.) Roll it one complete turn. There should

be no foil on top of the rolled portion. Gently pat the roll to even it out.

9. Continue rolling to cover the hot link slices, lifting up the foil and pushing the edge away from you. You should wind up with a compact log. Pat the log to even it out. Rewrap it in the foil, twisting the foil ends to enclose the log. Breathe a sigh of relief: The hard part is over. Refrigerate the log in the foil for at least 1 hour or up to 24 hours.

10. Set up your smoker following the manufacturer's instructions and preheat to 225° to 250°F. Add the wood as specified by the manufacturer.

11. Gently unwrap the torpedo and place it seam side down (where the bacon weave overlaps) on the rack in your smoker. Smoke the torpedo until browned on the outside and cooked through. To test for doneness, insert an instant-read thermometer through one end of the torpedo into the center. The temperature should be 160°F. Depending on your smoker and the weather, this will take about 2½ hours. Not surprisingly, the torpedo will release a lot of fat and shrink about 40 percent in size; this is normal.

12. Loosen the torpedo from the smoker rack (gently rock it back and forth with the edge of a spatula if it sticks). Transfer the torpedo to a cutting board. Let rest for 5 minutes, then cut crosswise into 1-inch slices, preferably with a serrated knife or an electric knife. Awesome would be an understatement.

WHAT ELSE: Burn Co. cooks their fatty in a woven bacon casing. This sounds more complicated than it really is: You might have mastered the weaving technique in first grade, making potholders (or later, making a lattice crust for a pie). It just takes a lot of words (in Step 2) to describe it.

There are lots of possible variations here: Use sweet or hot Italian sausage instead of breakfast sausage. Use chorizo or linguiça instead of hot links. Try smoked cheese instead of the pepper Jack and add jalapeño peppers. You get the idea. Leftovers make killer breakfast sandwiches when paired with eggs and biscuits.

SMOKED BRATWURSTS

YIELD: Makes 10 sausages

METHOD: Hot-smoking

PREP TIME: 5 minutes

SMOKING TIME: 30 to 45 minutes

FUEL: Hardwood of your choice—enough for 45 minutes of smoking (see chart on page 6)

GEAR: An instant-read thermometer

SHOP: Johnsonville is the gold standard of bratwurst in the United States, with the added advantage of being almost universally available. If your local butcher or wurst house makes a custom bratwurst, even better.

WHAT ELSE: Use the same technique for smoke-roasting any fresh sausage, such as Italian or chorizo.

You've seen the guy (it's usually a guy): Tongs in hand. Flames leaping from his grill. And trapped in the conflagration: bratwursts on their way to becoming charcoal. Allow me a little myth busting: The best way to cook bratwurst *isn't* the usual direct grilling. It's smoking. Smoke-roasting gives you terrific flavor (think bratwurst meets "hot guts"—Texas smoked beef sausage) with zero—I repeat zero—loss of juiciness. If you do it right, you'll get a smoke ring, and best of all, you'll eliminate the risk of a grill fire.

INGREDIENTS

10 bratwursts or other fresh sausages (2 to 3 pounds)

1 tablespoon extra virgin olive oil, or as needed

Hot dog buns or kaiser or semmel rolls (optional)

SUGGESTED TOPPINGS

Sauerkraut (see Note)

Onions, peeled and diced or thinly sliced

Mustard

Horseradish sauce, or better yet, horseradish mustard

1. Set up your smoker following the manufacturer's instructions and preheat to 275° to 300°F. (This is a little hotter than the low-and-slow method, but the heat helps crisp the sausage casings.) Add the wood as specified by the manufacturer.

2. Lightly brush the sausage casings on all sides with olive oil. Arrange them on the rack in the smoker. Smoke the brats until the casings are bronzed with smoke and the meat is cooked through (the juices will bubble under the casing), 30 to 45 minutes.

Another test: Insert the probe of an instant-read thermometer through one end of the sausage, toward the center. The internal temperature should be at least 160°F.

3. Transfer the smoke-roasted brats to buns, or arrange on a platter. Serve with your choice of toppings.

NOTE: Cool idea—place 1 pound of sauerkraut with its juices in a disposable aluminum foil pan in your smoker and smoke it while you're smoking the brats.

10 INDISPENSABLE TIPS
FROM SAUSAGE MASTER JAKE KLEIN

Jake Klein, owner of Jake's Handcrafted in South Slope, Brooklyn, is one of the most creative sausage makers in North America. And I'm not saying that just because he's my stepson. Jake has channeled Spanish paella, New Orleans oysters Rockefeller, Miami's cubano sandwich, and a New York deli Reuben into a sausage casing. His double-smoked brisket sausage is a "phenomenal piece of barbecue, packing more smoke into a sausage than I'd thought possible," wrote Pete Wells in the *New York Times*. To make it, Jake folds home-smoked burnt ends into ground fresh brisket meat, which he then cooks a second time in his smoker. Think of it as barbecue's second coming.

I asked Jake for his top 10 tips on making and grilling sausage.

1. Start with whole muscles like beef brisket, pork butt, leg of lamb, and turkey breast. The collagen helps give the sausage a supple texture.

2. Make sure your meat is super cold—almost frozen—before grinding. This will give you better texture, facilitate grinding, and help with the emulsification.

3. Use lots of liquid like water, beer, and wine. I push the limits on how much I incorporate. This will help make your sausages juicy and not greasy.

4. Use the right binder. In order to make great sausage you need to bind the meat and fat so they aren't greasy and crumbly. I find nonfat milk powder works well with red meat. Cornstarch is great for poultry.

5. Briefly blanch your sausages in a hot water bath (the water temperature should be no more than 150°F). Then shock them in ice water. This helps improve the texture and storage and shortens the cooking time.

6. Place your sausages in front of a fan for 10 minutes before cooking, or dry them, uncovered, in a single layer, overnight in the refrigerator. This will ensure a nice snap to the casing.

7. When cooking fresh (raw) sausages, allow them to come to room temperature before grilling. This will keep them from bursting on the grill.

8. When cooking sausages over an open fire or grill, I like to use a plancha or cast-iron plate. This minimizes the risk of flare-ups and gives you super snappy casings.

9. Take your time. Work over medium heat and allow some of the rendering fat to crisp the casings.

10. To speed up the cooking and assure even doneness, place an inverted stainless-steel bowl over the sausages as they grill. This helps the sausages cook from the top as well as the bottom.

And next time you're in Brooklyn, visit Jake's Handcrafted. Tell them Steven sent you.

POULTRY

Jamaican jerk. Barbecued chicken. Chinese tea-smoked duck. Some of the world's greatest poultry dishes owe their distinctive character to wood smoke. Here, you'll learn the fundamentals of smoking poultry—from curing and brining to hot-smoking and smoke-roasting; from spice-blasted rotisserie-smoked chicken to a double whiskey-smoked turkey you dish up with high drama for Thanksgiving. In this chapter, poultry goes up in smoke.

ROTISSERIE-SMOKED CHICKEN

The best way I know to cook a whole chicken is spit-roasting. Or is it smoking? This dish delivers the best of both methods—the self-basting, moisture-retaining, skin-crisping benefits of the rotisserie coupled with the flavor-boosting powers of wood smoke. The easiest way to do it is on a charcoal-burning kettle grill with a rotisserie ring (that would be a Weber, see page 262). Alternatively, use a straight wood-burning rotisserie or a gas grill rotisserie, plus one of the smoking devices on page 22.

INGREDIENTS

1 whole chicken (3½ to 4 pounds)

3 tablespoons barbecue rub (see Shop), or to taste

1 tablespoon extra virgin olive oil

1. Set up your grill for spit-roasting following the manufacturer's instructions, and preheat to medium-high (375°F). Yes, I know this is higher than the traditional low-and-slow smoking temperature, but the higher temperature crisps the skin.

2. Remove any giblets and large lumps of fat from inside the chicken. Place 1 tablespoon of the rub in the neck and main cavities. Tie the legs together with butcher's string or pin them together with a bamboo skewer. Fold the wing tips back and under the body of the chicken. Sprinkle the remaining rub over the outside of the chicken. Drizzle the bird with olive oil, rubbing it over the skin on all sides. Run the rotisserie spit through the chicken from side to side so the bird will spin head over tail evenly. (Why head over tail? You'll get a juicier bird with crisper skin. I can't explain the physics, but most of the world's grill cultures spit-roast chickens this way, and it works.) Tighten the nuts on the rotisserie forks.

3. Affix the spit with the chicken on the rotisserie. Place an aluminum foil drip pan under the bird. Toss the wood chips on the coals or otherwise add the wood as specified by the manufacturer. Turn on the motor.

4. Smoke-roast the chicken until the skin is dark brown and crisp and the meat in the thigh reaches 165°F on an instant-read thermometer. (Insert it into the deepest part of the thigh but not touching the bone.) This will take 1¼ to 1½ hours.

5. Transfer the chicken to a cutting board and let it rest for 5 to 10 minutes, then carve and dig in.

YIELD: Makes 1 chicken, enough to serve 2 to 4

METHOD: Spit-roasting

PREP TIME: 15 minutes

SMOKING TIME: 1¼ to 1½ hours

FUEL: With poultry I like fruitwood, such as apple or cherry wood chips—enough for 1½ hours of smoking (see chart on page 6).

GEAR: When smoking on a gas grill, you'll want a mesh or tube smoker (see On-grate smokers, page 22), a smoker box, or a cast-iron skillet filled with wood chips and lit charcoal; butcher's string; an instant-read thermometer

SHOP: As always, buy organic or local farm-raised chicken when possible. Use your favorite commercial rub, or for a Chinese accent, try the 5-4-3-2-1 Rub on page 100.

WHAT ELSE: Want a super easy dinner? Place potatoes, sweet potatoes, or other root vegetables (quartered lengthwise) with a couple of quartered shallots or a handful of garlic cloves (skins on) in a single layer in a 9-by-13-inch aluminum foil drip pan. Toss with 1 tablespoon olive oil and salt and pepper to taste. Place the pan under the chicken as it spit-roasts. The vegetables will roast in the dripping chicken fat. Stir from time to time so the veggies brown evenly. Amazing.

Variations

Don't have a rotisserie? Don't worry. Set up your grill for indirect grilling and preheat to 375°F. Toss the wood chips on the coals or use one of the smoking methods for gas grills on page 20. This will take 1¼ to 1½ hours.

Don't have a grill? Set up your smoker following the manufacturer's instructions. Preheat to 375°F (or as hot as the smoker will go if less than that). Smoke the chicken for 1¼ to 1½ hours, or until cooked as described previously.

POULTRY SMOKING CHART

FOOD	AMOUNT	SMOKER TEMP	TIME	INTERNAL TEMP/ DONENESS
Whole chicken (rotisseried)	3½-4 pounds (each)	375°F	1¼-1½ hours	165°-170°F
Spatchcocked chicken	3½-4 pounds (each)	275°F	2-2½ hours	165°-170°F
Chicken halves	1-1½ pounds (each)	225°-250°F	2-2½ hours	165°-170°F
Chicken thighs	5-6 ounces (each)	300°F	1-1½ hours	165°-170°F
Chicken wings (page 51)	3 pounds	375°F or 250°F	30-50 minutes or 1½-2 hours	165°-170°F
Chicken livers (page 46)	1 pound	300°F	30-40 minutes	Browned on the outside; pink in the center
Whole turkey	12-14 pounds	275°F	5-6 hours	165°-170°F
Turkey breast half	5-6 pounds	225°-250°F	2-3 hours	165°-170°F
Turkey drumsticks	1-1 ½ pounds (each)	225°-250°F	3-4 hours	170°F
Duck	5-6 pounds	225°-250°F (smoking)	3½-4 hours	175°F

SMOKED CHICKEN
WITH HORSERADISH DIP

From the day it was conceived in 1925, this smoky chicken has been an odd bird (excuse the pun) of American barbecue. The place: Big Bob Gibson's in Decatur, Alabama. The creator: a railroad-man turned pit master who had the idea to pair smoked chicken (unadorned with any special rub or seasoning) with a sauce concocted from cider vinegar and mayonnaise. Here's the Raichlen version—with pepper and horseradish to pump up the heat.

INGREDIENTS

2 chickens (3½ to 4 pounds each)

Coarse salt (sea or kosher) and freshly ground black pepper

2 cups mayonnaise, preferably Hellmann's or Best Foods

1 cup cider vinegar

¼ cup freshly grated horseradish or prepared white horseradish

1 to 2 teaspoons of your favorite hot sauce

1 teaspoon finely grated lemon zest

¼ cup bacon fat or 4 tablespoons (½ stick) butter, melted

1. Using poultry shears, cut the chickens in half: first cut out the backbones, then cut each bird through the breastbone. Rinse under cold water and blot dry with paper towels. Generously season both sides with salt and pepper.

2. Make the horseradish dip: Place the mayonnaise, vinegar, horseradish, hot sauce, lemon zest, 2 teaspoons salt, and 2 teaspoons pepper in a deep bowl and whisk until smooth. Refrigerate until serving.

3. Set up your smoker following the manufacturer's instructions and preheat to 225° to 250°F. Add the wood as specified by the manufacturer.

4. Arrange the chicken halves skin side up in the smoker. Smoke for 1 hour. Brush the chicken halves with bacon fat or butter. Continue smoking until the skin is bronzed and the meat is cooked and tender, 165° to 170°F on an instant-read thermometer inserted into a thigh, 1 to 1½ hours more.

5. Pour half the dip onto a deep platter. Place the chicken halves, skin side up, on top and let steep in the sauce for 3 minutes. Serve the remaining sauce on the side.

YIELD: Makes 2 chickens, enough to serve 4 to 6

METHOD: Hot-smoking

PREP TIME: 20 minutes

SMOKING TIME: 2 to 2½ hours

FUEL: Hickory or pecan wood—enough for 2½ hours of smoking (see chart on page 6)

GEAR: An instant-read thermometer

SHOP: Organic or local farm-raised birds. Freshly grated horseradish if you like your sauce hot; otherwise a good prepared white horseradish. Good-quality mayonnaise like Hellmann's or Best Foods.

WHAT ELSE: You can smoke the bird in any smoker. Upright barrel smokers (see page 263) work great.

JAMAICAN JERK CHICKEN

YIELD: Makes 2 chickens, enough to serve 4 to 6

METHOD: Hot-smoking

PREP TIME: 30 minutes

MARINATING TIME: 12 to 24 hours

SMOKING TIME: 2 to 2½ hours

FUEL: 2 cups pimento or other hardwood chips plus 3 tablespoons allspice berries. You'll need enough fuel for 2½ hours of smoking (see chart on page 6).

GEAR: A spice mill or clean coffee grinder; a small pot with heatproof handle; jumbo resealable heavy-duty plastic bags (optional); an instant-read thermometer

SHOP: Organic or local farm-raised chickens. You'll need a few special ingredients—chief among them, various parts of the pimento (allspice) tree. These include berries (about 25), leaves (think bay leaves that smell like allspice), and pimento wood sticks and chips. All are available from eXotic Wood Chips (pimentowood.com).

"**Y**ou need to sweat while you're eating jerk," Gary Feblowitz says. The Emmy-winning videographer (you've seen his work on the Food Network and on my *Project Smoke* show on Public Television) should know. Stranded unexpectedly in Jamaica for a few weeks (I can think of worse punishments), he became obsessed by the indigenous barbecue, jerk. So he started a company that imports pimento wood, leaves, and berries.

"Pimento" is what Jamaicans call allspice; this fragrant tropical tree is one of the defining flavors of jerk. To be strictly authentic, you use the berries and leaves for seasoning the meat, pimento wood sticks to fashion a grill grate, and pimento wood chips to generate smoke.

As for the ingredient that makes you sweat, we're talking scotch bonnet chiles—ranked at a tongue-tormenting 200,000 Scoville units. A Jamaican might use up to a dozen in the following recipe; I suggest starting with three or four, and to make the jerk even milder, you can remove the seeds.

Jamaicans like their jerk chicken very well done—even leathery—recalling another smoked food native to the Americas: jerky (page 52). Some scholars believe the terms are etymological cousins. I suggest serving the chicken a little less well done and juicier. And because there's so much flavor coming from the seasonings, this is a great dish to smoke on a gas grill. The only thing cooler than the way it looks is how authentic it tastes.

INGREDIENTS

2 whole chickens
  (3½ to 4 pounds each)

3 cups Jerk Seasoning (page 157), or
  your favorite commercial brand

25 pimento leaves or bay leaves

1 cup water

1. Using poultry shears, spatchcock the chickens: Cut down both sides of the backbone and remove it. Remove the breastbone and cartilage and open the chickens up like a book.

2. Spread half of the jerk seasoning across the bottom of a roasting pan large enough to hold both spatchcocked chickens opened up. Arrange the chickens on top. Spread

WHAT ELSE: This recipe calls for an ingenious technique that simulates a Jamaican jerk pit on a gas grill. You line the grate—either smoker or gas or charcoal grill—with pimento leaves. You arrange pimento sticks over them, and cook the chicken on top. The pimento wood chips and berries go into an aluminum foil smoking pouch set atop one of the lit burners to generate allspice smoke. And you place additional pimento leaves in a pot of water on the grill to keep the chicken fragrant and moist. This will be one of the coolest looking dishes you ever cook on your grill.

the remaining jerk seasoning over the birds. Cover the pan with plastic wrap and marinate the chickens in the refrigerator for 12 to 24 hours, turning them a couple of times so they marinate evenly. Alternatively, marinate the opened chickens in jumbo resealable plastic bags.

3. If using a gas or charcoal grill, soak the pimento wood chips and allspice berries in water to cover for 30 minutes, then drain. If using a gas grill, make a smoker pouch: Place the drained wood chips and berries in the center of a large sheet of heavy-duty aluminum foil. Fold over the foil to make a pouch. Fold the edges all around to seal the pouch. Poke a few holes in the top with a fork.

4. Make the steam pot: Place 5 pimento leaves and water in a small pot with a heatproof handle.

5. On a gas grill: Set up your grill for indirect grilling and preheat to medium-low (275°F). Place the pouch over the lit side of the grill; in a few minutes it will start to smoke. Arrange as many of the remaining pimento leaves on the grate away from the heat as are needed to cover an area the size of the opened chickens. Arrange 4 pimento wood sticks on the leaves, perpendicular to the grate and parallel to one another. Arrange the opened chickens skin side up on top of the sticks. Place the steam pot next to them. Cover the grill and indirect-grill the chickens until darkly browned and the internal temperature reaches 165° to 170°F on

an instant-read thermometer, 2 to 2½ hours. (Insert the thermometer into the deepest part of the thigh but not touching the bone.)

On a charcoal grill: Set up your grill for indirect grilling. Toss the drained wood chips and berries directly on the coals. Arrange as many of the remaining pimento leaves on the grate away from the heat as are needed to cover an area the size of the opened chickens. Arrange the pimento sticks on the grate away from the heat, over the drip pan. Arrange the opened chickens on top. Place the steam pot next to them, at the back of the grill. Cover the grill and cook as described previously.

In a smoker: Set up your smoker following the manufacturer's instructions and preheat to 275°F. Arrange the pimento leaves and sticks as described above on the smoker rack. Arrange the opened chickens on top of the sticks. Place the steam pot next to them. Add the pimento wood chips and berries as specified by the manufacturer. Cook as described previously.

6. Transfer the chicken to a platter or cutting board and let rest for 5 minutes, then chop or cut into pieces for serving.

JERK SEASONING

YIELD: Makes about 3 cups

This potent seasoning is the lifeblood of Jamaican jerk—a paste fiery with scotch bonnet chiles and fragrant with allspice and rum. It will keep for several weeks in a sealed jar in the refrigerator. (Line the lid with a double layer of plastic wrap so the chile fumes won't corrode the metal.)

INGREDIENTS

3 tablespoons Jamaican pimento berries or allspice berries

3 tablespoons black peppercorns

1 cinnamon stick (3 inches), broken into pieces, or 2 teaspoons ground cinnamon

1 whole nutmeg, or 2 teaspoons ground nutmeg

6 dried pimento leaves or 2 bay leaves, crumbled

2 to 8 scotch bonnet chiles (or their cousins, habanero chiles), stemmed (see Note)

2 bunches scallions, trimmed, white and green parts coarsely chopped

4 cloves garlic, peeled and coarsely chopped

1 piece (2 inches) fresh ginger, scrubbed and coarsely chopped

2 tablespoons fresh thyme leaves (strip them off the branches) or 1 teaspoon dried thyme

½ cup soy sauce

½ cup vegetable oil

½ cup distilled white vinegar

½ cup dark rum

5 tablespoons freshly squeezed lime juice

2 tablespoons molasses or brown sugar

Coarse salt (sea or kosher) and freshly ground black pepper

1. Place the pimento berries, peppercorns, cinnamon, nutmeg, and pimento leaves in a spice mill and grind to a fine powder. You may need to work in several batches.

2. Cut the scotch bonnets in half. For milder jerk, seed them; for more fiery jerk, leave the seeds in. Place the chiles, scallions, garlic, ginger, thyme, and the ground spices in a food processor and finely chop. Add the soy sauce, vegetable oil, vinegar, rum, lime juice, and molasses and process to form a thick paste. Add salt and pepper to taste.

NOTE: While no longer the world's hottest chiles, scotch bonnets are pretty fiery. Two give you a gentle heat; 8 put out the sort of firepower you'd find in Jamaica. Always wear gloves when handling scotch bonnets. You don't want the oils getting on your hands and then being transported to your eyes and/or other sensitive tissues.

BACON, HAM, AND CHEESE CHICKEN THIGHS

YIELD: Makes 8 thighs, enough to serve 4

METHOD: Hot-smoking

PREP TIME: 30 minutes

SMOKING TIME: 1 to 1½ hours

FUEL: Hickory or apple—enough for 1 hour of smoking (see chart on page 6)

GEAR: Butcher's string; an instant-read thermometer

SHOP: Look for skin-on, boneless chicken thighs. If unavailable, make a lengthwise slit in the inside face of the thigh with a sharp paring knife to remove the bone.

WHAT ELSE: Okay, so some people just don't like dark meat. Chicken breasts don't normally smoke well (they dry out), but layer them with ham and cheese and wrap them with bacon and they'll stay moist.

These bacon-wrapped smoked chicken thighs may sound like pure Americana, but the inspiration comes from Belgrade. In Serbia, grilled chicken and pork are routinely stuffed with smoked ham and piquant cheese. The thigh is the richest, juiciest part of the chicken, which makes it perplexing why most Americans profess to prefer the breast. But not our barbecuebible.com community. We like the big flavor of chicken thighs, and we like the price. We certainly like the smoke, salt, cheesy richness, and tart pickle crunch in these thighs.

INGREDIENTS

8 large skin-on boneless chicken thighs (6 ounces each, boneless; 8 ounces each, bone-in)

8 tablespoons Dijon mustard

8 ounces Gruyère cheese (preferably cave-aged), coarsely grated or cut into matchstick slivers

8 ounces sliced smoked ham, cut into matchstick slivers

16 dill pickle slices

Coarse salt (sea or kosher) and freshly ground black pepper

16 slices thin-sliced artisanal bacon (1 pound)

1. Place the chicken thighs on a cutting board and open them through the cut made to remove the bone. Spread the meat with mustard (1 tablespoon per thigh). Top each with an equal amount of cheese and ham and 2 pickle slices. Close the thighs to envelop the stuffing. Season the chicken with salt and pepper. Wrap each thigh with a strip of bacon, then another strip running perpendicular to the first. Tie the bacon in place with butcher's string.

2. Set up your smoker following the manufacturer's instructions and preheat to 300°F. (You'll smoke at a higher than normal temperature to crisp the bacon.) Add the wood as specified by the manufacturer.

3. Place the chicken thighs skin side up on the smoker rack. Smoke the chicken thighs until the outsides and bacon are browned, the cheese is melted, and the temperature in the center reaches 165° to 170°F on an instant-read thermometer, 1 to 1½ hours. Snip the string and remove before serving.

DOUBLE WHISKEY-SMOKED TURKEY

I've cooked our family turkeys most of my adult life, and I don't believe I've ever done it the same way twice. Over the years, I've tried indirect grilling, spit-roasting, spatchcocking, beer-canning, and more. But if I had to pick just one method, it would be this: whiskey-brined and whiskey barrel chip-smoked. The brine adds flavor and succulence, especially to the breast meat, which has a well-documented tendency to dry out. The whiskey barrel chips deliver a sweet musky smoke flavor. To keep the breast meat extra moist, I also inject it with melted butter and chicken stock. Once you put the bird in the smoker, you pretty much leave it there until it's done.

YIELD: Serves 8 to 10

METHOD: Hot-smoking

PREP TIME: 20 minutes

BRINING TIME: 24 hours

SMOKING TIME: 5 to 6 hours

FUEL: Whiskey barrel chips, such as Jack Daniel's or Jim Beam—enough for 5 hours of smoking (see chart on page 6)

GEAR: A large stockpot for brining; wire rack; an injector (see page 164); instant-read thermometer

SHOP: Ideally, an organic or heritage bird. Order it from Heritage Foods (heritagefoods.com), D'Artagnan (dartagnan.com), or via Local Harvest (localharvest.com). The meat has more chew and the flavor is infinitely better. A lot of industrially raised birds come injected with stock, water, and/or butter or vegetable oil—up to 15 percent of their weight. (Water is cheaper than meat, which is one reason processors do it.) This, coupled with your brine, would make the bird unbearably salty. If you can't find an organic bird, buy a non-organic bird that hasn't been previously injected.

INGREDIENTS

FOR THE TURKEY

1 turkey (12 to 14 pounds)

4 bay leaves

1 medium-size onion, peeled and quartered

4 whole cloves

1½ cups coarse salt (sea or kosher)

½ cup pure maple syrup

2 quarts boiling water

6 quarts cold water (2 gallons in all)

1 cup bourbon or rye whiskey

1 tablespoon whole black peppercorns

FOR THE INJECTOR SAUCE (OPTIONAL)

3 tablespoons butter

3 tablespoons low-sodium turkey or chicken stock (preferably homemade)

1 tablespoon whiskey or brandy

FOR SMOKING AND SERVING

4 tablespoons (½ stick) butter, melted

Turkey Jus (page 162), for serving

1. Thaw the turkey, if frozen. Remove the neck and giblets (liver, gizzard, and heart) and set aside. Be sure to empty both the front (neck) and main cavities of the bird. (Smoke the neck, gizzard, and heart to make a smoked turkey stock, and use the liver to make the Smoked Liver Pâté on page 47). Rinse the turkey inside and out with cold running water. Fold the wing tips behind the back.

2. Make the brine: Pin the bay leaves to the onion quarters with the cloves. Place the salt and maple syrup in a stockpot large enough to hold the turkey. Add the boiling water and whisk until the salt is dissolved. Whisk in the cold water, the whiskey, and the peppercorns. Add the turkey, legs up, and the onion quarters. Jiggle the turkey as needed so the brine flows into the main cavity and the whole bird is submerged. Put the lid on the stockpot and brine the turkey in the refrigerator for 24 hours. Turn the turkey over halfway through so it brines evenly.

3. The next day, remove the turkey from the brine. Discard the brine. Place the turkey on a wire rack over a rimmed baking sheet to drain and dry, 30 minutes. Truss the bird, if desired.

4. Meanwhile, make the injector sauce: Melt the butter in a saucepan. Stir in the stock and whiskey. Let cool to room temperature. Fill the injector with the sauce, then inject it in several places in the breast, thighs, and drumsticks.

5. Set up your smoker following the manufacturer's instructions and preheat to 275°F. Add the wood as specified by the manufacturer.

6. Full-smoke method: Place the turkey on the rack in the smoker. After 2 hours, start basting the turkey all over with melted butter and baste again every hour. Smoke the turkey until the skin is browned and the meat in the thigh reaches 165° to 170°F on an instant-read thermometer. (Insert it into the deepest part of the thigh but not touching the bone.). This will take 5 to 6 hours.

Smoke with the grill-finish method: This gives you the rich flavor of smoke with the crisp skin of a roasted turkey. Smoke the turkey as described above (without basting) until the skin is golden brown and the meat in the thigh reaches 145°F on an instant-read thermometer inserted into the thigh but not touching the bone, 3 to 4 hours. If your smoker operates at higher temperatures, increase the heat to 400°F. Otherwise, set up a grill for indirect grilling and preheat to medium-high (400°F). Transfer the turkey to the grill, over the drip pan. Baste the bird with melted butter. Roast the turkey until the skin is browned and crisp and the meat of the thigh reaches 165°F, 1 hour more or as needed, basting once or twice more.

7. Transfer the turkey to a platter and *loosely* drape a sheet of aluminum foil over it. (Don't bunch the foil around the bird.) Let rest for 20 minutes, then carve and serve with a gravy boat of Turkey Jus.

WHAT ELSE: How big a turkey should you buy? I like 12- to 14-pounders—even if you're serving a lot of people. You can always cook two birds if you're feeding a crowd. Smaller birds are moister and more tender, and it's easier to control the cooking. Figure on 1½ pounds per person. This will make you feel properly overfed—as you should at Thanksgiving—and leave you with welcome leftovers. Note: By way of a sauce, I suggest smoked Turkey Jus or gravy (see page 162).

TURKEY JUS

YIELD: Makes 2½ to 3 cups

Due to the brining, the drippings in the pan under the turkey may prove too salty for gravy. And there probably won't be enough. Unsalted chicken or turkey stock alleviates that problem and you smoke it alongside the turkey. Madeira adds a touch of sweetness to the jus. Omit it if you prefer the pure taste of turkey and wood smoke.

INGREDIENTS

3 cups turkey or chicken stock (preferably homemade)

½ cup smoked turkey drippings (optional)

2 teaspoons cornstarch (optional)

3 tablespoons Madeira (optional)

Coarse salt (sea or kosher) and freshly ground black pepper

1. Place the stock in a disposable aluminum foil pan in the smoker next to the turkey. Smoke for 2 hours.

2. When the turkey is cooked and resting, strain the turkey drippings into a large measuring cup. Depending on how much drippings you have and how salty they are, you'll use up to ½ cup skimmed of fat. Add enough of the smoked stock or more turkey or chicken stock to make 3 cups.

3. Bring the drippings and stock to a boil in a saucepan. For a slightly thickened jus, dissolve the cornstarch in 1 tablespoon of the Madeira and whisk into the boiling stock. It will thicken slightly. For an unthickened jus, add the Madeira and boil for 2 minutes. Whisk in salt and pepper to taste.

BRINING

When it comes to keeping foods moist on a smoker or grill, few techniques rival brining. A soak in a saline solution (which is what brine is) makes turkeys tender and succulent and pork chops plump and moist. Add a curing salt (like sodium nitrite—page 16) and brine gives pastrami its pinkish color and poultry or ham its umami richness.

So, how does brining work?

Muscles consist of long, bundled fibers. Moisture loss is inevitable when you hot-smoke or grill meat. The heat causes the muscle fibers to contract, wringing out the moisture—up to 30 percent of the meat's original weight.

The goal of brining is to get more water into the meat, but it's actually the salt that does the work by a process called denaturing. (Meat soaked in plain water will absorb moisture, but will not retain it during cooking.) Add salt to that water and the liquid enters and stays in the meat.

As anyone who has taken high school chemistry will remember, salt is comprised of two elements: sodium and chloride. When you dissolve salt in water, it breaks down into positive-charged sodium ions and negative-charged chloride ions. The sodium gives the meat its agreeable salty flavor.

When the chloride diffuses through the proteins in the meat, the negative ions repel each other, much like opposing magnets, pushing the meat fibers apart, creating gaps that are filled by water. It's this—not osmosis—that causes the water to enter the meat and stay there.

So what's the ideal ratio of salt to water for brine? Food scientists recommend 7 ounces of salt (roughly ¾ cup) per gallon of water. That gives you a salt concentration of 6 to 7 percent.

But there's more to making brine than simply dumping salt in a bowl of water. First the salt: I like sea salt, which contains minute traces of magnesium, calcium halides, algae, and other compounds. Others prefer the purity of kosher salt. Salt dissolves slowly in cold water, so I like to bring part of the water to a boil before whisking in the salt. Then I add the remaining water (it should be ice cold) to bring the brine back to room temperature. Never add food to warm brine.

To make basic brine, you need only salt and water. You can also add curing salts (such as sodium nitrite) and other seasonings, including sweeteners like sugar, honey, or maple syrup; aromatics like onion or garlic; and herbs and spices like bay leaves, juniper berries, and/or black peppercorns.

This brings us to a technique called equilibrium brining—advocated by food scientist and *Modernist Cuisine* visionary Nathan Myhrvold. The ultimate goal of brining is to give the food a salinity (salt content) of 0.5 to 1 percent. In traditional brining, you use a much saltier brine to achieve that salinity, then remove the excess salt by soaking and rinsing the meat with fresh water after brining. In equilibrium brining, you make the brine with the total amount of salt you want in the meat at the end. The advantage of equilibrium brining: more even brine dispersal and you never oversalt the meat. The disadvantage: The process involves elaborate calculations and measurements and takes considerably longer.

THE INS AND OUTS OF INJECTING

Afraid of needles? Don't let that deter you from the benefits of injecting. As the barbecue pros know, injecting is the most efficient way to add flavor and moisture to smoked, barbecued, or grilled meats. Think of injecting as marinating from the inside out.

Let me explain: Rubs, spice pastes, and glazes sit on the meat's surface. Marinades penetrate only a few millimeters into the meat. Brining solutions (see page 163) do reach the center, but require several days or even weeks to do so—a process that gobbles up real estate in your refrigerator. Injecting gets the flavor to the center of the food in seconds with the push of a plunger.

Injecting is a great way to accelerate the brining process with turkey, ham, or Canadian bacon. Inject part of the brine deep into the meat at 2-inch intervals. Other good candidates for injecting include chickens and game hens; whole hogs and pork shoulders; plus intrinsically dry meats like turkey breast and double-thick pork chops.

Most injectors look like oversize hypodermic needles. The syringe (plastic or stainless steel) typically comes with a 2- to 4-ounce capacity— enough for most barbecue projects. Use it for injecting broth, melted butter, and/or other liquid seasonings. For thicker flavoring mixtures like pesto or jerk seasoning, invest in a wide-mouth injector— often sold with a metal spike for making a deep hole in the meat into which you inject your spice paste.

To use an injector, fully depress the plunger and insert the needle into the injector sauce. Some needles are closed at the end but have holes along the sides; make sure the perforations are fully submerged in the sauce. Pull the plunger back to fill the syringe with liquid. Plunge the needle deep into the meat, then depress the plunger *slowly* and steadily. (A quick plunge may send streams of injector sauce squirting in the opposite direction.) Withdraw the needle gradually.

To minimize the number of holes you put in the meat (and hence the leakage), angle the needle in two or three directions using the same entry hole. Continue injecting until liquid begins leaking from the holes, indicating the meat cannot hold any more.

What should you inject with your injector? The short list includes broth or stock, melted butter, Cognac or whiskey, hot sauce, fish sauce or soy sauce, or, more often, a combination of these ingredients. For a touch of sweetness, add fruit juice or molasses or honey. (Warm molasses or honey so they flow easily.) On page 159, you'll find one of my favorite injector sauces.

Here's some additional injecting advice.

- Once you mix your injector sauce, transfer it to a deep, slender vessel to facilitate drawing the liquid into the syringe.

- Lubricate the rubber or silicone gasket on the end of the plunger with a little vegetable oil before using for the first time. Repeat after each washing to keep the rubber from drying out.

- Use low- or no-sodium broth when assembling injection sauces. This lets you control the salt content.

- Unless you own a needle with wide openings, avoid coarsely ground spices or similar ingredients that would clog the system. Strain out solids with a fine-mesh strainer or coffee filter.

- For better injector sauce dispersion, let the meat rest for an hour between injecting and smoking.

- Wash your injector by hand after each use, giving the needle special attention. Clean the tip with a straightened paper clip and run hot water through it. (The dishwasher may craze—produce fine cracks in—the syringe and dull the needle.) Some models are designed to store the needle(s) inside the syringe when not in use. Otherwise, replace the needle guard it came with, or push the tip into a small piece of wine cork between uses.

CITRUS-FENNEL TURKEY BREAST

M ost smoked turkey breast gets the ham treatment (brined with salt, sugar, and curing salts), or a pastrami crust of coriander seeds and black pepper (page 72). Here's a turkey breast bright with citrus (lemon, lime, orange, and grapefruit, pureed rind and all), with fennel pollen (or fennel seeds) for a licoricy sweetness—inspired by the Pig & Pickle in Scottsdale, Arizona.

INGREDIENTS

1 turkey breast half (preferably bone-in; 5 to 6 pounds)

1 lime, quartered

1 lemon, quartered and seeded

1 orange, quartered and seeded

¼ grapefruit, with rind, seeded and cut into 1-inch pieces

¼ cup coarse salt (sea or kosher)

¼ cup packed light or dark brown sugar

2 tablespoons cracked black peppercorns

1 tablespoon fennel pollen or fennel seeds

6 tablespoons extra virgin olive oil, or as needed

¼ cup water, or as needed

1. Rinse the turkey breast and blot dry with paper towels. If using a bone-in breast, trim off any visible rib tips. Place the turkey in a jumbo heavy-duty resealable plastic bag.

2. Make the citrus seasoning: Place the lime, lemon, orange, grapefruit, salt, sugar, pepper, and fennel pollen in a food processor and grind to a coarse paste. Grind in 4 tablespoons of the olive oil and ¼ to ½ cup of water—enough to make a thick but pourable paste. Pour this mixture over the turkey in the bag, massaging the bag to coat the meat evenly. Seal the bag and place it in a large aluminum

foil pan to contain any leaks. Marinate the turkey in this mixture in the refrigerator for 24 hours, turning the bag over several times so the meat marinates evenly.

3. Drain the turkey on a wire rack over a rimmed baking sheet. For a finished look, scrape off the marinade; for a more rustic look, leave it on. Let it dry in the refrigerator for 2 hours.

4. Set up your smoker following the manufacturer's instructions and preheat to 225° to 250°F. Add the wood as specified by the manufacturer.

YIELD: Serves 10 to 12

METHOD: Hot-smoking

PREP TIME: 20 minutes

MARINATING TIME: 24 hours

SMOKING TIME: 2 to 3 hours

FUEL: Any hardwood will work—enough for 3 hours of smoking (see chart on page 6)

GEAR: A jumbo heavy-duty resealable plastic bag; a large aluminum foil pan; a wire rack; an instant-read thermometer

SHOP: As always, my preference goes to organic turkey. Avoid turkey that comes pre-injected with water or brine. Fennel pollen is a coarse yellow powder with a sweet anise-like flavor. If unavailable, substitute fennel seeds.

WHAT ELSE: This citrus-fennel marinade also goes great with salmon: Marinate the fish for 6 hours. Rinse it off and dry and cold-smoke the salmon fillet as described on page 183.

5. Place the turkey breast in the smoker. After 1 hour, start basting the turkey with the remaining olive oil, and continue basting every 45 minutes. Smoke until the outside is bronzed with smoke and the internal temperature of the meat reaches 165°F on an instant-read thermometer. This will take 2 to 3 hours.

6. Transfer the turkey to a cutting board. To serve it hot, let it rest for 5 minutes, then thinly slice across the grain. To serve it cold (which is how we like it at my house), let the turkey breast cool to room temperature, then thinly slice. Store any extra in the refrigerator, where it will keep for at least 3 days.

NOTE: For crisper skin, smoke the turkey at 250°F without basting to an internal temperature of 130°F, 1½ hours. Then increase the smoker heat to 400°F. Brush the turkey with oil and cook until the skin is crisp and brown and the meat is cooked to 165°F, another ½ to 1 hour, basting once or twice with olive oil.

TURKEY HAM

YIELD: Makes 6 drumsticks; figure on 1 per person

METHOD: Hot-smoking

PREP TIME: 15 minutes

BRINING TIME: 48 hours

SMOKING TIME: 3 to 4 hours

FUEL: Hardwood of your choice (I like apple)—enough for 4 hours of smoking (see chart on page 6)

GEAR: An instant-read thermometer

Call them monster drumsticks. Or turkey ham. There's a lot to like about turkey legs: the affordable price, the moist and tender (but not *too* tender) meat, and a rich flavor that just doesn't quit. And like so much great barbecue, you get to eat them with your hands. This recipe gives turkey legs the ham treatment—a soak in a brown sugar brine followed by a slow-smoke with apple wood. Serve hot. Serve cold. Serve with your favorite barbecue sauce or chutney.

INGREDIENTS

4 quarts (1 gallon) water

¾ cup coarse salt (sea or kosher)

¾ cup packed light brown sugar

1 tablespoon pink curing salt (Prague Powder No. 1 or Insta Cure No. 1)

5 whole cloves

5 allspice berries, lightly crushed with the side of a chef's knife or cleaver

2 bay leaves, broken into pieces

2 cinnamon sticks (3 inches each), broken into pieces

1 tablespoon whole black peppercorns

6 turkey drumsticks (1 to 1½ pounds each)

1. Make the brine: Combine 2 quarts of the water, the sea salt, sugar, curing salt, cloves, allspice berries, bay leaves, cinnamon sticks, and peppercorns in a large stockpot. Bring to a boil over high heat, whisking to dissolve the salt and sugar. Remove from the heat and add the remaining 2 quarts water. Let cool to room temperature, then refrigerate until thoroughly chilled.

2. Rinse the turkey drumsticks in a colander under cold running water.

3. Add the turkey drumsticks to the brine, making sure they're completely submerged. You can hold them down with a dinner plate or a resealable plastic bag filled with ice. Brine the drumsticks in the refrigerator for 48 hours.

4. When you're ready to smoke, drain the drumsticks and discard the brine. Pick off and discard any clinging spices. Blot the drumsticks dry with paper towels.

5. Set up your smoker following the manufacturer's instructions and preheat to 225° to 250°F. Add the wood as specified by the manufacturer.

6. Place the drumsticks on the rack in the smoker. Smoke the turkey until darkly browned and very tender, 3 to 4 hours, or as needed. You're looking for an internal temperature of 170°F on an instant-read thermometer. (Make sure the probe doesn't touch bone, or you'll get a false reading.)

7. Do not be alarmed (on the contrary—be proud) if the meat under the skin is pinkish: That's a chemical reaction to the cure and the smoke. Serve hot or at room temperature. In the unlikely event you have leftovers, store in the refrigerator; the drumsticks will keep for at least 3 days.

SHOP: Look for large turkey drumsticks, weighing 1 to 1½ pounds each. You'll also need one special ingredient—a sodium nitrite-based curing salt called pink salt, Prague Powder No. 1, or Insta Cure No. 1.

WHAT ELSE: You could also brine and smoke turkey breast in this manner. It'll need 2 to 3 hours of smoking.

TEA-SMOKED DUCK

YIELD: Serves 2 or 3

METHOD: Hot-smoking

PREP TIME: 20 minutes

SMOKING TIME: 3 to 4 hours

FUEL: Cherry wood chips and the other smoking ingredients listed, plus enough wood for 4 hours of smoking (see chart on page 6)

GEAR: A sharp-tined fork or sharp skewer for pricking the duck skin (to help release excess fat). The tool I like the most is a large sewing needle stuck eye-end-first in a wine cork. (The cork prevents you from losing the needle—never a good thing to happen when you're handling food.) An instant-read meat thermometer.

SHOP: Most of the duck sold in the United States comes frozen, but if you're lucky, you may be able to find or order fresh duck at a farmers' market or your local butcher. If you do buy a frozen duck, allow at least 48 hours to thaw it in the refrigerator. Five-spice powder is a blend of star anise, fennel seed, cinnamon, pepper, and other spices—its flavor is licoricy and smoky. Asian (dark) sesame oil is a fragrant oil pressed from roasted sesame seeds.

Smoke figures minimally or not at all in most Asian cuisines. The reason may be as simple as the fact that, historically, North America possessed vast hardwood forests, while the more densely populated East (particularly China and Japan) did not. Which may explain the singular fuel and method used in Chinese tea-smoked duck. The traditional recipe uses not a single chip of hardwood: The duck (typically cut in pieces) is smoked in a wok over a mixture of black tea, orange peel, sugar, rice, cinnamon, and star anise. These utterly un-Western smoking ingredients add an otherworldly fragrance and, if you ever see the dish on the menu of a good Chinese restaurant, order it without fail.

I'm going to assume you're more likely to smoke in a stick burner (offset barrel smoker) or water smoker outdoors than in a wok, so I've reconfigured the recipe for a whole duck. The subtlety of the traditional Chinese smoking ingredients would get lost in a large-format smoker, so I've added some cherry wood to boost the smoke. There's an added advantage to cooking a duck by smoking: The bird makes a mess when roasted indoors; in an outdoor smoker, it puts out no more fat than a brisket. The aromatic tea smoke harmonizes elegantly with the dark, rich duck meat.

INGREDIENTS

FOR THE SMOKING MIXTURE

2 cups of cherry or other hardwood chips or chunks (unsoaked)

½ cup white rice

½ cup loose black tea (preferably Chinese)

½ cup packed light or dark brown sugar

3 cinnamon sticks (3 inches each)

3 whole star anise

3 strips (½ by 2½ inches) tangerine or orange peel

FOR THE DUCK AND RUB

1 duck (5 to 6 pounds), thawed if frozen, giblets removed

1 tablespoon granulated sugar

1 teaspoon coarse salt (sea or kosher)

1 teaspoon freshly ground black pepper

½ teaspoon Chinese five-spice powder

½ teaspoon ground coriander

¼ teaspoon ground cinnamon

About 1 tablespoon Asian (dark) sesame oil, plus extra as needed

Hoisin Barbecue Sauce (recipe follows; optional), for serving

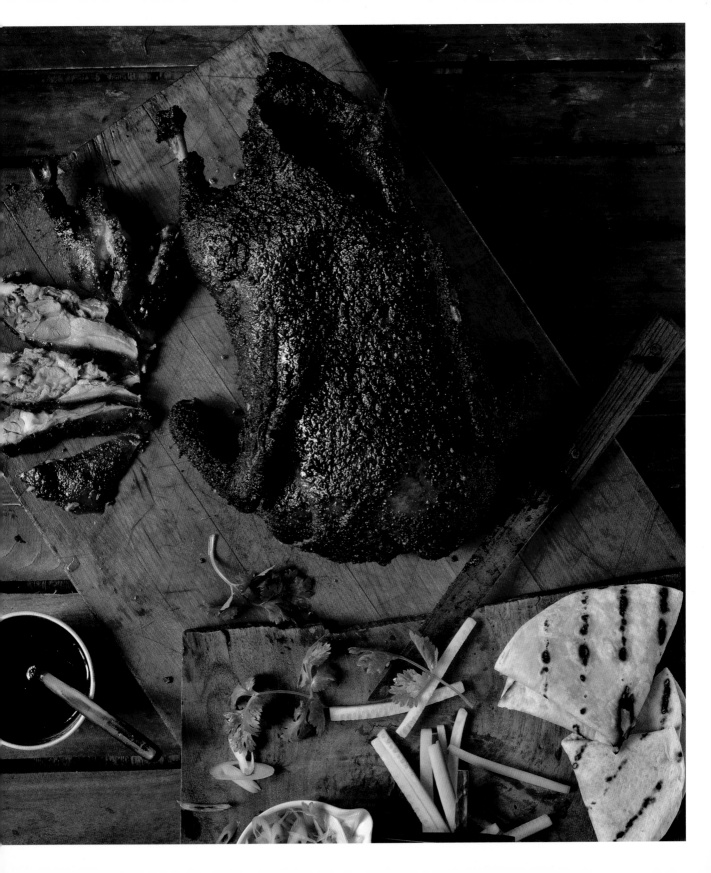

WHAT ELSE: The rub called for here is a variation on the 5-4-3-2-1 Rub on page 100, but if you have any extra of the latter (that recipe makes more than you need), by all means use it here. With this much smoke flavor, you don't really need a sauce, but if you want one, try the Hoisin Barbecue Sauce that follows.

1. Make the smoking mixture: Place the wood, rice, tea, sugar, cinnamon sticks, star anise, and tangerine peel in a bowl and stir to mix. Set aside. Rinse the duck inside and out under cold running water and blot dry with paper towels. Pull out and discard any excess lumps of fat from the cavities. Trim off the neck skin, leaving a 2-inch flap; fold and pin it to the back of the duck. Fold the wing tips back and under the duck. Prick the duck skin all over with a needle, piercing the skin but not the meat under it (this helps release the fat).

2. Make the rub: Combine the sugar, salt, pepper, five-spice powder, coriander, and cinnamon in a small bowl and stir to mix. Season the front (neck) and main cavities of the duck with half of the rub. Brush the outside of the duck all over with 1 tablespoon sesame oil. Sprinkle the outside of the duck all over with the remaining rub, rubbing it into the skin. I don't bother trussing the duck. Though it won't look as professional, it will get more exposure to the smoke if the cavity is left open.

3. Set up your smoker following the manufacturer's instructions and preheat to 225° to 250°F. Add half the wood and half the smoking mixture as specified by the manufacturer.

4. Place the duck on the rack with a drip pan underneath it. Smoke the duck until it reaches an internal temperature of 145°F on an instant-read thermometer inserted into the thickest part of the thigh, but not touching bone, 2 to 2½ hours.

5. Increase the smoker temperature to 350°F (if possible on your smoker). Brush the duck all over with fat from the drip pan or more sesame oil. Add the remaining cherry wood and smoking mixture and continue smoking until the skin is dark and crisp and the duck is cooked through, another 1 to 1½ hours. (The Chinese eat their duck well done.) There are two ways to test for doneness. Wiggle one of the drumsticks: The leg should move freely. Or check the internal temperature of the thigh meat with an instant-read thermometer; it should register 175°F. (Make sure the probe doesn't touch bone, or you'll get a false reading.)

6. Transfer the duck to a cutting board and let rest for 5 minutes, then carve and serve with the sauce on the side, if desired.

NOTE: If your smoker does not allow for temperatures higher than 250°F, increase the cooking time by 30 to 60 minutes.

HOISIN BARBECUE SAUCE

YIELD: Makes 1¼ cups

A sweet, salty, anise-flavored barbecue sauce in the tradition of Peking duck.

SHOP: As a reminder, hoisin sauce is a thick condiment made from soybeans. Rice wine is an alcoholic beverage made from fermented rice; if you can't find Chinese *shaoxing*, substitute sake or sherry.

INGREDIENTS

¾ cup hoisin sauce

2 tablespoons soy sauce

2 tablespoons rice wine (shaoxing), sake, or dry sherry

2 tablespoons honey

1 tablespoon Asian (dark) sesame oil

2 tablespoons chopped fresh cilantro

2 teaspoons minced fresh ginger

Combine the hoisin sauce, soy sauce, rice wine, honey, sesame oil, cilantro, and ginger in a saucepan and gently simmer over medium-low heat until thickened and richly flavored, 5 to 8 minutes, stirring from time to time to prevent scorching. Let the sauce cool to room temperature before serving.

SMOKED DUCK TACOS

YIELD: Makes 8 tacos, enough for 2 really hungry people, or 4 people when served with other food

Think of these duck tacos as Chi-Mex fusion finger food. Ridiculously delicious.

INGREDIENTS

1 Tea-Smoked Duck (page 168)

8 small flour tortillas

Hoisin Barbecue Sauce (above)

Vinegar Slaw (page 132)

2 scallions, trimmed, white and green parts thinly sliced crosswise

2 tablespoons toasted sesame seeds

Remove the skin from the duck. Scrape off and discard the fat from the skin and thinly sliver the skin. Remove the meat from the bones and thinly slice or shred. Warm the tortillas on a hot grill (10 seconds per side over high heat) or in a low oven. Top each tortilla with some sauce, duck meat, skin, slaw, scallions, and sesame seeds. Fold the tortilla in half or roll it around the duck and dig in.

SEAFOOD

Smoked seafood starts with a minimalist formula (fish plus salt plus wood smoke), but the result is anything but simple. Dozens of factors determine it, from the fish variety to the length of the cure to the drying, wrapping, and smoking. And that doesn't begin to factor in the smoker—its construction and age, and what type of wood it burns. In this chapter, you'll learn how to smoke shellfish, such as Danish and New Orleans-style shrimp. Smoke freshly shucked oysters over smoldering alder or hickory just long enough to impart flavor (but not so long you cook them through), and you wind up with a depth of flavor you never dreamt bivalves could possess. You'll also learn how to cold-smoke salmon, hot-smoke bluefish, and smoke bacon-wrapped trout on aromatic wood planks. Teach a man to smoke and he'll eat astonishing seafood the rest of his days.

OYSTERS SMOKED ON THE HALF SHELL

YIELD: Makes 24 oysters; serves 4 as a light starter, or 2 as a first course

METHOD: Hot-smoking or indirect grilling

PREP TIME: 30 minutes

SMOKING TIME: 15 to 20 minutes in a smoker; 5 to 8 minutes on a grill

FUEL: Hardwood of your choice—enough for 20 minutes of smoking (see chart on page 6)

GEAR: An oyster shucking knife; shellfish grilling rack or wire rack

SHOP: More than 1,000 different varieties of oysters are eaten worldwide—many hundreds in North America alone. Pick the oyster that is freshest in your area—for example, Pemaquid Point oysters from Maine, Katama Bays from Massachusetts, Blue Points from New York, Kumamotos from the Pacific Northwest.

WHAT ELSE: You can also smoke clams and mussels on the half shell this way. For clams you'll want tender littlenecks or cherrystones. My favorite wine with smoked bivalves is a well-chilled sauvignon blanc from New Zealand.

Smoked oysters used to mean salty, oily bivalves packed in cans like sardines. You likely wrapped them in bacon and broiled them (angels on horseback) or pureed them with cream cheese to make a dip. The modern approach involves fresh oysters—here smoked with nothing more than a simple pat of butter. Think bliss on the half shell and you'll never think about oysters—fresh or smoked—the same way.

INGREDIENTS

24 fresh oysters in the shell

4 tablespoons (½ stick) unsalted butter, cut into 24 equal pieces (each about ½ teaspoon)

Smoked Bread (page 56), for serving

1. Set up your smoker following the manufacturer's instructions and preheat to 225° to 250°F. Add the wood as specified by the manufacturer.

2. While the smoker is heating, carefully shuck the oysters, discarding the top shells. Pass the knife under each oyster to release it from the bottom shell. Leave the oysters in the shells. Arrange the oysters on a shellfish grilling rack or a wire rack, taking care not to spill the juices. Place a piece of butter on each oyster.

3. Place the rack with the oysters in the smoker. Smoke until the butter is melted and the oysters are warm but not fully cooked, 15 to 20 minutes, or as needed. Serve with grilled bread.

Variation

You can also smoke the oysters on a charcoal grill. Set it up for indirect grilling and preheat to 400°F. Arrange the oysters on their rack on the grate. Toss 1½ cups unsoaked wood chips (¾ cup on each side) or 2 wood chunks on the coals. Smoke the oysters as described above, 5 to 8 minutes, or as needed.

SMOKED SHRIMP COCKTAIL
WITH CHIPOTLE-ORANGE COCKTAIL SAUCE

Here's a Mexican twist on conventional shrimp cocktail, with smoke and fire coming at you from all directions. First from the shrimp, which you season with hot red pepper flakes and cumin and smoke over smoldering mesquite. Then from a cocktail sauce that features the sweet, smoky flavors of fresh orange juice and chipotle chiles. Add chiles to your liking—one for mildly spicy shrimp, two for pyromaniacs. Beats the traditional cold boiled shrimp cocktail hollow.

INGREDIENTS

FOR THE CHIPOTLE-ORANGE COCKTAIL SAUCE

1 cup ketchup

1 teaspoon finely grated orange zest

¼ cup fresh orange juice

1 tablespoon Worcestershire sauce

1 or 2 canned chipotle chiles, minced, plus 2 teaspoons adobo sauce

2 tablespoons finely diced white onion

2 tablespoons finely chopped fresh cilantro, plus 4 sprigs

FOR THE SHRIMP

1½ pounds jumbo shrimp, peeled with tails intact, and deveined

3 tablespoons chopped fresh cilantro

2 scallions, trimmed, white and green parts thinly sliced

1 to 2 teaspoons hot red pepper flakes

1 teaspoon ground cumin

Coarse salt (sea or kosher) and freshly cracked black pepper

4 tablespoons extra virgin olive oil, plus extra for oiling the rack

YIELD: Serves 4 as a starter

METHOD: Smoke-roasting or grilling

PREP TIME: 30 minutes

SMOKING TIME: 30 to 60 minutes in a conventional smoker or 4 to 6 minutes on a grill

FUEL: I like to smoke the shrimp with mesquite, but any hardwood will work. You'll need enough for 1 hour of smoking (see chart on page 6).

GEAR: Medium-size bamboo skewers (8 to 10 inches)

SHOP: Use fresh local shrimp when possible: Key West pinks if you're in Florida; spot prawns on the West Coast; Gulf shrimp in Louisiana; or Maine shrimp in New England. Size matters less than freshness.

WHAT ELSE: There are two options for smoking: traditional low-and-slow smoking, which gives you great flavor but a slightly rubbery texture, and high-heat smoke-roasting on a grill, which gives you a little more sizzle and crust.

1. Make the cocktail sauce: Place the ketchup, orange zest and juice, Worcestershire sauce, chipotles, adobo sauce, onion and chopped cilantro in a bowl and whisk to mix. Divide the cocktail sauce among four small bowls. Cover and refrigerate until serving. Place a cilantro sprig in the center of each just before serving.

2. Rinse the shrimp, drain, and blot dry. Place the shrimp, cilantro, scallions, hot red pepper flakes, cumin, and ½ teaspoon each of salt and pepper in a large bowl and toss to mix. Stir in 2 tablespoons of the oil, cover, and marinate for 15 minutes. Thread the shrimp onto bamboo skewers, 2 to a skewer. Leave ¼ inch exposed skewer at the point end and the bottom half of the skewer shrimp-free. Place the skewers on a lightly oiled wire rack if smoking.

3. Smoker method: Set up your smoker following the manufacturer's instructions and preheat to 225° to 250°F. Add the wood as specified by the manufacturer. Place the rack with the shrimp in the smoker and smoke until bronzed with smoke and firm to the touch, 30 to 60 minutes, or as needed. Baste with the remaining 2 tablespoons of the oil after 20 minutes.

Grill method: Set up your grill for direct grilling and preheat to high (450°F). Toss the wood chunks or chips on the coals. Direct grill the shrimp, turning them over once, until sizzling and brown on the outside and cooked through, 2 to 3 minutes per side. Slide a folded strip of aluminum foil under the exposed parts of the skewers to keep them from burning. Baste with the remaining oil after you turn the shrimp.

4. Serve the shrimp on the skewers with the Chipotle-Orange Cocktail Sauce for dipping.

SMOKE TIMES FOR SEAFOOD

FISH AND CUT	WEIGHT	SMOKER TEMP	TIME	INTERNAL TEMP/ DONENESS
Salmon fillet—cold-smoked	1½ pounds	Cold-smoke (under 100°F)	12-18 hours	Bronzed with smoke
Salmon fillet—hot-smoked	1½ pounds	225°-250°F	30-60 minutes	140°F
Trout	12 to 16 ounces each	350°F	15-25 minutes on a grill (10 minutes if direct grilling); 40-60 minutes in a smoker	140°F
Bluefish	1½ pounds	225°-250°F	30-60 minutes	140°F
Arctic char	1½ pounds	225°-250°F	30-60 minutes	140°F
Black cod	2 pounds	225°-250°F	30-60 minutes	140°F
Shrimp	1½ pounds	225°-250°F	30-60 minutes	Until firm
Oysters	1 dozen	225°-250°F	15-20 minutes	Until barely cooked

HOW TO BUILD A SMOKEHOUSE

Water smokers offer convenience, and stick burners (offset smokers) possess undeniable machismo. As you delve deeper into smoking, at some point you may want to make a more permanent commitment to the craft. Build a smokehouse.

It's not complicated and it indisputably establishes your bona fides as a smoke master. You can hot-smoke in a smokehouse, but it's especially well suited to cold-smoking.

To build my smokehouse, I enlisted the expertise of my carpenter friend and neighbor, Roger Becker. For the walls, we used a naturally water- and rot-resistant wood: cedar. For the base, we bought a 3-by-3-foot slab of bluestone. (You can also use the sort of concrete slab sold by hardware stores to go under outdoor air conditioning condensers.) You want a fireproof base to minimize the risk of setting your smokehouse on fire. For further fire resistance, we lined the lower 12 inches of the inside walls with WonderBoard, which is like Sheetrock made with cement.

The walls of my smokehouse rise 6 feet, with a slanted shingled roof to drain off rainwater. For food racks, I bought Metro shelving, installing the individual shelves 15 inches apart on horizontal slats. This way, they're easy to remove if I want to smoke a large hanging item like a ham. (I hang it from a hook in the ceiling.)

I attached the front panel with hinges, fitting the door of an old wood stove at the bottom to open for refueling. At the top in the front and back, I drilled a pair of 2-inch holes that could be partially covered with an adjustable wood damper to control the airflow.

To use the smokehouse for cold-smoking—my primary use—I drilled small holes in the back to accommodate a smoke generator like a Smoke

Daddy or Smoke Chief (see page 278). I drilled a hole in the front panel to install a thermometer. I attached a lean-to roof to one side to keep my wood dry. The materials cost less than $1,000. The pride it gave me was priceless.

SMOKED SHRIMP
WITH TWO DANISH DILL SAUCES

YIELD: Makes 2 pounds; enough to serve 6 to 8 as a starter, 4 as a main course

METHOD: Hot-smoking

PREP TIME: 10 minutes for cleaning the shrimp (if you decide to do so)

SMOKING TIME: 30 to 60 minutes

FUEL: Beech wood or alder—enough for 1 hour of smoking (see chart on page 6)

SHOP: Bornholmers use a small, preternaturally sweet shrimp from the Baltic Sea. The variety doesn't exist in North America, but fresh Maine shrimp, Key West pinks from Florida, or spot prawns from the West Coast and Hawaii give you an equal bang for the buck.

WHAT ELSE: So how do you clean shrimp with the shells on? Easy. Make a lengthwise slit down the back of each shrimp using kitchen scissors. Pull or scrape out the black vein using the tine of a fork or the point of a bamboo skewer.

The Røgerie Gudhjem is one of two dozen working smokehouse-restaurants scattered across Bornholm Island in Denmark. Founded in 1912, it now serves a thousand hungry people a day in summer. They flock here for house-smoked salmon and herring—the latter topped with raw onion and raw egg yolk and picturesquely christened *Sol over Gudhjem* (literally "sun over God's home"). For me, the Røgerie's star attraction is the hyper-sweet Baltic Sea shrimp smoked in the shell, with nothing more in the way of seasoning than smoke from local beech wood. Not even salt or pepper. The fireworks come from the pristine shrimp—and from a pair of piquant Danish sauces.

INGREDIENTS

2 pounds large shrimp (preferably fresh, with shells intact and heads on, if possible)

Vegetable oil, for oiling the rack

Lemon-Dill Sauce (recipe follows), for serving

Sweet Mustard-Dill Sauce (page 182), for serving

1. Set up your smoker following the manufacturer's instructions and preheat to 225° to 250°F. Add the wood as specified by the manufacturer.

2. Rinse the shrimp, drain, and blot dry. Arrange the shrimp on a lightly oiled wire rack and place in the smoker. Smoke until golden brown and cooked through (the shrimp will feel firm when squeezed), 30 to 60 minutes, or as needed (depending on the size of the shrimp).

3. Transfer the shrimp on their wire rack to a rimmed baking sheet to cool to room temperature. Or eat them hot out of the smoker, or chilled the next day. Dig in "peel-them-yourself-style" (twist to remove the heads and be sure to suck out the juices) with one or both of the sauces for dipping.

LEMON-DILL SAUCE

YIELD: Makes 1 cup

This simple sauce—bright with lemon zest and juice and fresh dill—goes great not only with shrimp, but with any smoked seafood.

INGREDIENTS

½ cup mayonnaise, Hellmann's or Best Foods or smoked mayonnaise (see page 204)

½ cup sour cream or smoked sour cream (see page 203)

2 tablespoons chopped fresh dill

1 tablespoon fresh lemon juice

1 teaspoon finely grated lemon zest

Coarse salt (sea or kosher) and freshly ground black pepper

Combine the mayonnaise, sour cream, dill, lemon juice, and lemon zest in a bowl and whisk to mix, adding salt and pepper to taste. Transfer to an attractive serving bowl and refrigerate until serving.

SWEET MUSTARD-DILL SAUCE

YIELD: Makes 1 cup

Another fresh dill sauce for smoked seafood. This one plays the spice of Dijon mustard against the sweetness of brown sugar.

INGREDIENTS

⅔ cup Dijon mustard

¼ cup packed light or dark brown sugar

2 tablespoons vegetable oil

1 tablespoons chopped fresh dill

Coarse salt (sea or kosher) and freshly ground black pepper

Combine the mustard, brown sugar, oil, and dill in a bowl and whisk to mix, adding salt and pepper to taste. Transfer to a serving bowl and refrigerate until serving.

BORNHOLM LAX
COLD-SMOKED SALMON LIKE THEY MAKE IT IN DENMARK

Cold-smoked salmon like Nova Scotia or *lax* requires a day or two of curing and a day or two of smoking—without the one element most of us associate with the smoking process: heat. So it wouldn't surprise me if the process intimidates you. It did me, and I've been hot-smoking salmon for decades. I have good news: It's surprisingly easy to turn out restaurant-quality cold-smoked salmon at home. You can do it in almost any sort of smoker. It helps to have one special piece of equipment—a smoke generator (see page 14)—and there are even workarounds if you lack that. The key is to cure the salmon in salt for at least a day (this both flavors and dehydrates the fish), then rinse it, dry it, and blast it with wood smoke, but—and this is a very important but—no heat. The low temperature (around 80°F) is crucial, for your goal is to smoke the salmon without cooking it. This gives you the translucent sheen, velvety texture, forthright smoke flavor, and briny marine tang (complete with a hint of iodine) characteristic of truly world-class cold-smoked salmon.

YIELD: Makes 2 pounds, enough to serve 10 to 12 as a starter or on bagels for breakfast

METHOD: Cold-smoking

PREP TIME: 20 minutes

CURING TIME: 24 hours

DESALTING AND DRYING TIME: About 2¼ hours

SMOKING TIME: 12 to 18 hours

RESTING TIME: 4 hours

FUEL: The Danes use beech wood; I'm partial to the alder burned in the Pacific Northwest. But you can use your favorite hardwood. You'll need enough wood for 18 hours of smoking (see chart on page 6).

GEAR: Kitchen tweezers or needle-nose pliers, to remove any fish bones; a smoke generator (see page 14); a large aluminum foil pan or other roasting pan (for ice) and a wire rack that fits on top of it, if smoking the fish on a warm day; unlined butcher paper (without a plastic coating)

INGREDIENTS

1 piece (2 pounds) fresh skin-on salmon fillet (preferably cut from the head end)

1½ cups coarse salt (sea or kosher)

Vegetable oil, for oiling the rack

1. Rinse the salmon and blot dry with paper towels. Run your fingers over the flesh side of the salmon fillet, feeling for the sharp ends of pin bones. Pull out any you find with kitchen tweezers.

2. Spread ½ cup of the salt over the bottom of a nonreactive baking dish just large enough to hold the fish. Lay the salmon fillet skin side down on top of the salt. (The salt should extend ½ inch beyond the edges of the fish on each side.) Spread the remaining 1 cup of salt on top so it covers the fish completely.

3. Cover the dish with plastic wrap and cure the fish in the coolest part of your refrigerator for 24 hours. (The fish will give off liquid as it cures. This is normal.)

SHOP: When you work with only two ingredients, both had better be great. My first choice is fresh wild king salmon from Alaska. All Alaskan salmon is wild; nearly all Atlantic salmon (the sort generally available on the East Coast of North America and in Europe) is farmed. Tradition calls for smoking whole sides of salmon, which can weigh 6 or 8 pounds each; I've scaled down the recipe to accommodate the 2-pound sections of salmon fillet typically found at fish markets. Choose a piece cut from the head end or middle of the fillet—these have more fat and tenderness.

WHAT ELSE: I like to leave the skin on—it gives the fish structure and protects it. I do remove the pin bones before smoking, although many smoked salmon masters leave the bones in.

4. Gently rinse the salt off the salmon under cold running water. Place the salmon in a large bowl with cold water to cover by 3 inches. Soak for 15 minutes (this removes any excess salt), then drain well in a colander.

5. Blot the salmon dry on both sides with paper towels. Arrange it skin side down on a lightly oiled wire rack over a rimmed baking sheet. Let the salmon air-dry, uncovered, in the refrigerator until it feels tacky, about 2 hours.

6. Set up your smoker for cold-smoking following the manufacturer's instructions. The smoker temperature should be no more than 80°F. To convert a hot-smoker into a cold-smoker, see page 203. Ideally, you'll be using a smoke generator to create the smoke.

7. If you're smoking the salmon on a hot day like we have so often in Florida (above 80°F), fill a disposable aluminum foil pan or roasting pan with ice and arrange the fish on the wire rack at least ½ inch above the ice. Otherwise, leave the wire rack on the baking sheet.

8. Cold-smoke the salmon until the exterior is bronzed with smoke and the salmon feels semifirm and leathery, 12 to 18 hours. Twelve hours of cold-smoking gives you very tasty smoked salmon (and allows you to get a good night's sleep). For even more smoke flavor, go 18 hours (see Note).

How will you know it's ready? Cut a slice from the wider end. The texture will be satiny. It will taste like, well, smoked salmon—cured and smoked, not raw.

9. Wrap the salmon in unlined butcher paper and let it rest in the refrigerator for at least 4 hours or as long as overnight before serving. The salmon will keep for at least 3 days in the refrigerator and for several months in the freezer.

10. To serve, using a long, slender, very sharp knife held sharply on the diagonal to the fish, cut the salmon off the skin into paper-thin slices.

NOTE: For the ultimate smoked salmon, smoke it for a full 24 hours. Make sure you have enough fuel.

TRADITIONAL SMOKED SALMON ACCOMPANIMENTS

So what's the best way to serve cold-smoked salmon? Russian style, on blinis (buckwheat pancakes)? French style, on toast points (preferably brioche)? Jewish style, on bagels with cream cheese? Or Danish style, as open-face sandwiches on rye bread? Winners, all, and you might also enjoy some or all of the following accompaniments. Arrange them in small bowls with spoons or on a large serving platter.

By the way, when serving smoked salmon for breakfast or as a starter, figure on 2 to 3 ounces per person.

- Sour cream
- Minced red onion
- Finely chopped hard-cooked egg whites
- Finely chopped hard-cooked egg yolks
- Finely chopped fresh flat-leaf parsley or dill
- Thinly sliced lemons or lemon wedges
- Brined capers (drained)
- Peeled, seeded, and finely diced cucumber, or thinly sliced cucumber

KIPPERED SALMON

Kippered salmon starts like cold-smoked salmon—with a salt (and often sugar) cure. But you cook the fish as well as smoke it, which gives you a completely different texture and taste. I've made it for decades—originally in a wok, then in a stovetop smoker (see page 275), and now in one of the dozens of smokers at Barbecue University and in my backyard. Many recipes start with a brine, but I prefer the texture you get with a dry cure. The rum wash gives the fish an extra layer of flavor.

You're probably wondering about the origin of the term "kipper." One theory holds that it comes from the Anglo-Saxon word for copper, *cypera*. (With a little imagination, smoked salmon does look copper colored.) Others cite the Old English *kippian* ("to spawn"), *kip* (the hooked lower jaw of a male salmon), or *kippen* ("to pull"—as in a fishing line).

YIELD: Makes 1½ pounds, enough to serve 8 to 10 as a starter

METHOD: Hot-smoking

PREP TIME: 15 minutes

MARINATING AND CURING TIME: 4½ hours

DRYING TIME: 2 hours

SMOKING TIME: 30 to 60 minutes

FUEL: I'm partial to cherry and alder, but any hardwood will work. You'll need enough for 1 hour of smoking (see chart on page 6).

GEAR: Kitchen tweezers
or needle-nose pliers for
removing any fish bones;
a wire rack; an instant-read
thermometer

SHOP: As always, buy fresh
wild salmon when you can get
it, preferably coho or king.

WHAT ELSE: By varying
the base ingredients, you
can create a dozen different
versions of kippered salmon.
Rinse with whiskey, vodka,
aquavit, or gin. Use maple
sugar, molasses, or honey
instead of brown sugar.
Add coriander and dill in
the manner of Scandinavian
gravlax. You get the idea.

INGREDIENTS

1 piece (1½ pounds) fresh
 skin-on salmon fillet
 (preferably a center cut)

1 cup dark rum

1 cup packed dark brown sugar

½ cup coarse salt (sea or kosher)

1 tablespoon freshly ground black
 pepper

Vegetable oil, for oiling the rack

1. Rinse the salmon fillet under cold running water and blot dry with paper towels. Run your fingers over the flesh side of the fillet, feeling for the sharp ends of pin bones. Pull out any you find with kitchen tweezers.

2. Place the salmon, skin side down, in a nonreactive baking dish just large enough to hold it. Add the rum, cover, and marinate in the refrigerator for 30 minutes, turning the fish twice. Drain the salmon well in a colander, discarding the rum, and blot the salmon dry with paper towels. Wipe out the baking dish.

3. Place the sugar, salt, and pepper in a bowl and mix well, breaking up any lumps in the brown sugar with your fingers. Spread ½ cup in the bottom of the baking dish. Arrange the salmon on top, skin side down. Sprinkle the remaining 1 cup of the cure over the salmon, patting it into the flesh with your fingertips. Cover with plastic wrap and cure in the refrigerator for 4 hours.

4. Rinse the cure off the salmon under cold running water and blot dry with paper towels. Arrange the salmon, skin side down, on an oiled wire rack over a rimmed baking sheet and let

air-dry, uncovered, in the refrigerator until tacky, about 2 hours.

5. Set up your smoker following the manufacturer's instructions and preheat to 225° to 250°F. Add the wood as specified by the manufacturer.

6. Transfer the salmon on its rack to the smoker. Smoke until golden brown, firm at the edges, and just cooked through, 30 to 60 minutes, or as needed. To test for doneness, press it with your finger; the flesh should break into clean flakes. Alternatively, insert the probe of an instant-read thermometer through one side of the fish into the center. The internal temperature should be about 140°F.

7. Transfer the salmon on its rack to a rimmed baking sheet and let cool to room temperature, then refrigerate, wrapped in plastic or aluminum foil, until serving. To serve, cut or break the salmon into flakes or chunks. It will keep in the refrigerator for at least 3 days or in the freezer for several months.

SALMON CANDY

You'll recognize it by its Old Master patina of wood smoke—usually alder. And by its sweet-salty flavor profile, the result of a salt-sugar cure and a generous basting of maple syrup or honey. The name says it all: salmon candy.

Tradition calls for cold- or cool-smoking the salmon candy, producing a chewy texture reminiscent of jerky. I opt for a higher temperature, which gives you crusty edges and a moist flaky texture. It's damn near irresistible, even for people who don't generally like smoked fish. Serve it with vodka or aquavit (it can stand up to the strongest spirits). Don't be intimidated by the overall preparation time—the actual work takes about 30 minutes.

INGREDIENTS

1 piece (1½ pounds) fresh skinless salmon fillet (preferably a center cut)

1 cup dark brown sugar or maple sugar

¼ cup coarse salt (sea or kosher)

¾ cup pure maple syrup (preferably dark amber or Grade B)

1 quart water

Vegetable oil, for oiling the rack

1. Rinse the salmon under cold running water and blot dry with paper towels. Run your fingers over the flesh side of the fillet, feeling for the sharp ends of pin bones. Pull out any you find with kitchen tweezers.

2. Using a sharp knife, slice the salmon widthwise into strips 1 inch wide and 4 to 5 inches long. Transfer the fish to a large heavy-duty resealable plastic bag and place the bag in an aluminum foil pan or baking dish to contain any leaks.

3. Combine the brown sugar, salt, and ½ cup of the maple syrup in a bowl. Add the water and stir until the sugar and salt dissolve. Pour this over the salmon and seal the bag. Cure in the refrigerator for 8 hours, turning the bag over several times to redistribute the brine.

4. Drain the salmon in a colander, discarding the brine, and rinse the salmon well under cold running water. Blot dry with paper towels. Arrange the salmon flesh side up on an oiled wire rack over a rimmed baking sheet and let air-dry in the refrigerator until tacky, 2 hours.

YIELD: Makes 1½ pounds, enough to serve 6 to 8 as a snack

METHOD: Hot-smoking

PREP TIME: 30 minutes

BRINING TIME: 8 hours

DRYING TIME: 2 hours

SMOKING TIME: 30 to 60 minutes

FUEL: Alder—enough for 1 hour of smoking (see chart on page 6)

GEAR: Kitchen tweezers or needle-nose pliers, to remove any fish bones, a large heavy-duty resealable plastic bag; a large aluminum foil pan; a wire rack; an instant-read thermometer

SHOP: As with all the smoked salmon in this book, ideally you'll use fresh wild salmon, preferably king or coho from Alaska or Washington State.

WHAT ELSE: For an interesting variation, glaze the salmon with honey instead of maple syrup. Warm the honey slightly so you can brush it more easily on the fish.

5. Set up your smoker following the manufacturer's instructions and preheat to 225° to 250°F. Add the wood as directed by the manufacturer.

6. Place the salmon on its rack in the smoker and smoke until the outside is bronzed with smoke and the salmon feels firm, 30 to 60 minutes. Start brushing the salmon with the remaining ¼ cup of maple syrup after 15 minutes, and brush several times until it's cooked (about 140°F on an instant-read thermometer). Transfer the salmon candy on its rack to a rimmed baking sheet to cool and brush one final time with maple syrup before serving. Serve at room temperature or cold.

7. In the unlikely event you have leftovers, store the salmon candy in a resealable plastic bag in the refrigerator; it will keep for at least 3 days.

Variation

To make traditional salmon candy that's chewy like jerky, set up your smoker or grill following the manufacturer's instructions and preheat to 175°F or as low as it will go. Add the wood as directed by the manufacturer. Place the salmon on its rack in the smoker and smoke until the outside is bronzed with smoke and the salmon feels firm, 4 hours, or as needed. Start brushing the salmon with the remaining ¼ cup of maple syrup after 2 hours, and brush several times until it's cooked. Transfer the salmon candy on its rack to a rimmed baking sheet to cool and brush one final time with maple syrup before serving. Serve at room temperature or cold.

SMOKED PLANKED TROUT

The mildly earthy flavor of trout makes it a staple on the world's smoked fish trail. When I smoke trout, I like to incorporate a popular grilling technique: planking. The plank—cedar, alder, hickory, your choice—adds a haunting wood flavor that's lighter and different from smoke. It also makes a convenient and handsome presentation for serving—you don't even need a plate. There's an added advantage: This method works equally well on a grill or in a smoker. Note: I work at a higher temperature than traditional low-and-slow smoking to crisp the bacon.

YIELD: Serves 4 as a main course

METHOD: Smoke-roasting

PREP TIME: 15 minutes

SMOKING TIME: 15 to 25 minutes on a grill (10 minutes if direct grilling) or 40 to 60 minutes in a smoker

INGREDIENTS

4 whole trout (12 to 16 ounces each), cleaned

Coarse salt (sea or kosher) and freshly ground black pepper

8 to 12 sprigs fresh dill

3 lemons, 1 thinly sliced and seeded, 2 cut in half crosswise

2 tablespoons (¼ stick) cold unsalted butter, thinly sliced

8 strips thin-sliced artisanal bacon (like Nueske's, or make your own, page 113)

1. Set up your grill for direct grilling and preheat to high (450°F). Lay the planks on the grill and grill until the underside is charred, 2 to 4 minutes. Let cool. If working on an offset barrel smoker, hold the planks with tongs over the fire in the firebox to singe them.

2. Rinse the trout inside and out under cold running water, then blot dry inside and out with paper towels. Make three diagonal slashes in each side of the trout with a single-edge razor blade or sharp paring knife. (This looks cool and helps the fish cook more evenly.) Generously season the trout inside and out with salt and pepper. Place a couple of dill sprigs, lemon slices, and butter slices in the cavity of each trout.

3. Tie 2 bacon strips to each trout, one on top, one on the bottom, using 4 pieces of butcher's string to secure them. Arrange the trout on the charred side of the grilling planks (align them on the diagonal) and place a lemon half on each plank.

4. Set up your smoker following the manufacturer's instructions and preheat to medium (350°F—or as hot as it will go). Add the wood as specified by the manufacturer.

5. Smoke-roast the trout until the bacon is sizzling and crisp and the trout is cooked through (about 140°F in the center), 15 to 25 minutes at 350°F, 40 to 60 minutes if your smoker runs cooler. Alternatively, direct grill the trout over a medium flame (this will take about 10 minutes). If the edges of the plank start to burn, spray with a squirt gun.

6. Serve the trout on the plank with the smoked lemon halves for squeezing.

FUEL: Hardwood of your choice—enough for 15 to 25 minutes of smoking on a grill, 40 to 60 minutes of smoking in a smoker (see chart on page 6)

GEAR: 4 cedar, alder, or other untreated wood planks, preferably 14 by 6 inches, available at grill shops and most supermarkets; butcher's string; an instant-read thermometer

SHOP: I like whole trout with the head intact, but you can certainly use headless, boneless trout to serve people with more delicate sensibilities.

WHAT ELSE: Conventional wisdom calls for soaking the plank in water prior to grilling or smoking on the theory that soaking keeps the plank from burning. You're going to do just the opposite: char the plank directly over the fire to bring out some of the flavor-producing carbonyls and phenols *before* adding the fish.

HONEY-LEMON SMOKED BLUEFISH

YIELD: Makes 1½ pounds (serves 6 to 8 as a starter)

METHOD: Hot-smoking

PREP TIME: 20 minutes

BRINING TIME: 8 hours

DRYING TIME: 2 hours

SMOKING TIME: 30 to 60 minutes

FUEL: I'm partial to maple wood, but cherry and alder also work great. You'll need enough wood for 1 hour of smoking (see chart on page 6).

GEAR: Kitchen tweezers or needle-nose pliers, to remove any fish bones; an instant-read thermometer (optional)

SHOP: Ideally, you're a fisherman and you'll smoke the bluefish you caught that morning. Otherwise, buy it from a trusted fishmonger the day it comes in.

WHAT ELSE: Warm the honey jar in a pan of simmering water. This makes it easier to pour. This cure works great for other oily fish like salmon and king mackerel. For a classic New England bluefish dip, see page 45.

More smoked bluefish pâté gets served at Martha's Vineyard cocktail parties than any other appetizer, period. (See the Smoked Seafood Dip on page 45.) The reason is simple—we have the best bluefish in North America, and catching it is an island obsession. (That obsession reaches a crescendo in September when normal life stops for a month-long fishing tournament called the Derby.) Many people dislike bluefish—or profess to—but that's because they've never tasted it fresh, just hours out of the water. (After more than one day, bluefish acquires an unpleasantly strong fish flavor.) The best way to boost bluefish's shelf life and tame its flavor is with a honey-lemon brine and hot-smoking.

INGREDIENTS

1½ pounds fresh skinless bluefish fillets

¼ cup honey

¼ cup coarse salt (sea or kosher)

1 tablespoon cracked black peppercorns

2 whole cloves

2 allspice berries

1 quart hot water

1 quart ice water

4 strips lemon zest (2 by ½ inch each; remove the zest with a vegetable peeler)

Vegetable oil, for oiling the rack

1. Run your fingers over the bluefish fillets, feeling for bones. Pull out any you find with kitchen tweezers. Trim off any dark red portions from the skin side of the fillets using a sharp knife. (This is where the "fishy" flavor resides.)

2. Place the honey, salt, peppercorns, cloves, allspice berries, and hot water in a large deep bowl and whisk until the honey and salt are dissolved. Whisk in the cold water and lemon zest. Add the fish, cover with plastic wrap, and brine in the refrigerator for 8 hours, turning several times. (Alternatively, place the fish and brine in a resealable heavy-duty plastic bag. Place the bag in an aluminum foil drip pan or baking dish to contain any leaks.)

3. Drain the bluefish in a colander and discard the brine and lemon zest. Rinse the bluefish well under cold running water; drain well and blot dry with paper towels. Place on an oiled wire rack over a rimmed baking sheet. Let the bluefish air-dry in the refrigerator until the surface is tacky, 2 hours.

4. Set up your smoker following the manufacturer's instructions and preheat to 225° to 250°F. Add the wood as specified by the manufacturer.

5. Smoke the bluefish on its wire rack in the smoker until bronzed with smoke and cooked through, 30 to 60 minutes. To test for doneness, press it with your finger; the flesh should break into clean flakes. Alternatively, insert the probe of an instant-read thermometer through one end of the fish into the center. The internal temperature should be about 140°F.

6. Transfer the bluefish on its rack to a rimmed baking sheet to cool to room temperature, then wrap in plastic wrap and refrigerate until serving. It will keep for at least 3 days in the refrigerator.

MAPLE-CURED AND SMOKED ARCTIC CHAR

YIELD: Makes 1½ pounds, enough to serve 6 to 8 as a starter or 3 to 4 as a main course

METHOD: Hot-smoking

PREP TIME: 10 minutes

CURING TIME: 1 hour

SMOKING TIME: 30 to 60 minutes

FUEL: Maple wood—enough for 1 hour of smoking (see chart on page 6)

GEAR: Kitchen tweezers or needle-nose pliers, to remove any fish bones; an instant-read thermometer (optional)

Arctic char is one of my favorite fish for smoking, offering the vivid color of salmon and the delicate texture of trout. (The flavor lies somewhere between them.) In keeping with its Canadian origins, I cure arctic char with maple sugar and smoke it with maple wood. You can make it start to finish in 2 hours—which is fast for smoked fish. Serve it any way you would Kippered Salmon (page 187).

INGREDIENTS

1 cup maple sugar

½ cup coarse salt (sea or kosher)

1 tablespoon freshly ground black pepper

1 teaspoon finely grated lemon zest

1½ pounds fresh arctic char fillets, skin on or off

Vegetable oil, for oiling the rack

1. Place the maple sugar, salt, pepper, and lemon zest in a bowl and mix well, breaking up any lumps in the sugar with your fingers. Spread ½ cup of the cure on a rimmed baking sheet. The salt should extend ½ inch beyond the edges of the fish on each side. Place the fillets on top, skin side down. Sprinkle the remaining 1 cup cure on top of the char, patting it into the flesh with your fingertips. Cover with plastic wrap and cure the fish in the refrigerator for 1 hour.

2. Run your fingers over the flesh side of the char fillets, feeling for bones. Pull out any you find with kitchen tweezers. Rinse the char fillets under cold running water. Drain the fillets and blot dry with paper towels. Arrange the fillets skin side down on an oiled wire rack over a rimmed baking sheet and let air-dry in the refrigerator for 30 minutes.

3. Set up your smoker following the manufacturer's instructions and preheat to 225° to 250°F. Add the wood as specified by the manufacturer.

4. Place the fish on its wire rack in the smoker. Smoke the fish until golden brown, crusty at the edges, and just cooked through, 30 to 60 minutes. To test for doneness, press it with your finger; the flesh should break into clean flakes. Alternatively, insert the probe of an instant-read thermometer through one of the ends of the fish into the center. The internal temperature should be about 140°F.

5. Transfer the fish to a wire rack over a rimmed baking sheet and let cool to room temperature, then refrigerate wrapped in plastic until serving. Serve it at room temperature or chilled. It will keep in the refrigerator for at least 3 days or in the freezer for several months.

SHOP: If you live in the American north or Canada, you'll probably find arctic char at your local fishmonger. Trout or small salmon could be cured and smoked the same way. Maple sugar is available in natural foods stores or online. Alternatively, use light brown sugar.

WHAT ELSE: When I make arctic char for myself, I don't bother to remove the skin. When I make it for my wife, I do.

SMOKED BLACK COD
WITH FENNEL-CORIANDER RUB

In delicatessens, it's called sablefish. If you live in the Pacific Northwest or Alaska, you know it as black cod. The mild flavor and high fat content endeared it to marquee chef Nobu Matsuhisa, who made black cod with miso a signature dish at his restaurants. Cure it with salt and sugar and smoke it with alder and you wind up with a fish that elevates a bagel with cream cheese, enlightens a toast point with cucumber, and tastes pretty darn good scarfed hot off the smoker rack with your fingers. I've eaten sablefish all my life, but never fully appreciated it until I pulled one out of Tutka Bay, Alaska, at the end of a fishing pole. (Less a tribute to my fishing skills than to black cod's fondness for herring.) The chef at the scenic Tutka Bay Lodge cures it Nordic style, with a fennel-coriander-brown sugar rub.

YIELD: Serves 4

METHOD: Hot-smoking

PREP TIME: 15 minutes

CURING TIME: 3 hours

DRYING TIME: 30 minutes

SMOKING TIME: 30 to 60 minutes

FUEL: Alder—enough for 1 hour of smoking (see chart on page 6)

GEAR: A spice mill or clean coffee grinder; a wire rack; an instant-read thermometer (optional); kitchen tweezers or needle-nose pliers, to remove any fish bones

SHOP: Black cod is widely available on the West Coast. Elsewhere, you may need to special-order. One good online source is the Pure Food Fish Market in Seattle (freshseafood.com).

WHAT ELSE: Can't find black cod? Try this rub on salmon, sturgeon, haddock, or cod.

INGREDIENTS

1 tablespoon fennel seeds

1 tablespoon coriander seeds

1 tablespoon white peppercorns

3 bay leaves, crumbled

⅔ cup coarse salt (sea or kosher)

¼ cup granulated sugar

¼ cup packed light or dark brown sugar

2 pounds black cod fillets (preferably skin on)

Vegetable oil, for oiling the rack

1. Heat a dry cast-iron skillet over medium heat. Add the fennel seeds, coriander, peppercorns, and bay leaves and roast, stirring, until fragrant and lightly browned, 2 minutes. Transfer to a small bowl and let cool. Grind the spices to a fine powder in a spice mill or clean coffee grinder. Return them to the bowl. Stir in the salt and both sugars.

2. Place the cure mixture on a large plate or platter. Crust each cod fillet on all sides with the cure, rubbing it into the flesh with your fingertips. Tightly wrap each fillet in plastic wrap and place on a rimmed baking sheet, skin side down. Refrigerate for 3 hours.

3. Rinse the cod fillets well under cold running water. Blot them dry with paper towels. Arrange the fillets on an oiled wire rack over the baking sheet and let air-dry in the refrigerator for 30 minutes.

4. Set up your smoker following the manufacturer's instructions and preheat to 225° to 250°F. Add the wood as specified by the manufacturer.

5. Place the cod on its wire rack skin side down in the smoker. Smoke the cod until golden brown, crusty at the edges, and just cooked through, 30 to 60 minutes. To test for doneness, press it with your finger; the flesh should break into clean flakes. Alternatively, insert the probe of an instant-read thermometer through one end of the fish into the center. The internal temperature should be about 140°F.

6. Transfer the cod on its rack to the rimmed baking sheet and let cool to room temperature. Run your fingers over the fillets, feeling for bones. Pull out any you find with kitchen tweezers. (The bones are easier to remove when the cod is cooked.) Refrigerate the smoked black cod until serving. It will keep in the refrigerator, wrapped in plastic wrap, for at least 3 days or in the freezer for several months.

SMOKED BLACK COD TOASTS WITH DILLED CUCUMBER RELISH

YIELD: Serves 4 to 6 as a starter

These simple toasts show off black cod in all its smoky, buttery glory, with cucumber for crunch and lemon and dill for brightness. For extra flavor, smoke the bread.

INGREDIENTS

1 medium cucumber, peeled, seeded, and cut into very fine dice

2 scallions, trimmed, white and green parts thinly sliced crosswise

1 tablespoon finely chopped fresh dill

½ teaspoon finely grated lemon zest

1 tablespoon fresh lemon juice, plus extra as needed

1 tablespoon extra virgin olive oil

Coarse salt (sea or kosher) and freshly ground black pepper

Smoked Bread (page 56), prepared without the seasoning

½ recipe Smoked Black Cod (page 197), flaked (about 2 cups)

1. Not more than 4 hours before serving, place the cucumber, scallions, dill, lemon zest and juice, and olive oil in a bowl. Do not mix.

2. Just before serving, grill the bread as directed in the recipe. Arrange the slices on a large platter. Toss the cucumber relish to mix, adding salt, pepper, and additional lemon juice, if desired, to taste.

3. To serve, top each toast with fish. Spoon the relish on top and dig in.

VEGETABLES, SIDE DISHES, AND MEATLESS SMOKING

The world of smoked foods is dominated by meat and seafood. Vegetables? Not so much. That's about to change when you smoke coleslaw and potato salad, hash browns and onions and creamed corn. No barbecue would be complete without baked beans, and yours will acquire an uncommon depth of flavor in the smoker. And while you're at it, breathe new life into that classic French bean dish, cassoulet. Vegans and vegetarians can get in on the action with my barbecued tofu and tofu "ham." Meatless smoking? It comes with the *Project Smoke* territory.

SMOKED SLAW

YIELD: Makes 1 quart, enough to serve 4 to 6

METHOD: Hot-smoking

PREP TIME: 15 minutes

SMOKING TIME: 10 to 15 minutes

FUEL: Hardwood of your choice—enough for 15 minutes of smoking (see chart on page 6)

GEAR: Two aluminum foil pans

SHOP: Lots of options for cabbage here, from commonplace green and red cabbage to crinkly Savoy cabbage or even napa cabbage. Organic or farmstand when possible.

WHAT ELSE: The quickest way to smoke the slaw is in a hot-smoker, but you can certainly use a cold-smoker. In that case, increase the smoking time to 45 minutes. For an even smokier slaw, use smoked mayonnaise.

Coleslaw (from the Dutch words for cabbage and salad) accompanies a lot of great American barbecue. This one makes you sit up and take notice, for you actually smoke the cabbage, carrots, celery—and optional apples—prior to mixing. The secret is to smoke the veggies long enough to flavor them, but not so long you cook them. Tip o' the hat to Martha's Vineyard chef and recipe tester Judy Klumick for the idea.

INGREDIENTS

1 small or ½ large green cabbage (about 1 pound), quartered and cored

1 small onion, peeled and quartered

2 carrots, trimmed and peeled

2 ribs celery, trimmed

1 apple, peeled, quartered, and cored

½ cup mayonnaise (preferably Hellmann's or Best Foods) or smoked mayonnaise (see page 204)

3 tablespoons cider vinegar, or to taste

3 tablespoons sugar

1 tablespoon prepared horseradish (don't drain)

½ teaspoon celery seeds, or to taste

Coarse salt (sea or kosher) and freshly ground black pepper

1. Set up your smoker following the manufacturer's instructions and preheat to 225°F. Add the wood as specified by the manufacturer.

2. Thinly shred the cabbage, onion, carrots, celery, and apple on a mandoline, in a food processor fitted with a slicing or shredding disk, or with a chef's knife. Spread out the vegetables and apple in a thin layer in 2 aluminum foil pans.

3. Place the vegetables in their foil pans in the smoker and smoke until lightly bronzed with smoke, but still raw, 10 to 15 minutes. Do not overcook. Let the vegetables cool to room temperature.

4. While the vegetables are cooling, make the dressing: Combine the mayonnaise, vinegar, sugar, horseradish, celery seeds, and salt and pepper to taste in a large bowl and whisk until the sugar is dissolved.

5. Stir the vegetables into the dressing. Correct the seasoning, adding salt or vinegar as desired; the slaw should be highly seasoned. Cover the slaw and refrigerate until serving. Try to serve within a couple of hours of mixing.

YOU CAN SMOKE *WHAT*?
28 FOODS YOU NEVER DREAMED YOU COULD SMOKE

By now, you've mastered barbecued ribs and brisket. I hope you've smoked salmon and bacon, and maybe even attempted a ham or a turkey. Ready to take your smoking skills to the next level? Here are 28 foods you may never have dreamed you could smoke—but you'll sure be glad you did.

BASIC SMOKING PROCEDURES

Most of the foods in this section are cold-smoked. Here's how to do it in a cold-smoker, a hot-smoker, and with a handheld smoker.

In a cold-smoker: Place the food in a shallow aluminum foil drip pan. (Spread or pour soft or liquid foods, like honey or ketchup, to a depth of ¼ inch.) If smoking perishable foods, like mayonnaise or cream, or smoking on a warm day, place the foil pan in a larger pan filled with ice and replenish the ice as it melts. Keep the smoker temperature at 80°F or less. Stir the food a few times so it smokes evenly. Smoke until well flavored by the smoke. (White foods like yogurt and mayonnaise will acquire a light golden brown film on the surface.) This can take as little as 1½ hours or as long as 6, depending on your smoker. The average is 3 to 4 hours.

Cold-smoking in a hot-smoker: Place the food in a shallow aluminum foil drip pan over a larger pan filled with ice, as above. Set the smoker temperature to 225°F or as low as it will go. Replenish the ice as it melts. Smoke the food until lightly bronzed with and well flavored by the smoke. This can take as little as 1 hour or as long as 3, depending on your smoker. The average is 1½ to 2 hours..

With a handheld smoker: Place the food in a large glass bowl and cover tightly with plastic wrap, leaving one edge open. Fill and light the smoker following the manufacturer's instructions. Insert

the tube of the smoker, fill the bowl with smoke, withdraw the tube, and tightly cover the bowl with the plastic wrap. Let infuse for 4 minutes. Stir the food to incorporate the smoke. Repeat 1 to 3 times or until the food is smoked to taste.

Alternate handheld smoker method: When smoking creamy or liquid condiments, like mayonnaise or ketchup, half empty the jar or bottle, cover with plastic wrap as above, fill the container with smoke, seal the plastic wrap, and let sit for 4 minutes. Screw on the lid and shake well. Repeat as necessary until the condiment has a pronounced smoke flavor.

YES, YOU CAN REALLY SMOKE THE FOLLOWING

Butter: Sometimes, an idea is so powerful it turns up simultaneously at opposite ends of the earth. Keenan Bosworth smokes house-churned butter at a gastropub called Pig & Pickle in Scottsdale, Arizona. Basque grill visionary Victor Arguinzoniz smokes goat's milk butter at his restaurant, Asador Etxebarri, in Spain's Basque country. Smoke using any of the described procedures.

Cream: Smoked heavy cream makes a great drizzle for soups or desserts, and you can whip it in a chilled metal bowl or with a nitrous oxide charger to make the world's most interesting whipped cream. (Note: If using a nitrous charger and a handheld smoker, you can pump the smoke right into the charger.) Smoke using any of the described procedures. Try it on the Smoked Chocolate Bread Pudding on page 231. Sour cream, half-and-half, and milk would be smoked the same way.

Ricotta cheese: Smoked ricotta drizzled with olive oil and spiked with pepper makes an astonishing spread for grilled bread. Use it to stuff ravioli,

(continued on next page)

(continued from previous page)

manicotti, or squash blossoms. Smoke using any of the described procedures. For the ultimate smoked ricotta, make it from scratch, wrap it in cheesecloth, and hang it from the ceiling of your smokehouse.

Salt: Excellent smoked salt is widely available these days, but when I started smoking, you had to smoke your own. For old times' sake, here's how I did it: Spread the salt (sea or kosher) in an aluminum foil drip pan in a layer ⅛ inch thick. Cold-smoke 10 to 12 hours, or hot-smoke 4 to 6 hours, stirring every half hour so the salt smokes evenly. (Vary the wood to vary the flavor.) You can smoke whole peppercorns the same way, but the smoke flavor is less pronounced.

Sugar, honey, maple syrup: I first smoked sugar for cocktails and fruit salads. It came out so awesome, I decided to smoke honey (to serve with biscuits and ham) and maple syrup for pancakes. Smoke using any of the described procedures on page 203. You can smoke cane syrup or agave syrup the same way.

To make smoked simple syrup, combine equal parts sugar and water (for example, 1 cup of each) in a saucepan. Boil until the sugar is dissolved. Let cool to room temperature, then smoke in an aluminum foil drip pan (or in a bowl covered with plastic wrap for a handheld smoker) as described on page 203. Store in a sealed jar.

Mayonnaise: Smoke imbues mayonnaise with umami flavors you never dreamed it could possess. Spread it on toast to make the ultimate BLT sandwich, or stir in capers, diced pickles, and chopped chives to make smoked tartar sauce. If cold-smoking or hot-smoking, keep the mayonnaise on ice at all times. Or use a handheld smoker, keeping the bowl with the mayonnaise over ice.

Mustard: You can smoke any mustard—I'm partial to Dijon. Great with pork and ham. Or mix with two parts regular or smoked mayonnaise to make

a sauce for grilled fish or seafood. Spread it in an aluminum foil drip pan to a depth of ¼ inch if cold- or hot-smoking, or use a handheld smoker.

Ketchup: The perfect condiment for the Hay-Smoked Hamburgers on page 136. Or mix 2 parts smoked ketchup with 1 part freshly grated or prepared horseradish (don't drain it) to make smoked cocktail sauce. Smoke using any of the described procedures on page 203.

Hot sauce: Puts smoke with the fire. Works particularly well with a thick hot sauce like sriracha. Smoke using any of the described procedures on page 203.

Olive oil: Amazing in salad dressings or drizzled over tomatoes or creamy cheese. Start with a fruity extra virgin oil. Smoke using any of the described procedures on page 203.

Tomato paste, tomato sauce, canned tomatoes: I originally smoked these to make smoked tomato sauce for pasta. Also great with smoked ricotta. Spread the tomato paste or pour tomato sauce in a ¼-inch layer in a small aluminum foil drip pan. Pour canned tomatoes with their juices into a large aluminum foil pan. Smoke using any of the described procedures on page 203.

Capers: Drain well, toss with a little olive oil, spread in a single layer in an aluminum foil pan, and smoke using any of the described procedures on page 203.

Olives: Smoke gives olives an otherworldly quality. Green olives hold the smoke better than black. Toss with a little olive oil, spread in a single layer in an aluminum foil pan or arrange directly on the smoker rack (if they're large enough to not fall through), and smoke using any of the described procedures on page 203.

Lemons: I often smoke lemons to serve with smoked or grilled fish. Cut in half crosswise, remove the seeds with a fork, and smoke the halves cut side up directly on the smoker rack. Smoke using any of the described procedures on page 203.

Garlic, shallots, onions: Smoke gives alliums a rich smokehouse flavor. To smoke garlic, peel the cloves, toss with a little olive oil, and spread in a single layer in an aluminum foil drip pan. (Alternatively, thread the garlic cloves on a bamboo skewer and smoke directly on the smoker rack.) Peel shallots, cut in half, and lightly brush with oil. Peel onions, cut into quarters, and lightly brush with oil. Both of these can go in a foil pan or be skewered and placed directly on the smoker rack. I prefer hot-smoking for these foods so they cook as well as smoke. Figure on 1 hour for garlic and 2 to 3 hours for shallots and onions at 225°F.

Sesame seeds: Sprinkle on salads, hummus, tacos, lamb shanks (page 128) and smoked ice cream (page 240) sundaes. Spread the seeds in a ⅛-inch-deep layer in an aluminum foil pan. Best hot-smoked, so you toast the seeds as well as smoke them. Figure on 30 to 45 minutes at 250°F.

Nuts: Infinitely superior to the "smoke-flavored" nuts you get on airplanes. Toss 2 cups of your favorite nuts with 1 tablespoon melted butter or olive oil. Stir in 1 tablespoon sugar; 1 teaspoon each sea salt, freshly ground black pepper, and smoked paprika; plus ½ teaspoon each ground cinnamon and cumin. Spread out in an aluminum foil pan and cold-smoke at 275°F until toasted and browned, 40 to 60 minutes, stirring several times.

Bologna, mortadella: "Oklahoma prime rib" is barbecue-speak for smoked bologna—traditionally served on a bun or white bread slices with barbecue sauce. Cut it crosswise into ½-inch slabs, lightly score the top in a crosshatch pattern (to improve smoke absorption), sprinkle with barbecue rub (optional), and arrange directly on the smoker rack. Smoke using any of the described procedures.

I also like to smoke mortadella, a large fine-textured Italian sausage speckled with cubes of pork fat. It comes from Bologna, Italy, and is an ancestor of American bologna. Smoke in ½-inch-thick slabs like bologna. Cut into cubes and serve on toothpicks.

Cinnamon sticks, vanilla beans: Sometimes used as an aromatic fuel for smoking—the Chinese, for example, burn cinnamon sticks for Tea-Smoked Duck (page 168). But you can also smoke cinnamon sticks and vanilla beans in a smoker, adding a smoky flavor to their sweet spiciness. Use smoked cinnamon sticks in Smoked Apples (page 239) or mulled cider. Use smoked vanilla beans in custards (like the Smoked Flan on page 233) and cocktails. Smoke using any of the described procedures on page 203.

Ice: Smoke ice and it will take your smoked cocktails (starting on page 244)—or any cocktail—over the top. Place regular ice cubes in an aluminum foil pan. Smoke using any of the described procedures on page 203. The ice will melt. It's supposed to. Pour the melted ice back into an ice cube tray and refreeze. *That's* how you smoke ice.

Water: Yes. You can even smoke water. Place it in an aluminum foil pan or bowl and smoke using any of the procedures described on page 203. Use it to make smoked lemonade or smoked iced tea.

SMOKED POTATO SALAD

YIELD: Serves 4 to 6

METHOD: Hot-smoking

PREP TIME: 30 minutes

SMOKING TIME: 1 to 1½ hours

FUEL: Bar Tartine uses alder, but any hardwood will work. You'll need enough for 1½ hours of smoking (see chart on page 6).

SHOP: You want boiling potatoes (less starchy than bakers). Good options include Red Bliss, Yukon Gold, or slender fingerling potatoes like French rattes or Russian banana potatoes.

WHAT ELSE: For even more smoke flavor, smoke the hard-cooked eggs as described on page 35.

N o barbecue is complete without potato salad. Bar Tartine in San Francisco takes potatoes to a new level by smoking them with alder wood. Fresh dill and ramps (wild leeks) give the dressing a vibrancy not found in your typical potato salad. Because fresh ramps are available only for a few weeks in the spring, I've substituted scallions, but use ramps if you can find them. (One seasonal online purveyor is earthydelights.com.) Here's my take on what may be the most soulful potato salad you've ever tasted.

INGREDIENTS

2 pounds boiling potatoes (preferably organic), scrubbed with a stiff brush

2 tablespoons extra virgin olive oil

Coarse salt (sea or kosher) and freshly ground black pepper

½ cup mayonnaise (preferably Hellmann's or Best Foods) or smoked mayonnaise (see page 204)

3 tablespoons Dijon mustard

1 tablespoon red wine vinegar, or more to taste

2 hard-cooked eggs, peeled and coarsely chopped

2 tablespoons chopped fresh dill

2 scallions, trimmed, white parts minced, green parts thinly sliced crosswise

8 pitted green olives or pimiento-stuffed olives, thinly sliced or coarsely chopped

8 cornichons (tiny tart French pickles) or 1 dill pickle, coarsely chopped (about 3 tablespoons)

1 tablespoon drained capers, or to taste

Spanish smoked paprika (pimentón), for sprinkling

1. Cut any larger potatoes in half or quarters; leave small ones whole. The idea is for all the pieces to be bite size, about 1 inch across. Arrange the potatoes in a single layer in an aluminum foil pan. Stir in the olive oil and season with salt and pepper.

2. Set up your smoker following the manufacturer's instructions

and preheat to 275°F. Add wood as specified by the manufacturer.

3. Place the potatoes in the smoker and smoke until tender (a bamboo skewer will pierce the spuds easily), 1 to 1½ hours, or as needed. Stir a couple of times so the potatoes brown evenly. Remove the potatoes and let cool slightly (they should be warm).

4. While the potatoes smoke, make the dressing: Combine the mayonnaise, mustard, and vinegar in a large bowl and whisk to mix. Whisk in the chopped eggs, dill, scallions, olives, pickles, and capers. Cover and refrigerate until the potatoes are ready.

5. Stir the warm potatoes into the dressing. Correct the seasoning, adding salt, pepper, and vinegar to taste; the salad should be highly seasoned. You can serve the potato salad warm or chilled (cover and refrigerate, or quick-chill the salad over a bowl of ice). Transfer to a serving bowl and dust with smoked paprika before serving.

DOUBLE-SMOKED POTATOES

B aked potatoes are good, stuffed potatoes are better, and nothing knocks it out of the park like hickory-smoked potatoes stuffed with smoky bacon, scallions, and smoked cheddar cheese—especially when you smoke the potatoes twice. You'll smoke the spuds at a higher temperature than you may be accustomed to; this gives you the crisp skin and airy interior characteristic of a great baked potato.

YIELD: Serves 4

METHOD: Smoke-roasting

PREP TIME: 15 minutes

SMOKING TIME: 1 hour, plus 15 to 20 minutes for re-smoking (see What Else, page 210)

FUEL: Hardwood of your choice—enough for about 1½ hours of smoking (see chart on page 6)

SHOP: Start with a proper baking potato like an organic russet or Idaho. True bakers are large and elongated with a rough brown skin.

INGREDIENTS

4 large baking potatoes (12 to 14 ounces each—preferably organic)

1½ tablespoons bacon fat or butter, melted, or extra virgin olive oil

Coarse salt (sea or kosher) and freshly ground black pepper

4 strips artisanal bacon (like Nueske's or the home-smoked bacon on page 113), cut crosswise into ¼-inch slivers

6 tablespoons (¾ stick) cold unsalted butter, thinly sliced

2 scallions, trimmed, white and green parts finely chopped (about 4 tablespoons)

2 cups coarsely grated smoked or regular white cheddar cheese (about 8 ounces)

½ cup sour cream

Spanish smoked paprika (pimentón) or sweet paprika, for sprinkling

1. Set up your smoker following the manufacturer's instructions and preheat to 400°F. Add enough wood for 1 hour of smoking as specified by the manufacturer.

2. Scrub the potatoes on all sides with a vegetable brush. Rinse well under cold running water and blot dry with paper towels. Prick each potato several times with a fork (this

WHAT ELSE: Smoked potatoes make a pretty awesome side dish. Even better if you serve them with smoked butter (see page 203) and smoked sour cream (page 203). So you could stop after Step 3. But that's not why you bought this book. No, you want the full Monty—a glorious, bubbling smoked potato packed with flavor and richness. Note: Some smokers won't get hotter than 275°F. In this case, increase the smoking time to 2 to 3 hours and the re-smoking time to 40 to 60 minutes.

keeps the spud from exploding and facilitates the smoke absorption). Brush or rub the potato on all sides with the bacon fat and season generously with salt and pepper.

3. Place the potatoes on the smoker rack. Smoke until the skins are crisp and the potatoes are tender in the center (they'll be easy to pierce with a slender metal skewer), about 1 hour.

4. Meanwhile, place the bacon in a cold skillet and fry over medium heat until browned and crisp, 3 to 4 minutes. Drain off the bacon fat (save the fat for future potatoes).

5. Transfer the potatoes to a cutting board and let cool slightly. Cut each potato in half lengthwise. Using a spoon, scrape out most of the potato flesh, leaving a ¼-inch-thick shell. (It's easier to scoop the potatoes when warm.) Cut the potato flesh into ½-inch dice and place in a bowl.

6. Add the bacon, 4 tablespoons of the butter, the scallions, and cheese to the potato flesh and gently stir to mix. Stir in the sour cream and salt and pepper to taste; the mixture should be highly seasoned. Stir as little and as gently as possible so as to leave some texture to the potatoes.

7. Spoon the potato mixture back into the potato shells, mounding it in the center. Top each potato half with a thin slice of the remaining butter and sprinkle with paprika. The potatoes can be prepared up to 24 hours ahead to this stage, covered, and refrigerated.

8. Just before serving, preheat your smoker to 400°F. Add enough wood for 30 minutes of smoking. Place the potatoes in a shallow aluminum foil pan and re-smoke them until browned and bubbling, 15 to 20 minutes. (Or you can heat them in a 400°F oven.)

POTATOES HIT THE SMOKER

It started with the smoked mashed potatoes at Wiley Dufresne's late iconoclastic restaurant, WD-50, on the Lower East Side in New York City. Then came the smoked potatoes with ramp (wild leek) aioli at Bar Tartine in San Francisco. Now there's hickory-smoked potato soup—tarted up with buttermilk and sherry vinegar—at the Mintwood Place in Washington, D.C.

Call it the latest outbreak of a smoke fever sweeping a nation hungry for barbecue beyond meat. Or call it the next big thing for one of the New World's great vegetable gifts to Planet Barbecue: potatoes hit the smoker.

What is it about spuds that makes them so irresistible for smoking?

- The mild flavor—think of the potato as a sort of sponge or blank canvas that readily absorbs any smoke, spice, or fire flavor you throw at it.

- The texture—or more precisely, the contrast of textures. For a smoke-roasted potato offers the perfect contrast of crustiness on the outside and a luscious, luxurious, soft and creamy center.

- The potato's natural affinity for the meats we love to smoke and grill: baked potatoes with steak; mashed potatoes with smoked meat loaf; potato

salad with pork shoulder and spareribs—all of them now smoked.

So how do you smoke a potato? Let me count the ways.

Smoke-roast a baking potato. Place on a kettle grill at a relatively high heat (400°F for 1 hour). Crisp skin, fluffy center.

Hot-smoke small new potatoes. Cut them in half and toss with olive oil, salt, and pepper. Hot-smoke in an aluminum foil drip pan, stirring from time to time, until easily pierced with a skewer, 1 to 1½ hours.

Ember-roast sweet potatoes. Lay sweet potatoes directly on a bed of wood or charcoal embers (they work better than white potatoes). As the skins char, they drive a powerful smoke flavor to the center.

Smoke with a handheld smoker. Cover the pan in which you made mashed potatoes with plastic wrap, leaving one edge open. Insert the rubber tube of a handheld smoker. Fill the pan with smoke and let stand for 4 minutes. Stir well and repeat once or twice, or until you've achieved the desired degree of smokiness.

SMOKED ROOT VEGETABLE HASH BROWNS

YIELD: Serves 2 or 3; can be multiplied as desired

METHOD: Smoke-roasting

PREP TIME: 15 minutes

SMOKING TIME: 40 to 60 minutes

FUEL: Hardwood chunks or soaked, drained chips of your choice—enough for 1 hour of smoking (see chart on page 6)

GEAR: A 10-inch cast-iron skillet or a large aluminum foil drip pan

SHOP: Sure, you could use straight potatoes and onions, but I like to boost the flavor with other root vegetables like carrots and sweet potatoes—preferably organic.

WHAT ELSE: This recipe calls for a technique I call smoke-roasting (see page 19), a higher-temperature smoking that delivers crisp, smoky vegetables, not to mention crisp-skinned poultry.

H ash browns on the smoker? This twist on an American breakfast classic not only endows the spuds with smoke flavor, but it also eliminates the mess of frying potatoes and onions on your stovetop—and, for that matter, continuous stirring to keep them from burning. For super-easy smoked hash browns, use the indirect grilling method outlined below. For crustier hash browns, set up your grill for direct grilling, again adding the wood chips to the coals; you'll need to stir more often to keep them from burning. Note: You'll need a grill or smoker that can cook at a high temperature (350° to 400°F), such as a kettle charcoal grill or pellet grill.

INGREDIENTS

2 pounds root vegetables (I like to use a combination of Yukon Gold potatoes, sweet potatoes, and carrots)

1 medium-size onion, peeled

2 tablespoons extra virgin olive oil, plus extra as needed

Coarse salt (sea or kosher) and freshly ground black pepper

2 teaspoons Spanish smoked paprika (pimentón; optional)

1 tablespoon butter

1. Rinse the root vegetables, scrubbing them with a stiff brush, and blot dry with paper towels. I leave the peel intact; you may need to trim away any blemishes. Cut the vegetables, including the onion, into ½-inch dice.

2. Place all the vegetables in a 10-inch cast-iron skillet or large aluminum foil pan, spreading them out in a single layer. Drizzle with olive oil and stir to mix. Season generously with salt and pepper and the paprika, if using, and stir again to mix. Add the butter.

3. Set up your grill for indirect grilling and heat to medium-high (400°F). Place the pan with the vegetables on the grill grate away from the heat. Toss the wood chunks or chips on the coals.

4. Cover the grill and smoke-roast the hash browns, stirring occasionally with tongs so they cook evenly, until browned and crisp, 40 to 60 minutes. If they start to dry out, add a little more oil. Serve directly from the skillet or pan.

CREAMED SMOKED CORN

Grilling corn caramelizes its natural sugars. And smoking gives this sweet vegetable a flavor that is at once familiar and exotic. The dark beer provides a pleasantly bitter counterpoint to the sweetness.

INGREDIENTS

FOR THE SMOKED VEGETABLES

4 ears fresh sweet corn, husks and silk removed, or 3 cups frozen corn kernels, thawed

1 small onion, peeled and quartered

2 tablespoons (¼ stick) butter, melted

Coarse salt (sea or kosher) and freshly ground black pepper

1 poblano pepper, stemmed, cut in half lengthwise, and seeded

FOR THE CREAMED CORN

1 tablespoon butter

1 tablespoon unbleached all-purpose flour

2 teaspoons Spanish smoked paprika (pimentón) or sweet paprika

½ cup dark beer

1 to 1½ cups half-and-half

1 tablespoon light or dark brown sugar

1½ cups coarsely grated cheddar cheese

YIELD: Serves 4 to 6

METHOD: Hot-smoking

PREP TIME: 30 minutes

SMOKING TIME: 30 to 40 minutes

FUEL: Hardwood of your choice—enough for 40 minutes of smoking (see chart on page 6)

WHAT ELSE: If using frozen corn kernels, spread them out in a large aluminum foil pan. You can smoke the corn, onion, and poblano pepper at an earlier smoke session. For even more flavor, spoon the creamed corn into a cast-iron skillet and warm it in your smoker before serving.

1. Set up your smoker following the manufacturer's instructions and preheat to 225° to 250°F. Add the wood as specified by the manufacturer.

2. Smoke the vegetables: Lightly brush the corn and onion with the butter and season with salt and pepper. Place the corn, onion, and poblano pepper on the smoker rack and smoke until lightly bronzed with smoke, 30 to 40 minutes. (If using frozen corn, see What Else.) Transfer to a cutting board and let cool. Cut the kernels off the cobs. Cut the onion and poblano into ¼-inch dice.

3. Finish the creamed corn: Melt the butter in a large saucepan over medium heat. Stir in the vegetables and cook until sizzling, 3 minutes. Stir in the flour and paprika and cook for 1 minute. Stir in the beer, increase the heat to medium-high, and boil for 1 minute (to cook off the alcohol). Stir in 1 cup half-and-half and the brown sugar and boil until thickened, 1 minute.

4. Reduce the heat and gently simmer the corn until thick and richly flavored, 5 to 8 minutes, stirring often. Stir in the cheese and cook just long enough to melt it. If the mixture seems too thick, add more half-and-half. Add salt, pepper, and additional sugar, if desired, and serve.

BARBECUED ONIONS

YIELD: Makes 4 onions

METHOD: Hot-smoking

PREP TIME: 20 minutes

SMOKING TIME: 2½ to 3 hours

GEAR: 4 grill rings (optional)

FUEL: Hardwood of your choice—enough for 3 hours of smoking (see chart on page 6)

SHOP: For the best results, use a sweet onion like Vidalia, Walla Walla, or Texas Sweet.

WHAT ELSE: To keep the onions upright during smoking, use grill rings or twisted, crumpled rings of aluminum foil.

If sweet onions stuffed with bacon, jalapeños, barbecue sauce, and cheese sounds like paradise, here's your hymnal. The preparation is infinitely customizable: You can substitute chorizo or other sausage for the bacon; diced pickles for the jalapeños; and use any of the barbecue sauces in this book. Or beyond. Honey instead of barbecue sauce? A different cheese on top? Share your favorite combination with us on barbecuebible.com.

INGREDIENTS

4 large (12- to 14-ounces each) sweet onions, peeled

3 tablespoons unsalted butter

4 strips artisanal bacon (like Nueske's or the Made-from-Scratch Bacon on page 113), cut crosswise into ¼-inch slivers

4 jalapeño peppers, seeded and diced (for spicier onions, leave the seeds in)

½ cup barbecue sauce (use your favorite)

½ cup grated cheddar or pepper Jack cheese (optional)

1. Using a sharp paring knife and starting at the top (opposite the root), cut an inverted cone-shaped cavity about 2 inches across the top and 2 inches deep in each onion. (The core should come out in a cone-shaped plug.) Chop the pieces you remove.

2. Melt 1 tablespoon of the butter in a medium-size skillet. Add the chopped onion, bacon, and jalapeños and cook over medium heat, stirring occasionally, until lightly browned, 4 minutes. Place a spoonful of the filling in the cavity of each onion. Divide the remaining 2 tablespoons of butter into 4 pats and place one on top of each onion. (The onions can be prepared several hours ahead to this stage. Place them on a plate, cover with plastic wrap, and refrigerate.)

3. Set up your smoker following the manufacturer's instructions and preheat to 225° to 250°F. Add the wood as specified by the manufacturer.

4. Place the onions on grill rings or in a shallow aluminum foil pan. Smoke until gently yielding when squeezed on the sides, about 2 hours.

5. Place 2 tablespoons of the barbecue sauce on each onion and top with 2 tablespoons of the cheese, if using. Continue smoking the onions for another 30 to 60 minutes. To test for doneness, squeeze the sides of the onion—they should be soft and easy to pierce with a metal skewer. Transfer the onions to a platter or plates for serving.

SMOKED MUSHROOM BREAD PUDDING

Here's my version of Thanksgiving stuffing; it meets all the holiday requirements while adding a flavor distinctly its own. You guessed it: the taste of wood smoke. Brioche and cream make it unabashedly rich, while pan-fried exotic mushrooms and sage add earthy autumnal flavors. (For even more seasonal flavor, add roasted chestnuts.) And you *don't* cook it inside the turkey, because cooking a stuffing inside the bird is something I've always found deleterious to both the bird and the stuffing.

INGREDIENTS

1 loaf (1 pound) day-old brioche, cut into 1-inch cubes (8 to 10 cups)

12 ounces mixed exotic mushrooms (see Shop)

6 tablespoons (¾ stick) unsalted butter

1 bunch scallions, trimmed, white and light green parts thinly sliced

1 rib celery, trimmed and chopped (optional)

8 fresh sage leaves, thinly slivered

1 cup coarsely chopped pecans or peeled roasted chestnuts

¼ cup Cognac or bourbon (optional)

5 large eggs (preferably organic)

3 cups heavy (whipping) cream

¼ teaspoon freshly grated nutmeg, or to taste

½ teaspoon coarse salt (sea or kosher), or to taste

½ teaspoon freshly ground black pepper, or to taste

YIELD: Serves 8

METHOD: Smoke-roasting

PREP TIME: 30 minutes

SMOKING TIME: 1 hour

FUEL: I like pecan, but any hardwood chunks or soaked drained chips will work. You'll need enough for 1 hour of smoking (see chart on page 6).

GEAR: A large aluminum foil pan, such as a turkey roasting pan; 12-inch cast-iron skillet

SHOP: Brioche is a French butter and egg-enriched bread. You'll want a firm, not soft-squishy loaf. (Stale brioche works great here.) Challah makes a good substitute. There are lots of options for mushrooms: morels, chanterelles, boletus, shiitakes, black trumpets, hen-of-the-woods—not to mention the more commonplace button mushrooms, cremini, and portobellos. Most are available at Whole Foods and many other supermarkets.

1. Set up your grill for indirect grilling and preheat to medium (350°F).

2. Arrange the brioche chunks in a single layer in a large aluminum foil pan. Place the pan on the grill grate away from the heat and cover the grill. For even more smoke flavor, add wood chunks or handfuls of wood chips to the coals. Indirect-grill the brioche, stirring occasionally so the cubes brown evenly, until toasted and golden brown, about 15 minutes. Set the pan of brioche aside to cool.

3. Meanwhile, trim the ends off the mushroom stems; remove and discard the stems if using shiitakes. Wipe the mushrooms clean with a damp paper towel. Cut large mushrooms into ¼-inch slices; leave small ones whole.

4. Melt 3 tablespoons of the butter in a 12-inch cast-iron skillet on the stove or grill side burner over medium-high heat. Add the scallions, celery, if using, and sage and cook, stirring often, until golden brown, 4 minutes. Add the mushrooms and pecans. Increase the

WHAT ELSE: You could cook the pudding in your smoker (add 1 to 2 hours to the cooking time), but I like the crisp crust you get at a higher temperature that comes with smoke-roasting on a kettle grill. Besides, your smoker is probably already occupied with your turkey (page 159).

heat to high and cook, stirring often, until the mushrooms brown and all their liquid evaporates, 5 minutes. Add the Cognac, if using, and boil until only 2 tablespoons of liquid remain, 2 minutes. Remove from the heat and let cool slightly.

5. Crack the eggs into a large bowl and whisk until smooth. Whisk in the cream. Stir in the mushroom mixture, then the brioche cubes. Grate in the nutmeg and stir in salt and pepper; the mixture should be highly seasoned. Spoon it back into the skillet and top with the remaining 3 tablespoons butter, cut into thin slices. (The pudding can be prepared several hours ahead to this stage; cover with plastic wrap or aluminum foil and refrigerate, if you have room. But the texture will be better if you cook it right away.)

6. If you shut down the grill after toasting the brioche, fire it up again for indirect grilling and preheat to 350°F. Add the wood chunks or chips to the coals following the manufacturer's instructions. Cover the grill and smoke-roast the pudding until puffed and browned on top and cooked through (a skewer inserted into the center should come out clean), about 45 minutes.

7. Serve it right from the skillet. Even more reason to give thanks for Thanksgiving.

SMOKEHOUSE BEANS

YIELD: Serves 6 to 8

METHOD: Hot-smoking

PREP TIME: 20 minutes

SMOKING TIME: 2 to 2½ hours

FUEL: Hardwood of your choice—enough for 2½ hours of smoking (see chart on page 6)

Frijoles charros. Fèves au lard. Bean hole beans. (Charros are Texas pinto beans. Fèves au lard are French-Canadian baked beans. Bean hole beans are cooked in a fire-heated subterranean pit in Maine and New Hampshire.) Every barbecue culture has a version of baked beans. Sure, you can give beans a mild smoke taste by adding the usual bacon or barbecue sauce, but nothing builds flavor and character like cooking the beans in your smoker.

INGREDIENTS

6 slices (6 ounces) artisanal bacon (like Nueske's or the Made-from-Scratch Bacon on page 113), cut crosswise into ¼-inch slivers

1 medium-size onion, peeled and finely chopped (about 1½ cups)

1 poblano pepper, stemmed, seeded, and diced

3 cans (15 ounces each) cooked beans, drained, rinsed, and drained again

¼ cup packed dark brown sugar, plus extra as needed

¼ cup molasses, or to taste

¼ cup barbecue sauce (use your favorite)

¼ cup ketchup

2 tablespoons Worcestershire sauce

1 tablespoon Dijon mustard

2 tablespoons cider vinegar, plus extra as needed

½ teaspoon liquid smoke (optional; no need to add it if you smoke the beans)

Coarse salt (sea or kosher) and freshly ground black pepper

SHOP: For convenience, I call for canned beans—ideally organic and low sodium. I like to use a mix of white (Great Northern), red (kidney), and black beans.

WHAT ELSE: For even more flavor, enhance the beans with burnt ends (see Sidebar, page 68) or a few boned chopped spareribs.

1. Cook the bacon in a heavy pot or Dutch oven over medium heat to render the fat, about 5 minutes. Spoon out and discard all but 2 tablespoons of the fat.

2. Add the onion and poblano to the bacon and cook, stirring often, until lightly browned, 5 minutes. Stir in the beans, sugar, molasses, barbecue sauce, ketchup, Worcestershire, mustard, vinegar, and liquid smoke, if using. Add salt and pepper to taste.

3. Set up your smoker following the manufacturer's instructions and preheat to 225° to 250°F. Add the wood as specified by the manufacturer.

4. Smoke the beans, uncovered, until thick and richly flavored, 2 to 2½ hours, or as needed, stirring from time to time so the mixture cooks evenly. If the beans start to dry out, stir in 1 cup of water, and cover the pot. Adjust the seasoning before serving, adding salt, sugar, and vinegar to taste.

SMOKED VEGETABLE CASSOULET

YIELD: Serves 4 to 6 as a main dish, 8 to 10 as a side

METHOD: Hot-smoking

PREP TIME: 1 hour

SMOKING TIME: 1 hour

FUEL: Paley uses Oregon's quasi-official smoking fuel, hazelnut shells. He also likes bay wood (from the tree that gives us bay leaves). If you can't get those, use hazelnut wood, apple, or oak. You'll need enough for 1 hour of smoking (see chart on page 6).

GEAR: A 12-inch cast-iron skillet (optional)

SHOP: Organic, homegrown, or farmers' market vegetables when possible

WHAT ELSE: This recipe may look complicated, but it's really just a series of simple steps. Paley cooks dried beans from scratch—you'll find instructions on how to do this following this recipe. (Start your beans at least one day before you make the cassoulet.) If you want to make the cassoulet in one afternoon, use good organic low-sodium canned beans—you'll need three 15-ounce cans.

I f the French did barbecue, cassoulet would be their baked beans. Picture a bean stew lavished with pork, sausage, goose or duck confit, and loads of garlic. (The fatty meats gave you energy in the winter.) The French would surely denounce the idea of a vegetarian cassoulet as heresy. Just don't tell Vitaly Paley. The French-trained owner of Paley's Place—a founding father of the Portland, Oregon, restaurant revolution—roasts duck and pork with the best of them, but his version of France's rib-sticking bean stew contains not a gram of meat. Not that you'll miss it, because smoking the cassoulet gives you the rich meaty flavors you associate with the French original. Serve with a gutsy red wine like a Côtes du Rhône.

INGREDIENTS

FOR THE VEGETABLES

6 to 8 tablespoons extra virgin olive oil

1 pound carrots, trimmed, scrubbed, and cut crosswise into 2-inch pieces

8 cloves garlic, peeled

Coarse salt (sea or kosher) and freshly ground black pepper

1 cauliflower, cut into 1-inch florets (discard the core)

1 pound broccolini or baby bok choy, trimmed and cut crosswise into 2-inch pieces

2 red or yellow bell peppers, or a combination, stemmed, seeded, and cut into 1-inch pieces

FOR THE BEANS

1 medium-size onion, peeled and finely chopped

1 medium-size leek, trimmed, rinsed thoroughly, white part finely chopped (save the leek greens if you cook dried beans from scratch)

1 rib celery, finely chopped

2 cloves garlic, peeled and minced

½ cup dry white wine

3 cans (15 ounces each) organic low-sodium white beans (preferably cannellini), drained, rinsed, and drained again, or drained Cooked Beans from Scratch (page 223)

2 to 3 cups vegetable stock, plus extra as needed

1 can (8 ounces) tomato sauce

2 sprigs fresh thyme, or 1 teaspoon dried

2 bay leaves

½ teaspoon hot red pepper flakes, or to taste

FOR THE CRUMB TOPPING

2 tablespoons (¼ stick) butter or extra virgin olive oil

2 cloves garlic, peeled and minced

¼ cup chopped fresh flat-leaf parsley

1 cup dried bread crumbs (preferably homemade)

1. Brown the vegetables: Heat 2 tablespoons of the olive oil in a Dutch oven, large pot, or 12-inch cast-iron skillet over medium-high heat. Add the carrots and 2 of the garlic cloves, and season with salt and pepper. Cook until lightly browned, 6 to 8 minutes. With a slotted spoon, transfer the carrots and garlic to a large bowl. Brown the cauliflower, broccolini, and peppers separately the same way, adding 2 garlic cloves, salt and pepper, and olive oil as needed to each batch. As each vegetable is done, transfer it to the bowl with the carrots. You should have about 3 tablespoons oil left in the pot; if there's less, add another tablespoon or two.

2. Start the beans: Heat the olive oil in the pan over medium heat. Add the onion, leek, celery, and garlic and cook, stirring with a wooden spoon, until golden brown, 6 to 8 minutes. Stir in the wine and boil until only 3 tablespoons remain, about 2 minutes. Stir in the beans, 2 cups stock, the tomato sauce, thyme, bay leaves, and hot red pepper flakes and bring to a boil. If the mixture looks dry (it should be moist but not soupy), add more stock.

3. Stir in the vegetables and bring back to a boil. Add salt and pepper to taste; the mixture should be highly seasoned. The cassoulet can be prepared up to a day ahead to this stage, covered, and refrigerated.

4. Make the crumb topping: Melt the butter in a large skillet over medium-high heat. Add the garlic and parsley and fry until fragrant but not brown, 2 minutes. Stir in the bread crumbs and cook until lightly browned, 2 minutes. Remove from the heat.

5. Set up your smoker following the manufacturer's instructions and preheat to 275°F. Add the wood as specified by the manufacturer.

6. Sprinkle the crumb topping over the cassoulet. Smoke the cassoulet until the crumb topping is browned, the cauliflower and other vegetables are tender, and the bean mixture is bubbling, 1 hour. Serve directly in the Dutch oven, spooning out crust and filling, dodging and discarding the bay leaves and thyme sprigs.

NOTE: I've made this recipe vegetarian, but a few strips of smoky bacon (dice and sauté with the carrots and garlic) will make a great cassoulet extraordinary.

COOKED BEANS FROM SCRATCH

YIELD: Makes about 5 cups

For the purist. Use a small white bean like cannellini or navy beans. The French would use Tarbais beans, which you can buy online from Purcell Mountain Farms (purcellmountainfarms.com).

2 cups dried cannellini beans

2 tablespoons extra virgin olive oil

1 small onion, peeled and quartered

1 carrot, trimmed, scrubbed, and cut into 2-inch chunks

3 cloves garlic, peeled

2 bay leaves

2 sprigs fresh thyme

3 inches of leek greens (from the Smoked Vegetable Cassoulet, page 220), rinsed thoroughly

2 quarts vegetable stock or water, plus extra as needed

1. The day before cooking, rinse the beans in a colander, sorting out any pebbles, and place in a large bowl with water to cover by 4 inches. Soak overnight in the refrigerator. Drain well.

2. Place the beans in a Dutch oven or large pot. Stir in the onion, carrot, and garlic. Wrap the bay leaves and thyme in the leek greens and tie into a bundle with butcher's string. Add this to the beans and stir in the stock. Gradually bring the beans to a boil over high heat. Reduce the heat and gently simmer the beans, covered, until tender, 1 to 1½ hours. Drain the beans. Remove and discard the leek-herb bundle.

SMOKED TOFU TWO WAYS

YIELD: Makes 1 pound, enough to serve 2 or 3

METHOD: Hot-smoking

PREP TIME: 20 minutes

BRINING TIME: 3 hours

SMOKING TIME: 1 to 1½ hours

FUEL: Hardwood of your choice—enough for 1½ hours of smoking (see chart on page 6)

GEAR: A large heavy-duty resealable plastic bag; a wire rack (optional)

SHOP: Extra firm tofu holds up best during curing and smoking.

WHAT ELSE: To make a grilled tofu "steak," chill the smoked tofu and slice it horizontally through the thickness to make two broad rectangles. Brush each with olive oil or melted butter and grill.

Vegetarians and vegans, Asian food fanatics, and the health-conscious need no special inducement to eat tofu. Here's a reason for the rest of us: Tofu absorbs spice and smoke flavors as readily as pork shoulder or brisket do. If you don't believe me, try the following smoked tofu dishes—one cured like ham and one smoked with barbecue rub. Their smoky depth of flavor may just make you a convert.

TOFU CURED LIKE HAM

The Mustard Seed Caviar on page 106 makes a killer accompaniment.

INGREDIENTS

1 pound fresh extra firm tofu	2 bay leaves
1 cup hot water	3 allspice berries
3 tablespoons honey	1 teaspoon black peppercorns
2 tablespoons coarse salt (sea or kosher)	1 cinnamon stick (about 2 inches long)
2 strips lemon or orange zest (½ inch by 1½ inches)	1 cup ice water
	Vegetable oil, for oiling the smoker rack

1. Rinse the tofu under cold running water and drain.

2. Combine the hot water, honey, salt, lemon zest, bay leaves, allspice berries, peppercorns, and cinnamon stick in a bowl and whisk until the honey and salt dissolve. Whisk in the ice water.

3. Place the tofu in a large resealable plastic bag in a baking dish. Add the brine and seal tightly. Brine the tofu for 3 hours in the refrigerator, turning the bag a couple of times so it marinates evenly.

4. Set up your smoker following the manufacturer's instructions and preheat to 275°F. Oil the smoker rack. Add the wood as specified by the manufacturer.

5. Drain the tofu in a colander, discarding the brine and flavorings. Rinse and blot dry with paper towels. Place the tofu in the smoker, directly on the rack, and cook until bronzed with smoke, 1 to 1½ hours.

6. You can eat the tofu hot, or transfer it to a wire rack placed over a rimmed baking sheet and let cool to room temperature, then refrigerate it until slicing and serving (see Note).

NOTE: Smoked tofu is soft-textured. To give it a satisfying crust, brown the tofu on both sides in melted butter or extra virgin olive oil in a hot pan. Sear until crusty on both sides, 2 to 3 minutes per side.

BARBECUED TOFU

No, it's not ribs or brisket, but a paprika-brown sugar rub and barbecue sauce take this smoked tofu solidly into smokehouse territory.

INGREDIENTS

Vegetable oil, for oiling the rack

1 pound fresh extra firm tofu

2 tablespoons butter, melted

About 2 tablespoons of your favorite barbecue rub

¼ cup of your favorite barbecue sauce (optional)

1. Set up your smoker following the manufacturer's instructions and preheat to 275°F. Oil the smoker rack with vegetable oil. Add the wood as specified by the manufacturer.

2. Cut the tofu into ¾-inch-thick slices and arrange on a wire rack. Brush each slice on both sides with melted butter and season generously on both sides with barbecue rub.

3. Place the tofu on its rack in the smoker. Tofu tends to be fragile, so the less you move it, the better. Smoke until bronzed, 1 to 1½ hours. Serve with the barbecue sauce on the side, if using. (See Note, above.)

TWO MORE WAYS WITH TOFU

BARBECUED TOFU ON THE GRILL

For even more flavor, set up your grill for direct grilling and preheat to high. Brush and oil the grill grate really well. (Tofu has a tendency to stick.) Brush the tofu pieces on both sides with barbecue sauce. Arrange on the grill. Direct grill the tofu until the sauce is sizzling and browned, 2 minutes per side. Serve with extra barbecue sauce on the side.

STOVETOP SMOKED TOFU

Tofu smokes really well in a stovetop smoker or wok. Set either up following the instructions on pages 275 and 276. You'll need about 20 minutes of smoking time.

DESSERTS

This chapter brings us to the last frontier in smoking: dessert. For even if salmon, brisket, and turkey fit your barbecue comfort zone, desserts may not. Just don't tell Michael Scelfo of Alden & Harlow restaurant in Cambridge, Massachusetts, who smokes chocolate bread pudding with hickory. Or Spanish grill visionary Victor Arguinzoniz, who smokes ice cream to go with—what else?—smoked apple crisp at his Michelin-starred restaurant, Asador Etxebarri. Smoke has been called the umami of barbecue, and in this chapter, you'll learn how it works miracles on cheesecake, flan, and two not-so-classic apple desserts.

SMOKED BACON-BOURBON APPLE CRISP

YIELD: Serves 8

METHOD: Smoke-roasting

PREP TIME: 30 minutes

SMOKING TIME: 45 minutes to 1 hour

FUEL: Apple wood, of course—enough for 1 hour of smoking (see chart on page 6)

GEAR: A 10-inch cast-iron skillet

WHAT ELSE: You can cook this crisp low and slow in a traditional smoker, but you'll get a crisper topping if you work at higher heat. This is a good dish to smoke-roast on a charcoal grill.

For years, I've been smoke-roasting blueberry and raspberry crumbles. I even smoked a crumble made with cactus pears on my *Primal Grill* TV show taped in the Sonoran Desert in Arizona. Here's the smoked version of an American classic—apple pie—and it was inspired by a restaurant in my summer stomping grounds, the Outermost Inn on Martha's Vineyard. "I think apple pie should step on the dark side," says its one-time chef and the recipe's creator, Michael Winkelman. "Give me bacon. Give me whiskey. Give me smoke. Give me a dessert that means business." I give you Winkelman's smoked apple crisp.

INGREDIENTS

FOR THE FILLING

2 strips artisanal bacon, like Nueske's or the Made-from-Scratch Bacon on page 113, cut crosswise into ¼-inch slivers

3 pounds crisp, sweet apples like Honeycrisps or Galas

⅓ cup packed light or dark brown sugar, or to taste

1½ tablespoons all-purpose flour

1 teaspoon finely grated lemon zest

1 teaspoon ground cinnamon

Pinch of salt

3 tablespoons bourbon

FOR THE TOPPING

8 tablespoons (1 stick) unsalted butter, cut into ½-inch pieces and placed in the freezer until icy cold

½ cup crushed gingersnap cookies or granola

½ cup all-purpose flour

½ cup granulated sugar

½ cup light or dark brown sugar

Pinch of salt

Smoked Ice Cream (page 240; use vanilla) or regular vanilla ice cream, for serving (optional)

1. Set up your grill for indirect grilling (see page 262) and preheat to 400°F.

2. Make the filling: Fry the bacon in a 10-inch cast-iron skillet over medium heat, stirring with a slotted spoon, until crisp and golden brown, 4 minutes. Transfer the bacon to a large bowl. Pour off and reserve the bacon fat for another use. Don't wipe out or wash the skillet.

3. Peel and core the apples and cut them into 1-inch pieces. Add them to the bacon. Stir in the sugar, flour, lemon zest, cinnamon, and salt. Stir

in the bourbon. Taste the mixture for sweetness, adding sugar as needed. Spoon the filling into the skillet.

4. Make the topping: Place the butter, cookie crumbs, flour, white and brown sugars, and salt in a food processor. Grind to a coarse mixture, running the processor in short bursts. Don't overprocess; the mixture should remain loose and crumbly like sand. Sprinkle the topping over the apples.

5. Place the crisp on the grill or smoker rack away from the heat. Add the wood to the coals and cover the grill. Smoke-roast the crisp until the topping is browned and bubbling, the apples are soft (they should be easy to pierce with a skewer), and the filling is thick, 45 minutes to 1 hour.

6. Serve the crisp hot off the grill or smoker. Extra points for topping it with Smoked Ice Cream.

SMOKED CHOCOLATE BREAD PUDDING

You may be surprised to not find chocolate on the long list of foods I've put in my smoker. The reason? Smoke gets lost in chocolate's already intense, bitter, earthy flavor. Here's the exception: a smoked chocolate bread pudding from the highly inventive Alden & Harlow restaurant in Cambridge, Massachusetts. Owner-chef Michael Scelfo makes strategic use of hickory smoke to raise a great bread pudding to the stratosphere. Moral of the story? Use smoke in desserts when it makes the whole greater than the sum of its parts.

YIELD: Serves 8

METHOD: Hot-smoking

PREP TIME: 30 minutes

SMOKING TIME: 30 to 45 minutes plus 40 minutes to 1½ hours, as needed

FUEL: Hickory—enough for 2¼ hours of smoking (see chart on page 6)

GEAR: A large disposable aluminum foil pan; 12-inch cast-iron skillet

SHOP: Brioche is a French butter- and egg-enriched bread. You'll want a firm, not soft-squishy, loaf. (Stale brioche works great here.) You'll also get good results with firm country-style white bread or challah. Use an intense bittersweet chocolate like Scharffen Berger.

INGREDIENTS

1 loaf (1 pound) brioche, cut into 1-inch cubes (about 8 cups)

3 cups heavy (whipping) cream

2 cups whole milk

1½ cups sugar

Pinch of salt

1 vanilla bean (optional—for an even smokier flavor, use a smoked vanilla bean, page 205)

8 ounces bittersweet chocolate, coarsely chopped

4 large eggs

2 large egg yolks

1 teaspoon pure vanilla extract (1½ teaspoons if not using the vanilla bean)

Butter, for buttering the skillet

Smoked Ice Cream (page 240; use vanilla), for serving (optional)

WHAT ELSE: Note the double smoking technique—first you toast the brioche cubes in the smoker, then you smoke the assembled bread pudding to cook it.

1. Set up your smoker following the manufacturer's instructions and preheat to 225° to 250°F. Add the wood as specified by the manufacturer.

2. Arrange the brioche cubes in a single layer in an aluminum foil pan and place in the smoker. Smoke, stirring occasionally so the cubes smoke evenly, until firm and toasted, 30 to 45 minutes.

3. Meanwhile, make the custard: Place the cream, milk, sugar, and salt in a heavy saucepan. Cut the vanilla bean, if using, in half lengthwise, and scrape the tiny black seeds into the cream. Then, add the vanilla bean halves. Bring to a boil over medium heat, whisking until the sugar dissolves. Remove the pan from the heat. Remove the vanilla bean halves; you can rinse, dry, and reuse them. Whisk in half of the chocolate until melted. (Return the pan to low heat if the chocolate needs help melting.)

4. Place the eggs, egg yolks, and vanilla extract, if using, in a large heatproof bowl and whisk until smooth. Gradually whisk in the hot cream mixture. Add it little by little so as not to curdle the eggs. Add the smoked bread cubes and fold until the bread has absorbed most of the custard.

5. Butter the skillet and spoon in the pudding mixture. Sprinkle with the remaining chopped chocolate, pushing the pieces into the bread pudding with a fork.

6. Increase the heat of your smoker to 325°F. Some smokers won't go that high; if not, increase the heat to 275°F. Smoke the bread pudding until puffed and browned on top and the custard is set, 40 to 60 minutes at the higher temperature, 1 to 1½ hours at the lower temperature. (Insert a metal skewer into the center of the pudding—it should come out clean when the custard is set.)

7. Serve the bread pudding hot (à la mode with Smoked Ice Cream, if desired).

SMOKED FLAN

Remember flan, aka crème caramel—that custard comfort dessert claimed with equal partisanship by the French, Spanish, and Latin Americans? You start by caramelizing sugar to coat the mold, which imparts an agreeably bitter smokelike flavor. You cook it in a hot water-filled pan (aka *bain marie*), which keeps the custard moist and prevents it from curdling. Sounds like some French version of low, slow, and smoky—which set me wondering what would happen if you actually cooked flan in a smoker. The wood smoke would play off the caramel flavor, and you wouldn't need to bother with a water bath. It's awesome and easy. And it makes you wonder why no one thought of it earlier.

INGREDIENTS

FOR THE CARAMEL

1 cup sugar

¼ cup water

FOR THE FLAN

½ cup sugar

3 large eggs

2 large egg yolks

Pinch of salt

1¼ cups whole milk

1 cup half-and-half

1 regular or smoked vanilla bean
    (see page 205), split, or 1 teaspoon
    pure vanilla extract

1. Make the caramel: Place the sugar and water in a heavy saucepan. Cover the pan and cook over high heat for 2 minutes. Uncover the pan and reduce the heat to medium. Swirl the pan so the sugar browns evenly, but don't stir, and watch it carefully so it doesn't burn or become bitter. (If it does, you'll need to start over.) Cook until the syrup is dark golden brown and caramelized, 4 to 6 minutes. Remove the pan from the heat immediately. Take care not to get any molten sugar on your hands.

2. Carefully pour the caramel into the ramekins, rotating each to coat the bottom and sides with it. (Wear grill gloves if necessary to protect your hands and arms.) Breathe a sigh of relief; the hard part is over. Let the caramel cool until hard. Arrange the ramekins on a rimmed baking sheet.

3. Make the flan: Place the sugar, whole eggs, yolks, and salt in a large heatproof bowl, and whisk just to mix. Combine the milk, half-and-half, and vanilla bean, if using, in a heavy saucepan and heat over medium heat

YIELD: Serves 6

METHOD: Hot-smoking

PREP TIME: 20 minutes

SMOKING TIME: 1 to 1¼ hours

COOLING TIME: 4 hours or overnight

FUEL: I'm partial to cherry, but any fruit wood will work. You'll need enough for 1¼ hours of smoking (see chart on page 6).

GEAR: 6 ramekins (straight-sided heatproof ceramic bowls), each with a 6-ounce capacity; an instant-read thermometer

SHOP: You probably have all the ingredients you need in your kitchen already.

WHAT ELSE: You can also cook one big flan in an 8-inch-diameter metal cake pan; smoke it for a little longer than you would individual flans. For extra smoke flavor, use a smoked vanilla bean (see page 205). The only remotely challenging thing about this recipe is cleaning the smoke-coated ramekins when you're finished. Soak them in soapy water for a couple of hours, then use a scouring pad to remove the smoke.

until very hot but not boiling. Slowly whisk the hot milk mixture into the egg mixture, ½ cup at a time. Strain into a large heatproof glass measuring cup, discarding the vanilla bean. (Or you can rinse it off, dry it, and reuse it another time). If using vanilla extract, whisk it in now. Let the custard cool slightly, then pour it into the caramel-coated ramekins.

4. Set up your smoker following the manufacturer's instructions and preheat to 225° to 250°F. Add the wood as specified by the manufacturer.

5. Place the baking sheet with the ramekins in the smoker and smoke until the custard is set, 1 to 1¼ hours. To test for doneness, poke one of the ramekins. When the flan jiggles (not ripples), it's cooked. The internal temperature measured on an instant-read thermometer should be 180°F.

6. Transfer the flans to a wire rack to cool to room temperature, then refrigerate for at least 4 hours or as long as overnight before serving.

7. To unmold, run the tip of a paring knife around the inside edge of each flan. Place a plate firmly over the ramekin, invert, and shake until the flan slips loose. Spoon any caramel left in the ramekin around the flan.

SMOKED CHEESECAKE

By now you probably realize you can smoke just about anything. But should you? Only if smoking adds something to a food or dish that makes it better or more interesting than it would be in its natural state. Which brings us to cheesecake. This is another dessert that you usually bake in a pan of simmering water, which cooks the filling while preventing it from cracking or curdling. In other words, low, slow, and moist. Sounds like a session in a water smoker to me. The smoke gives the cheesecake a haunting flavor—familiar yet exotic. This may just be the most interesting cheesecake you'll ever set fork to.

YIELD: Serves 8 to 10

METHOD: Hot-smoking

PREP TIME: 45 minutes

SMOKING TIME: 1½ to 2 hours

COOLING TIME: 1 hour, or as needed

FUEL: You want a mild smoking wood for this cheesecake. I'd go for a fruit wood like apple, peach, or cherry—enough for 2 hours of smoking (see chart on page 6).

INGREDIENTS

FOR THE CRUST

Vegetable oil, for oiling the pan

12 ounces gingersnaps (about 36) or chocolate icebox cookies (about 36)

3 tablespoons light brown sugar

8 tablespoons (1 stick) unsalted butter, melted

FOR THE FILLING

4 packages (8 ounces each) cream cheese, at room temperature

1 cup firmly packed light brown sugar

2 teaspoons pure vanilla extract

2 teaspoons finely grated lemon zest

1 tablespoon fresh lemon juice

2 tablespoons (¼ stick) unsalted butter, melted

5 large eggs

Burnt Sugar Sauce (recipe follows; optional)

GEAR: A 10-inch springform pan; a wire rack

SHOP: At our house we use organic cream cheese and a Meyer lemon.

WHAT ELSE: There are several ways to go with flavorings, from the classic lemon-vanilla to butterscotch or orange. Whichever you use, go easy. What you really want to focus on is the smoke.

1. Set up your grill for indirect grilling and preheat to medium-high (400°F). Or preheat your oven to 400°F. Lightly oil the springform pan with vegetable oil and wrap a sheet of aluminum foil around the outside.

2. Make the crust: Break the cookies into pieces and grind with the brown sugar to a fine powder in a food processor. You'll want about 1¾ cups of crumbs. Add the melted butter and run the processor in short bursts to obtain a crumbly dough. Press the mixture evenly across the bottom and halfway up the sides of the springform pan. Indirect-grill or bake the crust until lightly browned, 5 to 8 minutes. Transfer the pan to a wire rack and let cool.

3. Make the filling: Wipe out the food processor bowl. Add the cream cheese, brown sugar, vanilla, lemon zest, lemon juice, and butter, and process until smooth. Work in the eggs one by one, processing until smooth after each addition. (You can also use a stand mixer, beating the cream cheese mixture until smooth and beating in the eggs one at a time.) Pour the filling into the crust. Gently tap the pan on the countertop a few times to knock out any air bubbles.

4. Set up your smoker following the manufacturer's instructions and preheat to 225° to 250°F. Add the wood as specified by the manufacturer.

5. Place the cheesecake in the smoker. Smoke until the top is bronzed with smoke and the filling is set, 1½ to 2 hours. To test for doneness, gently poke the side of the pan—the filling will jiggle, not ripple. Alternatively, insert a slender metal skewer in the center of the cake; it should come out clean.

6. Transfer the cheesecake in its pan to a wire rack to cool to room temperature. Refrigerate until serving; the cheesecake can be made up to 8 hours ahead. Run a slender knife around the inside of the springform pan. Unclasp and remove the ring. (You'll serve the cheesecake off the bottom of the pan.) Let the cheesecake warm slightly at room temperature before serving.

7. If serving with the sauce, pour some of it over the cheesecake and the rest into a pitcher. Cut into wedges and pass the remaining sauce.

Variation

For a tropical flavor, substitute 2 teaspoons finely grated fresh ginger for the vanilla extract, lime zest for the lemon zest, and lime juice for the lemon juice.

BURNT SUGAR SAUCE

YIELD: Makes 2 cups

What could be more appropriate for a smoked cheesecake than a sauce of burnt sugar (aka caramel)?

INGREDIENTS

1½ cups sugar

½ cup water

1 cup heavy (whipping) cream

1 teaspoon pure vanilla extract

1. Place the sugar and ½ cup water in a deep heavy saucepan. Cover the pan and cook over high heat for 3 minutes. Uncover the pan and reduce the heat to medium. Swirl the pan so the sugar browns evenly, but don't stir. Watch it carefully so it doesn't burn or become bitter. (If it does, you'll need to start over.) Cook until the syrup is dark brown and caramelized, 4 to 6 minutes. Remove it from the heat immediately. Take care not to get any molten sugar on your hands.

2. Add the cream. The mixture will bubble up like Mount Vesuvius—it's supposed to. Return the pan to the heat and whisk until the cream is completely blended in. Whisk in the vanilla.

3. Remove from the heat and let the sauce cool to room temperature. Pour it over the cheesecake or serve it on the side, or do a little of both.

SMOKED APPLES

Here's a second smoked apple dessert—a smoke-blasted remake of a classic comfort food—baked apples. Smoking adds complex caramel flavors to an apple's straightforward fruity sweetness. The upright cinnamon stick and roasted marshmallow provide additional flavor and whimsy. Especially when served with Smoked Ice Cream (page 240) or whipped smoked cream (see page 203).

INGREDIENTS

6 firm, sweet apples like Honeycrisps or Fuji

6 tablespoons (¾ stick) unsalted butter, at room temperature

¼ cup firmly packed dark brown sugar

¼ cup dried currants

¼ cup gingersnap crumbs, graham cracker crumbs, or ground almonds

½ teaspoon ground cinnamon

¼ teaspoon freshly grated nutmeg

1 teaspoon pure vanilla extract

6 cinnamon sticks (each 2 to 3 inches long)

3 large marshmallows, halved horizontally (optional)

Smoked Ice Cream (page 240; use vanilla), or regular vanilla ice cream, for serving (optional)

YIELD: Serves 6

METHOD: Hot-smoking

PREP TIME: 30 minutes

SMOKING TIME: 1 to 1½ hours

FUEL: Apple wood, what else?—enough for 1½ hours of smoking (see chart on page 6)

GEAR: An apple corer, melon baller, or fixed-blade vegetable peeler for coring the apples; grilling rings for holding the apples upright (or make your own grilling rings with crumpled twisted aluminum foil)

SHOP: You want a firm sweet apple like a Honeycrisp or Fuji

WHAT ELSE: Pears and quinces can be stuffed and smoked the same way

1. Set up your smoker following the manufacturer's directions and preheat to 275°F.

2. Core the apples, but don't cut all the way through the bottom; the idea is to create a cavity for stuffing.

3. Beat the butter and brown sugar in a medium-size bowl until fluffy. Beat in the currants, cookie crumbs, ground cinnamon, nutmeg, and vanilla. Divide the filling evenly among the apples. Stick a cinnamon stick upright through the filling of each apple and place a marshmallow half on top, if using.

4. Arrange the apples on grill rings on the smoker rack or balance them directly on the smoker rack. Smoke the apples until the sides are soft, but not collapsing, 1 to 1½ hours. If the marshmallows start to brown too much, loosely tent the apples with aluminum foil. Serve the smoked apples hot with ice cream on the side, if desired.

SMOKED ICE CREAM

YIELD: Makes 1 quart

METHOD: On a grill, in a smoker, or with a handheld smoker

PREP TIME: 5 minutes

SMOKING TIME: 6 to 10 minutes on a grill; 30 to 45 minutes in an offset smoker; 15 minutes with a handheld smoker

FUEL: Wood chips (unsoaked)—enough for 5 minutes of smoking, or hardwood sawdust of choice—enough for 15 minutes of smoking

SHOP: To make your life easier, start with a good commercial vanilla ice cream like Ben & Jerry's, Häagen-Dazs, Graeter's, or Talenti.

WHAT ELSE: You have three ways to smoke ice cream. Use a charcoal grill or smoker: you want to add a lot of dry chips to the fire to generate dense smoke quickly before the ice cream melts. (Chips start smoking faster than chunks or logs and dry chips start smoking faster then wet chips.) You place the ice cream in a bowl of ice to keep it from melting while you smoke it. Alternatively, use a handheld smoker.

He's been called the mad scientist of barbecue. His Michelin-starred restaurant, Asador Etxebarri, in Spain's Basque country, draws cutting-edge chefs from all over the world. His name is Victor Arguinzoniz, and no food is safe from Victor's one-of-a-kind grills and smokers. Not *kokotxa*—hake throat, which tastes like fish and slithers down your throat like an oyster. Not butter, which Arguinzoniz smokes over oak to spread on—what else?—grilled bread. Not even milk, which he smokes in a wood-burning oven to make a smoked ice cream that, like everything he serves, will take your breath away.

Ice cream may seem like the last food you'd smoke, but wood smoke gives it a haunting quality. Sure, you could smoke the cream (see page 203) and churn the ice cream from scratch, but there's a far easier way to do it: Use a charcoal grill or smoker. Or use a handheld smoking device, like a Smoking Gun or Aladin, to smoke your favorite premium commercial ice cream. Smoked ice cream makes an awesome à la mode with the Smoked Bacon-Bourbon Apple Crisp on page 228 or the Smoked Chocolate Bread Pudding on page 231. It's equally outrageous eaten straight off the spoon.

INGREDIENTS

1 quart best-quality ice cream (vanilla or your favorite flavor), slightly softened

Place the ice cream in a shallow bowl over a large flameproof bowl of ice. Keep this in the freezer until you're ready to smoke the ice cream.

On a charcoal grill: Set up your grill for indirect grilling and preheat to medium-high (400°F). Place the ice cream over its bowl of ice on the grill. Add 2 cups unsoaked wood chips to the mounds of embers. Cover the

grill and smoke until you see a light patina of smoke on the ice cream, 3 to 5 minutes. Turn the ice cream over with a spatula and smoke the other side the same way. Remove the ice cream from the grill. If it melted too much, refreeze it.

In a smoker: Set up your smoker following the manufacturer's instructions. Place the ice cream over its bowl of ice in the smoker. Add the unsoaked wood chips to the fire. Smoke as described previously. You may need a bit longer to put a patina of smoke on the ice cream.

With a handheld smoker: Place the ice cream in a large glass bowl and cover tightly with plastic wrap, leaving one edge open. Place the bowl over a pan of ice. Fill and light the smoker following the manufacturer's instructions. Insert the tube of the smoker, fill the bowl with smoke, withdraw the tube, and tightly cover the bowl with the plastic wrap. Let infuse for 5 minutes. Repeat once or twice more, until the ice cream is as smoky as you like. If the ice cream starts to melt, refreeze it.

COCKTAILS

Somewhere between the Penicillin—ginger, honey, lemon, and Scotch, concocted by bartender Sam Ross at Milk & Honey in New York City in 2005—and the bourbon-based Dragon's Breath (page 247) I drank from a mesquite smoke-filled brandy snifter at a cocktail lounge in Scottsdale, the American cocktail got smoked. Literally—using an ingenious handheld smoker like the Smoking Gun or Aladin smoker. Or indirectly by adding a smoke-scented spirit like Mexico's mezcal (distilled from smoke-roasted agave) or single-malt Scotch whisky (made with peat-smoked barley). In this chapter, you'll learn how wood smoke can turn a cocktail you've sipped a hundred times into a beverage that will fill you with wonder. Think of it as barbecue you can drink. Cheers.

SMOKY MARY

YIELD: Serves 1; can be multiplied as desired

METHOD: Smoking with a handheld smoker

PREP TIME: 10 minutes

SMOKING TIME: 8 minutes, or as needed

FUEL: 1 teaspoon oak or hickory sawdust, or as needed

GEAR: Handheld smoker

SHOP: For tomato juice, I like Sacramento. For mezcal, I like Del Maguey or Sombra.

WHAT ELSE: Don't have a handheld smoker? Pour the tomato juice into a shallow aluminum foil pan and hot- or cold-smoke it in a conventional smoker, following the instructions on page 203.

The Raichlen twist on the traditional Bloody Mary burns it up with fresh horseradish and sriracha. You'll smell smoke—literally—thanks to a flavorful blast of hickory from a handheld smoker. I know it sounds like heresy, but to reinforce the smoke flavor, use mezcal (a smoky cactus spirit from Mexico) in place of the usual vodka.

INGREDIENTS

¾ cup tomato juice

2 ounces (4 tablespoons) mezcal

2 teaspoons fresh lemon juice

1 teaspoon freshly grated or undrained prepared horseradish

1 teaspoon sriracha or other hot sauce

1 teaspoon Worcestershire sauce

4 to 6 ice cubes (1 cup; for even more flavor use smoked ice cubes—see page 249)

1 strip Sriracha Beef Jerky (page 52) or 1 rib celery (preferably from the heart, with leaves still attached)

1. Place the tomato juice, mezcal, lemon juice, horseradish, sriracha, and Worcestershire in a shaker glass or metal shaker and stir well to mix.

2. Load the handheld smoker following the manufacturer's instructions.

3. Cover the shaker glass with plastic wrap, leaving one edge open for the smoker tube. Insert the tube into the glass above the top of the liquid and fire the smoker to fill the glass with smoke. Quickly remove the tube and seal the top of the glass with the plastic wrap. Let stand for 4 minutes, then stir in the smoke with a bar spoon. Repeat once more, or until the desired degree of smokiness is achieved.

4. Place the ice cubes in a highball glass. Add the Smoky Mary and stir to mix. Insert the beef jerky or celery and serve.

NOTE: Some people like to rim the Bloody Mary glass with flavored salt or spices. Options include celery salt, Old Bay seasoning, or Tabasco Spicy Salt (a mix of Avery Island salt and the lees from Tabasco sauce). Spread out the salt and spices in a shallow dish. Rub the rim of the glass with cut lime and dip it in the spices. You'll need to smoke the Bloody Mary in a shaker, then pour it into the spice-rimmed glass, taking care not to dislodge the seasonings.

SMOKED MANHATTAN

YIELD: Serves 1; can be multiplied as desired

METHOD: Smoking with a handheld smoker

PREP TIME: 5 minutes

SMOKING TIME: 6 to 8 minutes, or as needed

FUEL: 1 teaspoon oak or hickory sawdust (or as needed)

GEAR: Handheld smoker

SHOP: You can use rye or bourbon for this Manhattan. For the former, I like Old Overholt or Rittenhouse; for the latter, Eagle Rare or Bulleit. The vermouth of choice would be Dolin or Carpano Antico. For cherries, use an artisanal brand, like Luxardo maraschino.

WHAT ELSE: For a smoky bacon flavor, make the cocktail with the Bacon Bourbon on page 257.

The Manhattan is one of North America's bedrock cocktails. It's about to get more interesting thanks to—you guessed it—a shot of wood smoke. Extra points if you chill it with smoked ice (see page 205). One sip justifies the expense of acquiring a handheld smoker.

INGREDIENTS

2 ounces (4 tablespoons) rye whiskey

1 ounce (2 tablespoons) red vermouth

4 to 6 ice cubes (1 cup; for even more flavor, use smoked ice cubes—see page 249)

Dash of bitters (I like Peychaud's)

1 strip orange zest (½ inch by 1½ inches)

1 maraschino cherry (see Shop)

1. Chill a cocktail glass. Load the smoker with sawdust following the manufacturer's instructions.

2. Place the whiskey and vermouth in a shaker glass or metal shaker. Cover the glass with plastic wrap, leaving one edge open for the smoker tube. Insert the tube above the top of the liquid and fire the smoker to fill the glass with smoke. Quickly remove the tube and seal the top of the glass with the plastic wrap. Let stand for 4 minutes, then stir in the smoke with a bar spoon. Repeat once more, or until the desired degree of smokiness is achieved.

3. Add the ice cubes and stir vigorously for 30 seconds. Strain the Manhattan into the chilled cocktail glass. Add a dash of bitters. Rub the rim with the orange zest (shiny side down). Drop the orange zest and cherry in the drink and serve.

GEAR FOR SMOKING COCKTAILS

Yes, a handheld smoker (see page 276) is the latest weapon in a mixologist's (not to mention barbecue fanatic's) arsenal, and smoked cocktails are turning up at cutting-edge bars from Brooklyn to Berkeley. Smoke adds a complexity and depth of flavor that can make a respectable cocktail great and a great cocktail a masterpiece.

Handheld smokers come in two basic models (both work on a similar principle). You can also smoke a cocktail in a conventional smoker.

Weapon #1: The Smoking Gun by PolyScience. It looks like a black plastic pistol. Place hardwood sawdust in the smoke chamber. Switch on the battery-powered fan and light the sawdust with a match or lighter. The smoke flows through a rubber tube into your glass, shaker, or pitcher where it flavors the drink or food. Cover with plastic wrap and fill with smoke. Repeat as necessary.

Weapon #2: The Aladin smoker. Yes, I know it looks like a bong. But, the smoke it generates is fragrant hickory or pungent mesquite. The upright metal cylinder has a fan in the bottom section, a sawdust holder at the top, and a flexible rubber tube for directing the smoke. Bartenders and chefs find it equally indispensable. Operate as described in Weapon #1.

Weapon #3: A conventional smoker; you can use any of the smokers starting on page 262. Pour fruit puree (fresh pineapple works great) into an aluminum foil pan to a depth of ¼ inch. Place in a larger pan filled with ice. Cold-smoke for 1½ to 2 hours or hot-smoke for 30 to 40 minutes. You can also smoke vermouth or wine this way. Refrigerate until using, but try to use within a few hours of smoking. (Note: You can freeze smoked fruit puree in ice cube trays for future use.)

DRAGON'S BREATH

Here's a cocktail that smokes—literally—thanks to an inverted brandy snifter filled with mesquite smoke. It comes from a Moldovan bartender named Aleks Karavay who I met in Scottsdale, Arizona. The Cointreau and St-Germain provide sweet-sour notes of fruitiness. "Slay your inner beast," Karavay says. Amen.

INGREDIENTS

4 to 6 ice cubes (1 cup; for even more flavor, use smoked ice cubes—see page 249)

2 ounces (4 tablespoons) bourbon (use your favorite)

1 teaspoon St-Germain

1 teaspoon Cointreau (or other orange-flavored liqueur)

1 teaspoon simple syrup or smoked simple syrup (see Note, page 252)

YIELD: Serves 1; can be multiplied as desired

METHOD: Smoking with a handheld smoker

PREP TIME: 5 minutes

SMOKING TIME: 2 minutes

FUEL: 1 teaspoon mesquite sawdust

GEAR: Handheld smoker

SHOP: St-Germain is an elderflower liqueur. Everything else should be on your bar shelf.

1. Load the smoker with sawdust and fire it up following the manufacturer's instructions.

2. Hold a brandy snifter upside down. Insert the smoker tube into the glass and fill it with smoke until you can't see through the glass. Tightly cover the glass with a coaster to hold in the smoke and turn it upright.

3. Place the ice cubes in a shaker. Add the bourbon, St-Germain, Cointreau, and simple syrup and stir rapidly for about 20 seconds.

4. Uncover the snifter and immediately strain the cocktail into it. Serve at once, with the smoke still spilling from the glass.

WHAT ELSE: For extra flavor, use smoked simple syrup (see page 204).

HOW TO INFUSE SMOKE INTO A COCKTAIL

There are six ways to infuse smoke into a cocktail.

1. Use a smoked spirit. Scotch whisky has a distinctive smoke flavor—the result of being distilled from smoked barley. *Rauchbier* (German-style smoked beer) is also brewed from smoked barley. Mezcal is made from fire-roasted agave cactus hearts. All three make killer smoked cocktails.

2. Coat the inside of the glass with smoke. Fill an inverted bar glass with smoke. Place a coaster over the mouth of the glass (now facing downward) to cover it tightly. Now turn the glass back upright and let stand covered for 1 minute. Pour in the cocktail and serve while the glass is still smoking. Try this for the Dragon's Breath on page 247.

3. Infuse smoke directly into the cocktail. Mix your drink in a bar glass or shaker. Cover the top with plastic wrap, leaving one edge open. Load your handheld smoker with hardwood sawdust, following the manufacturer's instructions. Insert the smoking tube into the glass above the drink. Fire the smoker to fill the glass with smoke. Withdraw the tube and tightly cover the glass with the plastic wrap. Let stand for 4 minutes, then uncover and stir in the smoke with a bar spoon. Repeat as needed

to achieve the desired degree of smokiness. Try this with the Smoky Mary on page 244.

4. Smoke a large batch of cocktails at once. Mix your ingredients in a large glass pitcher or bowl and cover with plastic wrap, leaving one edge open. Insert the handheld smoker tube above the drink and fill the pitcher with smoke. Remove the tube and tightly cover the glass with plastic wrap. Let stand for 4 minutes, then stir and repeat as needed, as for a single cocktail.

5. Smoke the garnish. Use a smoky garnish like a crisp strip of bacon or home-smoked beef jerky (page 52), as a swizzle stick.

6. Smoke your ice cubes. Place regular ice cubes in an aluminum foil pan. Cold-smoke for 1½ to 2 hours or hot-smoke for 20 to 30 minutes (keep the temperature as low as possible). Yes, the ice will melt. Refreeze the water in ice cube trays. Bingo—smoked ice cubes. (I learned this trick from the bartenders at the Broadmoor in Colorado Springs, where I run Barbecue University.) Alternatively, place the ice in a bowl over another bowl of ice. Cover with plastic wrap and smoke using a handheld smoker, as described above. Repeat as necessary.

MEZCALINI

Cross a margarita with a mojito and you get a Mezcalini. Add smoke and you achieve nirvana, not to mention notoriety—especially if you brandish the handheld smoker in front of your guests. It may be the most refreshing cocktail ever to slake your thirst (cucumber and *yerba buena* will do that). I discovered it at the rooftop dining room of the sophisticated Casa Oaxaca Hotel in this colonial city in south-central Mexico. No, you likely won't be able to replicate it exactly—unless you have access to the *chinicuiles* (fried cactus worms) that are nibbled along with fried grass-hoppers and crickets in this part of Mexico as bar snacks. Said worms (think miniature Cheetos that taste of bacon and butter) are ground with salt and dried chiles to make a rub for the glass rim. Smoked salt (see page 204) works fine for rimming the glass in the United States. By the way, don't miss dinner at the Casa Oaxaca: chef Alejandro Ruiz's refined Oaxacan cuisine will blow you away.

YIELD: Serves 6

METHOD: Smoking with a handheld smoker

PREP TIME: 10 minutes (yes, it can be made ahead)

SMOKING TIME: 6 to 8 minutes (optional)

FUEL: 1 teaspoon mesquite or oak sawdust, or as needed (optional)

GEAR: Handheld smoker (optional)

SHOP: *Yerba buena* ("good herb," literally) is one of the many Mexican wild herbs that go into mole verde and other green sauces. It has a distinctive, pungent, mild anisy flavor, like a cross between spearmint and Thai basil. Look for it at Mexican markets. Spearmint or peppermint makes a reasonable approximation.

WHAT ELSE: Mezcal is tequila's smoky cousin: a spirit made in central Mexico from fire-roasted agave cactus hearts. Good brands include Del Maguey, Sombra, and Montelobos. Avoid the cheap stuff with the worm in the bottle.

INGREDIENTS

1 cup mezcal

1 cup fresh lime juice (it must be fresh)

¾ cup simple syrup or smoked simple syrup (see Note)

2 tablespoons Cointreau (or other orange-flavored liqueur)

1 medium-size cucumber, peeled, seeded, and cut into ¼-inch dice (about 1 cup)

1 bunch fresh yerba buena, spearmint, or peppermint, rinsed, shaken dry, and separated into sprigs

½ cup smoked salt (use a good commercial brand or make your own following the instructions on page 204) or kosher salt

1 lime wedge, for moistening the glass rims

6 jumbo ice cubes (see Note) or 18 to 20 regular or smoked ice cubes (page 249)

1. Combine the mezcal, lime juice, simple syrup, and Cointreau in a pitcher, cover, and refrigerate until serving. You can do this several hours ahead.

2. Just before serving, place the cucumber and *yerba buena* in a mortar or bowl and lightly crush them with a pestle or muddler. Stir this mixture into the pitcher. If you make the Mezcalini right before serving, you can muddle the cucumber and *yerba buena* right in the pitcher using a long-handled wooden spoon.

3. Optional—for even more smoke flavor, smoke the Mezcalini with a handheld smoker: Cover the pitcher with plastic wrap, leaving one edge open for the smoker tube. Just before serving, load the smoker with sawdust following the manufacturer's instructions. Insert the tube and fill the pitcher with smoke. Quickly remove the tube, seal the pitcher with plastic wrap, and let stand for 4 minutes. Stir well with a bar spoon and repeat once more.

4. To serve, spread out the smoked salt in a shallow bowl. Moisten the rims of 6 large glasses with the lime wedge, then dip them in the salt. Shake off the excess.

5. Place 1 jumbo or 3 to 4 regular-size ice cubes in each glass. Pour the Mezcalini into the glasses. Spoon some of the cucumber and *yerba buena* into each glass, taking care not to drip on the salt.

NOTES: The beauty of jumbo ice cubes is their slow melt, which means less dilution of your drink. Look for molds for spherical and cube ice at bar supply stores or Williams-Sonoma.

To make simple syrup, combine equal parts (1 cup and 1 cup for example) sugar and water in a saucepan. Bring to a boil over high heat and cook until clear, 2 to 4 minutes. Let cool to room temperature, then transfer to a bottle or jar. Instructions for making smoked simple syrup are found on page 204.

THE MYSTIQUE OF MEZCAL

Call him the still seeker. Since 1995, Ron Cooper has crisscrossed remote villages in the mountains around Oaxaca searching for distillers of small-batch artisanal mezcal. In the process, the Taos, New Mexico, artist-turned-mezcal-mogul and founder of Del Maguey (pronounced *dell ma gay*) has helped elevate Oaxaca's indigenous alcohol from a harsh cactus-based firewater once infamous for the worm in the bottle to a prestige spirit poured at top cocktail lounges from Tokyo to New York.

Mezcal is a spirit distilled from fire-roasted *maguey* (the indigenous term for agave cactus). It takes five to fifteen years for the plant to reach maturity. Harvesting is done by hand with a machete, often on hillsides too steep even for donkeys. Shorn of their spiky leaves, the hearts resemble pineapples—*piñas* in local parlance. It takes 15 to 25 pounds of piñas to make a single quart of mezcal.

So what distinguishes Del Maguey's mezcals from tequila or from the mass-produced mezcals?

I embarked on a bone-jarring two-hour ride over twisting dirt roads to the village of Santa Catarina Minas to find out.

Luis Carlos Vasquez greeted us next to a cone-shaped earthen mound, its perimeter blackened with wood smoke—the *horno* where a fresh batch of agave hearts had been roasting in an oak-fired, stone-lined pit for four days. His dark, weathered face had the features you see in bas reliefs of Zapotec kings. Vasquez comes from a long line of *mezcaleiros*. His father, mezcal legend Loreano Carlos, has a distillery a few miles down the road.

"Distillery" is a grand word for this open-air shack with its dirt floor and corrugated tin roof. If you're expecting the gush of alcohol you'd find flowing from a still at a tequila factory, you'd be surprised, even underwhelmed, by the thin trickle of liquid that flows from the bamboo tube. Here, as at all of Ron Cooper's distilleries, everything is done by hand, from harvesting the agave to building the fire pit to crushing the roasted cactus hearts, and of course, to stoking and operating the still.

When we entered the still house, one worker cut the fire-charred piñas into fist-size chunks while another pounded them to a fibrous pulp with a giant wooden pestle. It's grueling work—the pestle must weigh 40 pounds. At most distilleries, the grinding is done by a horse- or mule-powered millstone. But Vasquez believes an animal's presence would leave an odor detectable in the final mezcal.

The next step is fermentation: The pounded maguey hearts are pitchforked into man-high wooden tanks where they ferment in the open air under the hot sun for a week or more, loosely covered with rush mats. Fruit flies and bees buzz in lazy circles around the tanks.

Once fermented, the sweet, sticky sludge is transferred to what may be the most low-tech still operating in North America. (Most mezcal distilleries now use copper stills.) The "boiler" is a large clay pot irrigated with a steady stream of cold water and topped with a shallow clay bowl. The alcohol condenses on the bottom of the bowl, where it's funneled through bamboo tubes into plastic demijohns.

The first distillation produces a tart, peppery liquid, which is distilled a second time to bring it to about 45 percent alcohol. But you won't find a hygrometer or a single scientific measuring instrument in Vasquez's still house. The cutting (to remove the peppery "heads" and impurity-filled "tails") is done using sight, smell, and taste. An hour at the still house left my clothes smelling like I'd been sitting downwind of a campfire.

Traditionally, you drink mezcal the way it emerges from the still—unblended, unaged, and unflavored. It is a fine spirit—potent but mellow, with a complex flavor of plant sugars, minerals, and wood smoke. That flavor varies depending on the agave variety, the microclimate, the local water, and of course the distiller's experience and art. For this reason, since starting his company in 1995, Cooper has specialized in single village mezcals—clearly labeled as such—without the blending typical of the industrial product.

It is often said that the Spanish brought distillation to the New World—a claim that Ron Cooper strongly disputes. Seeing Vazquez's still, fashioned entirely from clay pots, wooden bowls, and bamboo tubes, it was easy for me to believe that the Zapotecs perfected distillation long before the arrival of the conquistadores.

LIMONEIRO
MEZCAL WINE COOLER WITH GINGER AND ROSEMARY

YIELD: Serves 1; can be multiplied as desired

PREP TIME: 5 minutes

SHOP: You'll want an artisanal mezcal for this cocktail like Del Maguey or Sombra.

Daniel Avila, barman of Los Danzantes restaurant in Oaxaca, won a national Mexican mixology contest with this flavor-packed mezcal-based cocktail. Riffing on Brazil's caipirinha, Avila muddles diced lime and fresh ginger then adds white wine, mezcal, and rosemary. Think of it as the ultimate wine cooler, and don't dream of a summer smoke session without it.

INGREDIENTS

1 lime, cut into ¼-inch dice (rind and all)

1 piece (1 inch) fresh ginger, peeled and cut into ¼-inch dice

2 ounces (4 tablespoons) mezcal

1 ounce (2 tablespoons) dry white wine

1 tablespoon fresh lime juice

1 tablespoon simple syrup or smoked simple syrup (see Note, page 252)

4 to 6 ice cubes (1 cup; for even more flavor use smoked ice cubes—see page 249)

1 large sprig rosemary, for garnish

Place the lime and ginger in the bottom of a shaker and muddle well. Add the mezcal, wine, lime juice, simple syrup, and ¾ cup ice cubes and shake vigorously for 1 minute. Strain into a tall glass filled with ice. Garnish with the rosemary sprig and serve.

GREEN SMOKE

YIELD: Serves 4

PREP TIME: 15 minutes

You often serve Mexican spirits with salsa verde, but this is the only cocktail I know that combines fresh tomatillos and smoky mezcal in a single drink. (It comes from the edgy Alden & Harlow restaurant in Cambridge, Massachusetts.) Tomatillos belong to the gooseberry family, and possess a fragrant acidity that's as much in the realm of fruit as vegetable.

INGREDIENTS

4 cups regular ice cubes or smoked ice cubes (see page 249)

6 ounces (¾ cup) mezcal

4 ounces (½ cup) Tomatillo-Coriander Puree (recipe follows)

3 ounces (6 tablespoons) fresh lime juice

2 ounces (¼ cup) Kronan Swedish Punsch

⅛ teaspoon coarse or fine salt (sea or kosher)

Place the ice in a large pitcher. Add the mezcal, tomatillo puree, lime juice, Punsch, and salt. Stir vigorously for 1 minute, then strain into chilled cocktail glasses.

SHOP: For mezcal, Alden & Harlow uses Del Maguey Vida. Kronan Swedish Punsch is a West Indian cane spirit—popular in the United States before Prohibition, and currently enjoying a resurgence. If it's not available, substitute dark rum or Brazilian cachaça.

WHAT ELSE: Tomatillos come with a papery husk around a round green fruit. Peel it off with your fingers and discard.

TOMATILLO-CORIANDER PUREE

YIELD: Makes about 1¼ cups

This makes more puree than you need for the Green Smoke. It freezes well—freeze it in ice cube trays so you always have 1-ounce portions on hand.

INGREDIENTS

¾ cup coarsely chopped tomatillos (3 or 4 medium-size tomatillos, stemmed, husked, and rinsed)

½ cup sugar

1 tablespoon coriander seeds

½ cup water

Place the tomatillos, sugar, and coriander seeds in a food processor and puree to a paste. Add the water, and process in short bursts until smooth. Refrigerate, covered, for at least 3 days, or freeze in ice cube trays. (If using the latter, once frozen transfer to a resealable plastic bag for longer storage—up to 3 months.)

BACON BOURBON

Here's one more manifestation of the bacon mania sweeping Planet Barbecue, not to mention an ingenious way to make America's most beloved spirit even more amiable. The infusion technique comes from chef Megan Neubeck of Terzo Piano at the Art Institute of Chicago. (The smoke flavor comes from the bacon fat.) Manhattans and Old Fashioneds just got insanely better. Better still, serve them with a bacon strip garnish.

INGREDIENTS

8 ounces smoky bacon, cut crosswise into ¼-inch slivers

1 bottle (750 milliliters) bourbon or whiskey (use your favorite)

1. Place the bacon in a cold medium-size skillet over medium-high heat on the stove (or on a grill set up for direct grilling and preheated to medium-high, 400°F). Cook the bacon, stirring often with a wooden spoon, until the bacon has browned and the fat has rendered, 5 minutes.

2. Remove the pan from the heat and let the bacon cool slightly, then pour the fat through a fine-mesh strainer into a large metal bowl. Save the bacon pieces for another use, like sprinkling on a salad or topping Deviled Smoked Eggs (page 36).

3. Pour the bourbon into the warm bacon fat and whisk to mix; reserve the bottle and cap. Let the bourbon infuse at room temperature for 2 hours, then cover and place in the freezer overnight.

4. Remove the bourbon from the freezer. The bacon fat will have risen and congealed on the surface. Skim it off; you can use it for cooking and basting.

5. Line a funnel with a paper coffee filter. Place the funnel in the neck of the bourbon bottle and strain the bourbon back into the bottle. Recap before storing. It will keep at room temperature for several weeks (not that it will last that long).

YIELD: Makes 1 (750 ml) bottle

PREP TIME: 15 minutes

GEAR: Funnel; coffee filter

INFUSING TIME: 12 hours

SHOP: Neubeck uses KOVAL Four Grain whiskey distilled in Chicago. Other good candidates include Maker's Mark, Knob Creek, Blanton's, or even Wild Turkey bourbon, or a Tennessee whiskey like Jack Daniel's. For bacon, use a good artisanal brand like Nueske's, or make your own following the instructions on page 113.

WHAT ELSE: Intense sipped straight. Excellent for cocktails and adding to barbecue sauce.

BLOOD AND SAND

YIELD: Makes 1 drink; can be multiplied as desired

PREP TIME: 5 minutes

SHOP: Blood oranges are in season from December through March. Look for them at Whole Foods or order online through Melissa's (melissas.com).

WHAT ELSE: There are lots of candidates for single malt Scotches: Laphroaig and Lagavulin have the most intense smoke flavor. The vermouth of choice would be Dolin or Carpano Antico. Cherry Heering is a cherry liqueur invented in the late eighteenth century by Danish master distiller Peter Heering.

Smoke works wonders in multiple ways—even inspiring the comeback of a vintage cocktail. The Blood and Sand takes its name from a 1922 bullfighter movie starring Rudolph Valentino. It's in this book because the principal spirit, single malt Scotch whisky, is distilled from peat-smoked barley. Relax: The only blood shed in this recipe comes from a blood orange, a citrus fruit with a strawberry-orange flavor.

INGREDIENTS

1 blood orange

1 ounce (2 tablespoons) single malt Scotch whisky

1 ounce (2 tablespoons) red vermouth

1 ounce (2 tablespoons) Cherry Heering

4 to 6 ice cubes (1 cup; for even more flavor use smoked ice cubes—see page 249)

1. Chill a cocktail glass.

2. Using a vegetable peeler, remove a 1- by 1½-inch strip of the blood orange zest and set aside. Cut the fruit in half widthwise and cut a ¼-inch-thick slice off the wide end of one half. Remove any seeds from the slice, then make a slit along the radius so you can hang it on the glass rim. Set aside. Juice the rest of the blood orange into a shaker or bar glass. You need 1 ounce (2 tablespoons).

3. Add the whisky, vermouth, Cherry Heering, and the ice cubes to the shaker. Shake well, then strain into the cocktail glass. Wipe the rim with the orange zest strip (shiny side down) and place the reserved orange slice on the rim.

CONVERSION TABLES

Please note that all conversions are approximate but close enough to be useful when converting from one system to another.

OVEN TEMPERATURES

FAHRENHEIT	GAS MARK	CELSIUS
250	½	120
275	1	140
300	2	150
325	3	160
350	4	180
375	5	190
400	6	200
425	7	220
450	8	230
475	9	240
500	10	260

NOTE: Reduce the temperature by 20°C (68°F) for fan-assisted ovens.

APPROXIMATE EQUIVALENTS

1 stick butter = 8 tbs = 4 oz = ½ cup = 115 g

1 cup all-purpose presifted flour = 4.7 oz

1 cup granulated sugar = 8 oz = 220 g

1 cup (firmly packed) brown sugar = 6 oz = 220 g to 230 g

1 cup confectioners' sugar = 4½ oz = 115 g

1 cup honey or syrup = 12 oz = 350 g

1 cup grated cheese = 4 oz = 125 g

1 cup dried beans = 6 oz = 175 g

1 large egg = about 2 oz or about 3 tbs

1 egg yolk = about 1 tbs

1 egg white = about 2 tbs

LIQUID CONVERSIONS

US	IMPERIAL	METRIC
2 tbs	1 fl oz	30 ml
3 tbs	1½ fl oz	45 ml
¼ cup	2 fl oz	60 ml
⅓ cup	2½ fl oz	75 ml
⅓ cup + 1 tbs	3 fl oz	90 ml
⅓ cup + 2 tbs	3½ fl oz	100 ml
½ cup	4 fl oz	125 ml
⅔ cup	5 fl oz	150 ml
¾ cup	6 fl oz	175 ml
¾ cup + 2 tbs	7 fl oz	200 ml
1 cup	8 fl oz	250 ml
1 cup + 2 tbs	9 fl oz	275 ml
1¼ cups	10 fl oz	300 ml
1⅓ cups	11 fl oz	325 ml
1½ cups	12 fl oz	350 ml
1⅔ cups	13 fl oz	375 ml
1¾ cups	14 fl oz	400 ml
1¾ cups + 2 tbs	15 fl oz	450 ml
2 cups (1 pint)	16 fl oz	500 ml
2½ cups	20 fl oz (1 pint)	600 ml
3¾ cups	1½ pints	900 ml
4 cups	1¾ pints	1 liter

WEIGHT CONVERSIONS

US/UK	METRIC	US/UK	METRIC
½ oz	15 g	7 oz	200 g
1 oz	30 g	8 oz	250 g
1½ oz	45 g	9 oz	275 g
2 oz	60 g	10 oz	300 g
2½ oz	75 g	11 oz	325 g
3 oz	90 g	12 oz	350 g
3½ oz	100 g	13 oz	375 g
4 oz	125 g	14 oz	400 g
5 oz	150 g	15 oz	450 g
6 oz	175 g	1 lb	500 g

THE VARIOUS TYPES OF SMOKERS

CHARCOAL GRILLS

If you own a charcoal grill, you already have a smoker. Charcoal is the easiest fuel to smoke with—a lot easier than propane in a gas grill. Simply set up the grill for indirect grilling, add wood chips or chunks to the coals, and you're in business. Note: You need a charcoal grill with a tall, tight-fitting lid for smoking.

Advantages:
- Charcoal grills are widespread, space efficient, and inexpensive. (You may well own a kettle already.)

Drawbacks:
- Because kettle grills are designed for grilling, it's harder to maintain an even heat at lower temperatures.
- The relatively small cooking grate limits how much meat you can smoke at one time.

Tips:
- Place the food on the grate, then add the wood chips or chunks. If you add the wood first, you'll have to maneuver through clouds of eye-stinging smoke.
- Use tongs to add wood to the fire, laying it gently on the coals. Don't drop or toss in the wood or you'll stir up ash, which will land on the food. This holds for any charcoal-burning smoker.

HOW IT WORKS:

Light your charcoal in a chimney starter and load the side baskets of your kettle grill for indirect grilling or smoke-roasting. For smoke-roasting (high-heat smoking), use a full chimney of charcoal; for low-heat smoking (low and slow), use a half to a third chimney of lit coals (about 10 coals per side). For cold-smoking, use a smoke generator or smoking tube or mesh smoking pouch.

Place an aluminum foil drip pan between the ember baskets.

Install the grill grate.

Soak the wood chips in water to cover prior to smoking.

Add soaked wood chips to the coals to generate smoke. There is no need to soak wood chunks.

HOW TO ROTISSERIE-SMOKE ON A KETTLE GRILL

If you have a Weber kettle, invest in a rotisserie ring, spit, and motor. This enables you to turn the grill into a "smoke-tisserie," which combines the best of smoking and spit-roasting. The ring also elevates the grill lid by several inches—useful for smoking whole turkeys or beer can chickens.

HOW IT WORKS:

Install the metal rotisserie ring on the kettle grill. Place the coals in the coal baskets on opposite sides, as you would for indirect grilling. Here a chicken is being spit-roasted over a vegetable-filled drip pan in the center.

UPRIGHT BARREL SMOKERS / COOKERS (AKA DRUM SMOKERS)

Why has the upright barrel cooker (sometimes called **drum smoker**) become one of America's bestselling smokers? By what paradoxical law of thermodynamics can a rack of ribs hover two inches above the fire without burning? And how do manufacturers pack so much performance into a smoker-grill combo that typically retails for less than $300?

The upright barrel smokers start as an upright steel drum with a charcoal basket at the bottom. The food cooks vertically, suspended from metal bars stretched across the top. Air enters the cooker through a vent at the bottom and exits through small holes at the top. Like a grill, the food cooks directly over the charcoal (with no water pan acting as a barrier). Like a smoker, it operates as a sealed system, with smoke generated by wood chips or chunks added to the charcoal. Thus, the heat is both radiant and convective, so food smokes faster in an upright barrel smoker than it would in a conventional smoker.

Advantages:

- Upright barrel smokers are inexpensive, space efficient, extremely easy to use, and versatile—use for smoking, roasting, and direct grilling (for the latter, remove the lid).
- The closed cook chamber seals in moistness. The vertical position of the food helps drain off fat. The meat juices produce extra flavor when they hit the coals.

Drawbacks:

- These smokers have relatively limited cooking space, making them better for cooking for small to medium-size gatherings than for a large crowd.
- The smoke flavor is a bit less pronounced than in a water smoker or an offset smoker.

HOW IT WORKS:

Load the coal basket three quarters of the way with unlit coals.

Pour the lit coals from the chimney starter on top of the unlit coals.

Place a few wood chunks on the coals to generate smoke.

(More on the next page.)

Once the coal basket has been lowered to the bottom of the Pit Barrel, insert the crossbars for hanging the food.

Hang the food to be smoked from one of the crossbars. Note the wooden handle with the eyelet for grabbing the hot hook.

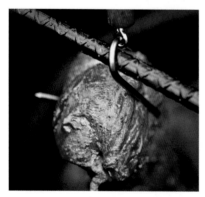

The genius of an upright barrel smoker: the food cooks vertically over the coals, just as it would in an Indian tandoor.

Tips:

• Most upright barrel smokers come with vents in a preset position. When cooking and smoking at high altitude, open the bottom vent a bit more to let in more air.

• Any time you want to spike the temperature (to crisp chicken skin, for example, or power through a brisket stall), set the lid ajar by ½ to 1 inch.

OFFSET SMOKERS (AKA OFFSET BARREL SMOKERS OR "STICK-BURNERS")

Nothing says you mean business like a stick-burner. For years these hardcore smokers—the technical term is offset smoker or offset barrel smoker—have dominated the competition barbecue circuit. Now, mass-market models sold at Home Depot and Lowe's bring their own particular machismo to American and European backyards.

Legend has it that oilfield workers in Texas and Oklahoma built the first offset smokers from oil pipes or steel drums. Modern offset smokers follow the same design—a lidded horizontal barrel-shaped or boxlike smoking/cooking chamber with a firebox connected to and lower from one end (hence the name "offset"). In some models the firebox is located beneath or behind the smoke chamber. A grease drain at the bottom of the smoke chamber funnels excess fat to a bucket.

Whatever the configuration, the heat and smoke flow through a portal into the cook chamber where they circulate around the food and exit through the chimney. This flow of hot air and wood smoke is one of the defining features of the offset smoker, producing ribs and pork shoulders with exceptionally crisp "bark" (crust) and deep red smoke rings.

Advantages:

• Offset smokers burn real wood—logs for the large ones; wood chunks or chips on a bed of charcoal in smaller models. No pellets, propane, or electricity allowed.

• The substantial size of the cook chamber allows you to smoke large quantities of food—even whole hogs. And you don't need to open the smoke chamber to add the wood, so you never experience a drop in heat. Thanks to the offset design, stick-burners rarely overheat.

- There's no electrical circuitry to burn out or moving parts to replace. However, the steel will rust if the smoker is left uncovered.

Drawbacks:

- Even modest-size offset smokers can weigh hundreds of pounds, making them difficult to maneuver without assistance. They also have a large footprint—a challenge for people with limited space.
- The entry-level cost is relatively high—figure on $1,000 or more for a well-built unit.
- It can take an hour or more to bring your pit up to temperature. After that, you'll need to check on it frequently. This is not a set-it-and-forget-it smoker (nor is it practical for a quick after-work smoke session), and it takes practice to obtain consistent results.
- Performance can be affected by wind, rain, or cold weather.
- The market is flooded with inexpensive and poorly built offset smokers. Hinges break, paint flakes, metal rusts, and target temperatures are difficult to maintain. Some assembly is usually required. Check the reviews online.

Tips:

- Run the smoker a couple times to burn off any factory grease or protective coatings *before* your smoke your first batch of food.

- Remember: The smoke chamber will be hotter at the firebox end. Start with the larger, fattier end of the brisket or pork shoulder toward the fire. Rotate the meat from the hot end to the cooler end every hour or so—so it will cook evenly.
- Another way to equalize the internal cooking temperature is to buy a smoker with reverse flow technology or a **convection plate**. The former channels hot air to the far end of the smoke chamber, then back again via a chimney positioned close to the firebox. The latter uses a heavy metal plate (often perforated) under the grate to help equalize the temperature in the cook chamber and shield the food closest to the fire from some of the heat.
- Buy the right size smoker for your entertaining style. If you cook a whole hog once a month, you'll need a different smoker than if you smoke the occasional ribs or pork shoulder. But buy more smoker than you think you'll need—this will inspire you to stretch your imagination and grow your skill set.
- The thicker the metal, the better the heat retention and more even the cooking: ¼-inch-thick steel is the gold standard.
- Other useful options include a grill grate you can position over the firebox (to turn your smoker into a grill); a counterweight on the smoke chamber lid; and front or bottom work shelves.

HOW IT WORKS:

For larger units, build a wood fire in the firebox (see How to Smoke with Straight Wood on page 26). Start smoking when you have a hot bed of coals, adding logs to generate smoke. For smaller units, light charcoal in a chimney starter and spread the embers over the charcoal rack at the bottom of the firebox. Once the food is on, add small logs or wood chunks or chips (about 2 to 4 cups per hour) to generate smoke. Control the heat by opening or closing the vents. Note: Follow the manufacturer's instructions for seasoning a new smoker.

The air intake vent and the chimney vent should be fully open. Pour a chimney of hot coals into the firebox.

Rake the coals into an even layer with a grill hoe.

(More on the next page.)

Place a couple of logs on the burning charcoal.

Thanks to the hot charcoal, the logs catch fire quickly.

Close the lid—make sure the cooking chamber lid is closed as well—and preheat the smoker to the desired temperature (usually 225° to 275°F).

Adjust the convection plate to equalize the heat and smoke flowing into the cook chamber.

Use the push rod outside the firebox to move the convection plate.

At the smoker, cutting up a rack of cooked ribs.

CERAMIC COOKERS / SMOKERS (AKA KAMADO-STYLE SMOKERS)

For years I've called them an evangelical army of ceramic cooker enthusiasts who have a cultlike attachment to their Big Green Eggs or Kamodo Kamados and a messianic fervor to spread the gospel to every corner of the world. The fact is, kamado-style cookers (the name comes from a traditional Japanese oven) have taken the planet by storm. Picture a large upright ceramic egg or ovoid with a hinged dome-shaped lid. You burn charcoal at the bottom (often enhanced with wood chunks or chips), controlling the heat by opening or closing the large vents at the top and bottom.

Advantages:
- Versatility: The ceramic cooker functions as a smoker, a grill, and an oven. Use it for everything from smoking pork shoulder to baking pizza to grilling a steak.
- Excellent temperature control and thermodynamics: The venting and airflow systems allows you to go from 225°F

for smoking to a searing 700°F for direct grilling in a matter of minutes. Thanks to those thick ceramic walls, once you get a ceramic cooker up to temperature, it holds the heat—even in an Alaskan winter.

- Fuel efficiency: Properly regulated, a single 5-pound load of charcoal will burn as long as 18 hours or even more in some models.
- The thick clay walls retain heat and moisture in a way that other grills don't. The felt gasket between the lid and body helps hold in moisture, too.

Drawbacks:

- Ceramic cookers have a relatively small cooking area—262 square inches on a large Big Green Egg, for example. Compare that with the more than 1,200 square inches on an offset smoker, like a 20-inch Horizon Marshall. (But note: The XXL Egg has 672 square inches.)
- Refueling: Unlike offset smokers or front-loading grills, you need to remove the grate and any food on it, and sometimes the **heat diffuser** (a heavy ceramic plate also called a **plate setter**), in order to replenish the charcoal or wood chips. On the other hand, thanks to the design—especially when you use an **airflow regulator** (see Tips on page 268), you don't need to refuel very often.

- The smoke flavor isn't quite as pronounced as with a water smoker or offset barrel smoker.
- Weight: Ceramic cookers weigh a lot (162 pounds for a large Egg; about 400 pounds for the XXL), which makes them difficult to transport (although that doesn't

HOW IT WORKS:

Arrange unlit lump charcoal in the bottom of the cooker, interspersing wood chips throughout the coals.

Place 1 or 2 paraffin fire starters in the center of the coals.

Steeple a few coals over the fire starters.

Light the fire starters. The fire will spread gradually from the center to the periphery, burning the wood chips as it goes.

Install the ceramic convector plate to shield the food from direct exposure to the fire.

(More on the next page.)

Install the grill grate.

Adjust the top vent to control the airflow and thus the heat. The more open the vent, the greater the airflow and thus the heat.

Adjust the bottom vent to control the airflow and thus the heat. The less open the vent, the lower the airflow and thus the heat.

stop people from bringing them to tailgate parties).

- Expense: The starting price for a large Big Green Egg is around $800. Tables and metal stands—called "nests"—are sold separately.

Tips:

- Light the charcoal directly in the bottom of the cooker. No chimney starter or lighter fluid needed.
- Once the cooker is hot, "burp" it a few times before opening the lid completely. That is, raise the lid a few inches to release some of the heat, then lower it. This keeps you from getting blasted by a fiery flashback.
- To further control the heat, invest in an **airflow regulator** with a thermostat (see Temperature and Draft Controllers on page 14). This battery-powered device regulates the airflow through the bottom vent, allowing you to control the cooking temperature almost to the precise degree.

WATER SMOKERS

The water smoker delivers big performance in a small space at an affordable price. Shaped like the Star Wars robot R2-D2 (or an upright bullet—nickname of the popular Weber Smoky Mountain), the water smoker has a bowl-shaped metal firebox on legs at the bottom. Atop that sits a cylindrical smoke (cook) chamber with an access door in the front for adding wood and charcoal. A large metal water bowl fits between the fire at the bottom and the smoke chamber. Over the water bowl are one or more wire racks to hold the food and a dome-shaped lid to hold in the heat and smoke.

Advantages:

- The water smoker's defining feature—the water pan—keeps food moist, even after 12 hours of smoking.
- The tri-part construction makes it easy to add charcoal and wood to the fire, access the meat, and clean the smoker.
- The unique design and thermodynamics almost guarantee a consistent smoking temperature of 225° to 275°F.
- The water smoker has a small footprint (about the size of a kettle grill)—useful for people with limited space. Most weigh

less than 50 pounds, making them portable for tailgating.

- There are few moving parts and no electronics to malfunction—cleaned regularly and protected from the elements, water smokers will last for years.

Drawbacks:

- The cooking area is somewhat limited when compared to offset smokers (although some models double the cooking space with upper and lower racks).
- Thin-gauge steel construction makes it challenging to maintain the cooking temperature in cold, windy, or wet weather.
- Water smokers are designed to burn charcoal with wood chips, chunks, or smoking pellets added to generate smoke. The purist who insists on smoking solely with wood would be better off with an offset smoker.

HOW IT WORKS:

Fill the firebox (the bottom section of the smoker) with lit coals. Note the perforated metal ring to corral the coals.

Place the smoke chamber (the center section of the smoker) atop the firebox.

Install the water pan.

Fill the water pan with water that's at least 2 inches deep.

Install the lower rack. Water smokers like this one allow you to cook on two levels.

Install the upper rack.

(More on the next page.)

Install the front door panel.

Install the domed lid.

Make sure the lid fits snugly, with the thermometer facing front.

Open the front door panel and add the wood chips to the coals. Gently place them on the coals so as not to stir up ash.

Adjust the top and bottom vents to control the heat. As always, the wider the vents are open, the greater the airflow and the heat.

Tips:

- Line the water bowl with heavy-duty aluminum foil to facilitate cleanup.
- You'll need to replenish the charcoal and wood chips every hour or so. If using lump charcoal, add it directly to the fire and leave the access door open for a couple of minutes to allow the charcoal to ignite. If using briquettes, light them in a chimney starter, then add *lit* coals to the fire. (Unlit briquettes often release an acrid smoke.)
- Replenish the liquid in the water bowl as needed—there should be at least two inches at all times. (The easiest way to do this is from a pitcher.) Add cool water when firing up the smoker (to cool the initial hot burn). Add hot water once you're cooking (so you don't cool down the smoke chamber).
- There are times when you *don't* want to add liquid to the water pan—to crisp the skin on smoked chicken, for example, or when you want to smoke meats like pork loin or duck at a higher temperature. Without liquid, temperatures in the smoke chamber can climb to 350°F or more.
- When cooking two different proteins on stacking racks at one time, think about what will be dripping onto what. Chicken fat dripping on potatoes—or salmon for that matter—rocks! Salmon drippings on brisket, not so much
- Keep the smoker covered when not in use to prevent chipping.

GAS SMOKERS / BOX SMOKERS

Propane-fueled smokers offer the convenience of push-button ignition and turn-of-a-dial temperature control for an investment as low as a couple hundred dollars. Advanced models can cost thousands. Picture a metal box with a gas burner/heating element at the bottom surmounted by a metal pan or tray to hold the wood chunks, chips, or sawdust. Some models come with a water pan over the wood tray to moderate the heat and keep the smoke chamber moist.

Advantages:

- Small footprint—especially compared to offset smokers.
- Portability. Unlike electric smokers, you don't need a power outlet. Some models run on the 14-ounce canisters used to fuel a blowtorch.
- Smoking temperatures are easy to maintain, and with much less labor than with a wood- or charcoal-burning smoker.

Drawbacks:

- The same as with gas grills— they don't burn wood or charcoal.
- No internal airflow—which helps form bark (the crust).
- Some widely available brands are poorly constructed using thin-gauge metals. They leak smoke and do not perform well in cold or windy weather conditions.

HOW IT WORKS:

Place the wood chips, pellets, or sawdust (depending on the model) in the smoker box.

Add water to the water pan.

Light the burner with the igniter. Turn the thermostat to set the heat.

Wait for the smoke chamber to fill with smoke.

Once the smoke chamber fills with smoke, add the food—here salmon over ice for cold-smoking.

(More on the next page.)

Adjust the top vent to ensure a steady smoke flow.

Tips:
- Choose a model that's wide or tall enough to accommodate a brisket or full rack of ribs (you may need to hang the latter). Otherwise, you'll need to cut them in half, which doesn't look nearly as impressive.
- Long smoke sessions may exhaust your propane. Always have a backup cylinder/canister on hand.

ELECTRIC SMOKERS

If you're a purist who likes splitting logs, messing with fires, and checking the smoker every 30 minutes (even during a 16-hour smoke session), an electric smoker is not for you. But, it's hard to beat the convenience of push-button ignition, thermostatic temperature control, and an electric heating element that turns sawdust disks or wood shavings into fragrant wood smoke reliably every time. Sophisticated models let you program the temperature and the length of the smoke session and monitor the internal temperature of what you're smoking (with an alarm to let you know when the meat is cooked).

Advantages:
- Convenience and consistency.
- Electric smokers allow you to maintain consistent low temperatures—something that's very difficult to do in a wood- or charcoal-burning smoker.

Drawbacks:
- You must work near an electrical outlet, so you can plug the smoker in.
- Limited internal airflow—which helps form "bark" (the crust).
- Most models aren't wide enough to accommodate a packer brisket or full rack of ribs. You may need to cut these items in half.
- No fire, no fun.

Tips:
- Cooking ribs or other slow-cooked foods? If your smoker has hooks at the top, smoke them vertically.
- Electric smokers are excellent for smoking bacon, jerky, salmon, and other foods you smoke at a low temperature.

HOW IT WORKS:

Assemble the smoker, with the controller mounted to the smoke chamber. The controller allows you to set the temperature, cooking time, and smoking time.

Insert the sawdust disks (bisquettes) in the hopper.

As the sawdust disks move through the smoker mechanism, they're burned on a heated plate, then discarded in the water bowl.

Adjust the top vent to control the smoke flow.

PELLET GRILLS / SMOKERS

Pellet grills represent one of the fastest-growing segments of the smoker market. It's hard to beat their versatility (you can barbecue, smoke, roast, bake, braise, and, on some models, grill on a pellet grill). Then, there's their set-it-and-forget-it convenience. Picture a classic offset barrel smoker or gas grill with a side- or rear-mounted hopper replacing the firebox. You fuel it with food-grade cylindrical wood pellets—each about 1 inch long and ¼ inch wide—composed of compressed hardwood sawdust.

When you plug a pellet grill in and turn on the digital controller, a rotating augur delivers pellets from the hopper to a fire chamber housing an igniter rod. The rod glows red hot for several minutes, igniting the pellets. Heat and smoke from the combusting pellets are diffused by a blower fan as well as metal plates under the grill grate. At lower temperatures (200° to 250°F), pellet grills operate as smokers. At higher temperatures, they function more like an outdoor oven.

Advantages:
- Like gas grills, pellet grills preheat quickly—15 to 20 minutes. Some pellet grills allow you to regulate temperatures in five-degree increments, giving you ovenlike heat control.
- The design discourages flare-ups. And because a pellet grill works like a convection oven, you can load up the cook chamber without fear of uneven cooking.
- It's almost impossible to over-smoke food on a pellet grill. The smoke flavor is more subtle than with a water smoker or stick-burner.
- Pellet grills come in a wide range of sizes, from small models for home use to commercial-size units that can accommodate a whole hog.

Drawbacks:
- Pellet grills don't put out quite the intense smoke flavor you get with a water smoker or stick-burner. The higher the cooking temperature, the less smoke the unit generates. You'll get the most smoke flavor at temperatures below 250°F.
- Pellet grills run on electricity, so you have to use them near a power source.
- Though they are marketed as "grills," it is difficult to get a good sear or grill marks on most pellet grills. A few pellet grills, such as the Memphis Wood Fire Grill, have removable metal plates over the firebox so you direct grill over a live pellet fire.
- Any grill or smoker with moving parts and electrical components is more prone to breakdowns than charcoal or wood burners.

Tips:
- Pellets come in a variety of flavors—hickory, pecan, alder, mesquite, cherry, apple, maple, bourbon, and more—and can be mixed or changed in minutes. Under normal circumstances, a pellet grill burns about ½ pound of pellets per hour on the smoke setting and 2½ pounds at higher temperatures—more in cold or rainy weather.
- If exposed to moisture, pellet fuels will disintegrate. If you live in a humid climate, store pellets in airtight containers—preferably indoors.
- For additional wood smoke flavor, you can position hardwood chunks or pouches of soaked wood chips directly on the heat diffuser plate.

HOW IT WORKS:

Wood pellets ready for loading in the pellet grill.

Dropping pellets into the hopper.

Pellets burning in the burn chamber produce both heat and smoke.

- If your model has a drip tray/diffuser plate, cover it with heavy-duty aluminum foil to facilitate cleanup.
- Some companies, such as Traeger, offer cold-smokers as an accessory—perfect for cheese or Nova Scotia-style salmon.

WOOD-BURNING GRILLS

Most of the smokers in this section have lids to hold in the smoke. But you can also smoke on an open grill—provided it burns wood. This brings us to Argentinean-style grills, which burn logs under a grate you can raise and lower using a flywheel. Wood grilling gives you a different flavor than traditional smoking—cleaner, lighter, more subtle—but you do get a distinctive smoke flavor, nonetheless.

Advantages:
- Designed as grills, thus excellent for steak, chops, and vegetables, and you're not restricted to low heat.
- Fueled solely with wood.

Drawbacks:
- They lack a lid, so much of the smoke dissipates.

HOW IT WORKS:

Build a wood fire with kindling or a charcoal base. Control the heat by raising or lowering the grate with the flywheel.

Tips:
- For smokier meats, start grilling while the logs still flame. For less smoky meats, burn the logs down to embers before putting on the food.
- To capture more of the smoke flavor, place a pie pan, overturned roasting pan, or metal wok lid over the steak or fish you're grilling. This is usually done once the bottom side is seared and you've turned the meat over.
- To smoke larger cuts that you would normally indirect-grill, like prime rib or pork shoulder, cook them on the rotisserie of your wood-burning grill.

STOVETOP SMOKERS

This brings us to smokers to use indoors. The Nordic Ware 365 Kettle Smoker uses a process similar to wok-smoking in China. Then there's the Camerons Stovetop Smoker cooker—a device of ingenious simplicity consisting of a rectangular metal box with a drip pan at the bottom, a wire food rack on top of it, and a tight-fitting lid. You fuel it with hardwood sawdust and heat it on the stove. I often use it for making kippered salmon.

Advantages:

- Simple and effective with no moving parts and it gives you real hardwood smoke flavor indoors.
- Good for smoking small pieces of food, such as shrimp and mushrooms, that might get lost in a large outdoor smoker.
- Runs at a higher temperature than most outdoor smokers, so it cuts down on the smoking time.

Drawbacks:

- Because of the small size, you're limited as to how much you can smoke. Good for salmon, scallops, and chicken parts. Not so good for whole racks of ribs or brisket. However, you can smoke a whole chicken or turkey by covering the smoker with a large sheet of heavy-duty aluminum foil instead of the lid.
- Indoor smokers invariably produce smoke in your kitchen, which may set off your smoke alarm. If you do disconnect the alarm while smoking (not that I say you should), remember to *reconnect* it afterward.

Tips:

- With use, the smoker lid may warp, allowing smoke to escape. To seal any leaks, place a heavy object, like a cast-iron skillet, on top.
- Remember, the bottom of the smoker will be *extremely* hot when it comes off the fire. Place it on a heatproof surface or trivet.

HOW IT WORKS:

Place 1 to 2 tablespoons of hardwood sawdust at the bottom of the smoker.

Insert the drip pan (line it with aluminum foil to facilitate cleanup) and food rack (lightly oiled).

Place the food on the food rack.

Close the lid, leaving a 1-inch gap. Place the smoker on the burner and heat until you see smoke (about 30 seconds), then close the lid. Adjust the burner to the desired temperature, and smoke until the food is cooked. For larger foods, you may need to replenish the sawdust.

HANDHELD SMOKERS

Maybe you've sipped a smoked cocktail like the Dragon's Breath on page 247. Perhaps you've dined at a restaurant where the food arrives in a cloud of smoke under a glass bell jar. Meet the cool tool that makes it possible: the handheld smoker. One popular model looks like a pistol; another like a bong; both use a burner, blower, and rubber tube to deliver fragrant wood smoke to your drink or food. You'll definitely want to add one to your smoker collection.

Advantages:

- Handheld and completely portable. Delivers smoke in a highly focused manner.
- The flexible rubber tube directs smoke anywhere you point it—even into spaces you don't normally associate with smoking, like mayonnaise jars and whiskey bottles.
- Great for quick cold-smoking, as the smoke doesn't heat or cook the food.

Drawbacks:

- Better for small-portion dishes, like cocktails, soups, and salads. Too small for large cuts of meat.

Tips:

- Use a clear glass bowl or bottle so you can see how much smoke you have in it.
- To smoke whiskey or another spirit, empty the bottle halfway. Insert the smoke tube. Seal the bottle with plastic. Swirl the bottle to stir in the smoke. Repeat as needed.
- To smoke mayonnaise, empty the jar halfway. Smoke as above. Shake vigorously or stir to diffuse the smoke.
- Load hardwood sawdust in the burn chamber. Switch on the blower and hold a match or lighter to the sawdust to light it. Once you see smoke, direct the smoke through the hose to where you want it.
- Have the food or drink you want to smoke in a bowl, pitcher, or glass covered with plastic wrap (leave one edge open so you can insert the smoker tube). Switch on the fan and fill the bowl with smoke, switch on the blower, and pull the plastic tight to cover the container. Let the smoke infuse the food or drink for 4 minutes. If working with a liquid ingredient, stir well. Taste and repeat 1 or 2 times or until the smoke flavor is as pronounced as you desire.

HOW IT WORKS:

Load the smoke chamber with sawdust.

Light the sawdust.

Switch on the fan motor to propel the smoke through the rubber smoking tube.

Insert the smoking tube into a pitcher or bowl covered with plastic wrap. Let the smoke infuse the cocktail for 3 to 4 minutes. Stir and repeat as necessary.

ADDITIONAL SMOKING ESSENTIALS

SMOKE GENERATORS AND GRILL INSERTS

- **Smoke Daddy:** Designed by smoke master Dennis Correa, this clever cold-smoke generator consists of an upright metal cylinder with wire mesh at the bottom for holding the wood chips and removable caps at the top and bottom. Place a lit charcoal in the canister, then fill the canister with un-soaked wood chips or pellets. (Alternatively, remove the bottom cap and light the wood from below with a blowtorch.) Switch on the blower motor: air conducted by a flexible hose blows the smoke into your smoker (smokedaddyinc.com).

- **Smoke Chief:** An electric cold-smoke generator brought to you by the folks who manufacture the Little Chief and Big Chief Smokers in Hood River, Oregon. You load the hopper with wood pellets, which are ignited by an electric heating element. Depress the plunger to push the pellets toward the igniter. Note: Clean the metal smoke pipe often (it fills with tars), using the screw-like tool provided for this purpose (smokehouseproducts.com).

- **Smokenator 1000:** A lot of us started our smoking careers on the ubiquitous Weber kettle grill. The kettle works great for smoke-roasting, but it's more challenging to maintain a consistent low temperature of 225°F for true low-and-slow smoking. Enter the Smokenator—a stainless-steel insert with a charcoal partition and a water pan, which turns your kettle grill into a water smoker. The Smokenator 1000 enables you to smoke low and slow for up to 6 hours on a single load of charcoal (smokenator.com).

FREESTANDING SMOKER BOXES

Many companion sell a variety of stainless-steel, cast iron, and nonstick smoker boxes for wood chips and pellets. These smoker boxes are often used on gas grills.

UNDER-GRATE SMOKER BOXES

- **Companion Group V-Shaped Gas Grill Smoker Box with Pellet Tube:** Has an ingenious slender metal chute that lets you refill the smoker with pellets during grilling without having to remove the grate (companiongroup.com).

- **Best of Barbecue Disposable Gas Grill Smoker Box with Chips:** Fit between the Flavorizor ™ bars of a Weber gas grill (barbecuebible.com).

- **Smoke in a Cup:** A disposable heavy aluminum foil cup filled with hardwood sawdust. Position it under the grate over one of your burners. Run the grill on high until you see smoke, then reduce the heat (companiongroup.com).

OVER-GRATE SMOKERS

- **A-Maze-N Tube Smoker:** Fill the perforated metal tube with hardwood pellets. Light one end (use your blowtorch) and place it next to the food: the pellets will smoke as they burn to the other end. Available in 6-, 12-, and 18-inch models that produce smoke for up to 6 hours. Use on gas grills for hot- and cold-smoking and for boosting the smoke in pellet grills. The company also manufactures a metal mesh maze smoker designed to burn hardwood sawdust or pellets for cold smoking (amazenproducts.com).

- **Mo's Smoking Pouch:** A metal mesh bag you fill with wood chips or pellets and place directly on the grill grate. Position on the grate next to the food (mossmokeandsauce.com).

- **Best of Barbecue Smoke Pucks:** Movable puck-shaped metal smoke boxes with vents for directing the smoke (barbecuebible.com).
- **Smoke Daddy Vortex Cold Smoker:** The flying saucer design keeps pellets burning for up to 10 hours of cold smoking (smokedaddyinc.com).
- **GrillGrates:** For years, grillers have sworn by these raised rail aluminum grates to improve grill marks, sear temperature, and overall grilling performance. But you can also use them for smoking: simply sprinkle hardwood pellets or chips in the valleys between the raised grill rails (grillgrate.com).
- **Moistly Grilled Smoking Platform:** Food smokes best in a moist environment. Picture a flat metal box you fill with wood chips or pellets, with a perforated metal grate for the food and reservoirs on the ends to hold water or other liquid to generate steam (companion-group.com).

THERMOMETERS

INSTANT-READ THERMOMETERS

- Pro-Temp and 2 Way Thermocouple Thermometer by Maverick (maverickhousewares.com)
- Thermapen and ThermoPop by Thermoworks (thermoworks.com)

REMOTE/WIRELESS THERMOMETERS

- Redi-Chek, Remote Smoker Thermometer, Wireless Barbecue Thermometer Set, and Wireless BBQ & Meat Thermometer by Maverick (maverickhousewares.com)
- ChefAlarm, ThermaQ 2-Channel Alarm, and Dot Cooking Alarm by Thermoworks (thermoworks.com)
- iGrill Mini, iGrill Mini Pro Ambient Temperature Probe, and iGrill Pitmaster by iGrill (idevicesinc.com)
- Talking BBQ Thermometer by Oregon Scientific (oregonscientific.com)
- Long Range Wireless Dual 2 Meat Probe BBQ Smoker Meat Thermometer by Ivation (myivation.com)
- Temperature Monitoring System by Tappecue (tappecue.com)

TEMPERATURE AND DRAFT CONTROLLERS

These work on most ceramic cookers and charcoal water smokers.

The industry leader is BBQ Guru (bbqguru.com), manufacturer of the DigiQ DX2 and PartyQ and a proprietary brand for Big Green Egg. The BBQ Guru works great: I've used it to get 14-hour burns on a single batch of charcoal in a Big Green Egg. Another brand is the Pitmaster IQ (pitmasteriq.com).

TOOLS FOR GETTING FLAVOR INTO MEAT AND SEAFOOD

- **Vacuum marinating canisters:** Check out the FoodSaver System (foodsaver.com) and Polyscience External Vacuum Sealing System 150 (polyscienceculinary.com).
- **Vacuum tumblers:** Check out the Marinade Express (marinadeexpress.com).

NONSTICK SILICONE MESH MATS

Use these mats for cooking small or fragile foods. Two good brands are: **Frogmats** (frogmats.com) and **Bradley Smoker Magic Mats** (bradleysmoker.com): They withstand heats up to 500°F, and are good for smoking and indirect grilling.

INJECTORS

- **The SpitJack Magnum Meat Injector Gun:** This top-of-the-line injector has a rubberized pistol grip and a strong ratcheted injection system with calibrated dial to deliver precise amounts of injection sauces deep into the meat via a series of 5.5 inch specialty needles—slender, wide, multi-hole, and so on (spitjack.com).

- **The F. Dick Marinade Brine Injector:** An industrial strength marinade/brine injector equipped with several feet of tubing with a terminal valve on one end that can be submerged in a large container of injector liquid. Good for whole hogs (dick.de).
- **Bayou Classic Cajun Injector:** The syringe has a 2-ounce capacity and is made of stainless steel for durability (thebayou.com).
- **Best of Barbecue Marinade Injector and Spice Paste Injector:** My own brand. The latter has a wide tip to accommodate thick liquids like pesto or jerk seasoning, and a metal spike for making fill holes in the meat (barbecuebible.com).

PHOTO/ILLUSTRATION CREDITS

All photos by Matthew Benson unless otherwise credited below.

Courtesy Use: Aladin pg. 4 (handheld), pg. 276 (handheld smoker, right); Big Green Egg pg. 266 (ceramic smoker); Bradley pg. 4 (electric smoker), pg. 14 (electric smoke generator), pg. 22 (electric cold smoker), pg. 272 (electric smoker); Camerons pg. 275 (stovetop smoker); Char-Broil pg. 4 (front-loading charcoal grill); Companion Group pg. 13 (shovel), pg. 13 (electric fire starter), pg. 13 (suede gloves), pg. 13 (grate grabber), pg. 15 (basting brushes), pg. 15 (barbecue mop), pg. 15 (grill humidifier), pg. 15 (rib rack), pg. 16 (meat claws); Landmann-USA pg. 271 (gas smoker); Horizon pg. 4 (offset smoker); Kalamazoo pg. 4 (wood-burning grill), pg. 274 (wood-burning grill, top right); Komodo Kamado pg. 4 (ceramic); Maverick pg. 14 (remote digital thermometer); Memphis pg. viii (btm right), pg. 4 (pellet grill), pg. 273 (pellet grill), pg. 274 (top left), pg. 274 (middle left), pg. 274 (btm left); Nordic Ware pg. 4 (stovetop smoker); Pit Barrel Cooker Co. pg. 4 (upright barrel smoker), pg. 263 (upright barrel smoker); PolyScience pg. 276 (handheld smoker, left); Southern Pride pg. 4 (carousel-style smoker); SpitJack pg. 15 (injector); ThermoWorks pg. 14 (instant-read thermometer); Weber pg. 4 (kettle-style), pg. 4 (water smoker), pg. 262 (charcoal grill), pg. 268 (water smoker); Yoder pg. 4 (big-rig offset), pg. 264 (offset smoker).

Fotolia: fablok pg. 9 (sawdust); Givaga pg. 9 (logs); Kurt Holter pg. 9 (chips); ras-slava pg. 11; Yeko Photo Studio pg. 9 (pellets).

Author Photos: pg. viii (top right), pg. 1, pg. 4 (home-built smokehouse), pg. 179.

Illustration: James Williamson pg. 5.

INDEX

Chicken:
  doneness tests, 29–30
  Jamaican jerk, 154–56, *155*
  livers, smoked, 46
  red hot wings with Pac-Rim seasonings, *50,* 51–52
  rotisserie-smoked, 150–52, *151*
  shopping for, 18
  smoked, with horseradish dip, 153
  smoked liver pâté, 47
  smoking chart, 152
  thighs, bacon, ham, and cheese, 158
Chilies:
  chipotle, adding smoke flavor with, 37
  chipotle-orange cocktail sauce, 177
  jerk seasoning, 157
  see also Jalapeños
Chimney, 5
Chimney starters, 13, 27
Chinatown spareribs with Beijing barbecue sauce, 98–100, *99*
Chinese barbecued pork strips (smokehouse char siu), 107–8
Chipotle(s):
  adding smoke flavor with, 37
  -orange cocktail sauce, 177
Chocolate bread pudding, smoked, *230,* 231–32
Chops, monster pork, smoked and grilled in the style of Butcher and the Boar, 109–10, *111*
Chowder, smoked fish, 59
Cinnamon sticks:
  how to smoke, 205
  smoking foods with, 11
Citrus fennel turkey breast, 165–66
Cold-smoked eggs, 35

Cold-smoked salmon like they make it in Denmark (Bornholm lax), 183–84, *185*
Condiments:
  mustard seed caviar, 106
  pairing with food, 18
  see also Sauces
Convection plate, 5, 266
Cook chamber, 5
Cooked beans from scratch, 223
Coriander:
  -fennel rub, smoked black cod with, 197–98
  spice rub for pastrami, 72
  -tomatillo puree, 255
Corn:
  creamed smoked, 213
  -tomato salsa, smoked, 39–41
Crab-bacon poppers, 55
Cream, how to smoke, 203
Creamed smoked corn, 213
Cucumber(s):
  lamb belly banh mi, 132
  relish, dilled, smoked black cod toasts with, 199
  smoked gazpacho, 57–58
Curing food, 16

D

Desserts:
  smoked apples, 239
  smoked bacon-bourbon apple crisp, 228–30, *229*
  smoked cheesecake, 235–38, *236*
  smoked chocolate bread pudding, *230,* 231–32
  smoked flan, 233–35, *234*
  smoked ice cream, 240–41
Deviled smoked eggs, *34,* 36

Dill(ed):
  cucumber relish, smoked black cod toasts with, 199
  -lemon sauce, *181,* 182
  -mustard sauce, sweet, *181,* 182
  sauces, serving with seafood, 18
Dips:
  smoked seafood, 45
  smoked tomato-corn salsa, 39–41
Double-smoked potatoes, *208,* 209–10
Double whiskey-smoked turkey, 159–61, *160*
Dragon's breath, 247–49, *248*
Drinks:
  bacon bourbon, *256,* 257
  blood and sand, 258
  dragon's breath, 247–49, *248*
  green smoke, 254–55
  infusing smoke into, 249, 276–77
  limoneiro (mezcal wine cooler with ginger and rosemary), 254
  mezcalini, *250,* 251–52
  smoked Manhattan, 246
  smoking, gear for, 247
  smoky mary, 244, *245*
Drum smokers, 263–64
Duck:
  smoked, tacos, 171
  smoking chart, 152
  tea-smoked, 168–70, *169*

E

Eggplant parmigiana, smoked, 44
Egg(s):
  cold-smoked, 35
  deviled smoked, *34,* 36
  pickled smoked quail, in the style of Noma, 38–39

Mezcalini, *250,* 251–52

Monster pork chops smoked and grilled in the style of Butcher and the Boar, 109–10, *111*

Montreal meatballs with maple-mustard barbecue sauce (boulettes fumées), *140,* 141–42

Mop sauces, 17

Mortadella, how to smoke, 205

Mozzarella, hay-smoked, 42–44, *43*

Mulberry wood, 10

Mushroom bread pudding, smoked, *216,* 217–18

Mustard:

    deviled smoked eggs, *34, 36*

    -dill sauce, sweet, *181,* 182

    how to smoke, 204

    -maple barbecue sauce, 142

    seed caviar, 106

    vinegar sauce, 118

Mutton, doneness tests, 29–30

N

Nachos, smoked, 48, *49*

Nuts, how to smoke, 205

O

Oak-smoked cherry-glazed baby back ribs, *94, 95*–96

Oak-smoked top round, 65

Oak wood, 10

Offset smokers, 264–66

Olive oil, how to smoke, 204

Olives, how to smoke, 204

Olive wood, 11

Onions:

    barbecued, 214, *215*

    how to smoke, 204–5

Orange(s):

    blood and sand, 258

    -chipotle cocktail sauce, 177

Orange wood, 10

Orchard woods, 6, 10

Oysters:

    smoked on the half shell, 174, *175*

    smoke times, 178

P

Palochina wood, 11

Panini, smoked mozzarella, 44

Pastrami:

    about, 74

    home-smoked, 72–75, *73*

Pâté, smoked liver, 47

Peach wood, 10

Pear wood, 10

Pecan wood, 10

Pellet grills, 273–74

Pellets, 9

Peppers:

    smoked gazpacho, 57–58

    smoked vegetable cassoulet, 220–22, *221*

    see also Chilies

Pickled smoked quail eggs in the style of Noma, 38–39

Pimentón, adding smoke flavor with, 37

Pimento wood, 11

Pine or spruce needles, smoking with, 11

Plate setter, 5, 267

Plum wood, 10

Pork:

    baby back ribs, about, 97

    belly, barbecued, 116–18, *117*

Chinatown spareribs with Beijing barbecue sauce, 98–100, *99*

chops, monster, smoked and grilled in the style of Butcher and the Boar, 109–10, *111*

country-style ribs, about, 97

doneness tests, 29–30

heritage, buying, 18

how to smoke a whole hog, 92–93

Montreal meatballs with maple-mustard barbecue sauce (boulettes fumées), *140,* 141–42

oak-smoked cherry-glazed baby back ribs, *94, 95*–96

ribs, buying, 97

ribs, 3-2-1 cooking method, 103

ribs, removing membrane from, 97

ribs, smoking, tips for, 97

ribs, types of, 97

rib tips, about, 97

shoulder, smoked, pulled, and vinegar-sauced in the style of North Carolina, 88–90, *89*

smoked, layers of flavor in, 91

smoke-roasted cherry-glazed baby backs, 96

smoking chart, 108

spareribs, about, 97

St. Louis-cut ribs, about, 97

St. Louis ribs with vanilla-brown sugar glaze, 101–3

strips, Chinese barbecued (smokehouse char siu), 107–8

see also Bacon; Ham; Sausage(s)

Potato(es):

    double-smoked, *208,* 209–10

    how to smoke, 211

    smoked, salad, 206–9, *207*

    smoked fish chowder, 59

smoked root vegetable hash
    browns, 212
Poultry:
    doneness tests, 30
    smoking chart, 152
    see also Chicken; Duck; Turkey
Prime rib, smoked, 78–80, *79*

R

Rauchbier, adding smoke flavor
    with, 37
Red hot wings with Pac-Rim
    seasonings, *50,* 51–52
Remote digital thermometers, 14
Reverse searing, 83
Rib racks, 15, 97
Ribs:
    baby back, about, 97
    baby back, oak-smoked cherry-
        glazed, *94,* 95–96
    baby backs, smoke-roasted
        cherry-glazed, 96
    beef, plate, smoked salt-and-
        pepper, 62–64, *63*
    buying, 97
    Chinatown spareribs with
        Beijing barbecue sauce,
        98–100, *99*
    country-style, about, 97
    ham, honey-cured, *104,* 105–6
    lamb, barbecued, with fresh
        herb wet rub, 133
    removing membrane from, 97
    rib tips, about, 97
    smoking, tips for, 97
    spareribs, about, 97
    St. Louis, with vanilla–brown
        sugar glaze, 101–3
    St. Louis-cut, about, 97
    3-2-1 cooking method, 103
    types of, 97

Rice, smoking with, 11
Rosemary:
    and ginger, mezcal wine cooler
        with (limoneiro), 254
    smoking with, 11
Rotisserie-smoked chicken,
    150–52, *151*
Rubs:
    about, 17
    5-4-3-2-1 (Asian barbecue rub),
        100
    spice, for pastrami, 72
Rum:
    jerk seasoning, 157
    kippered salmon, *186,* 187–88

S

Salads:
    smoked caprese, 44
    smoked potato, 206–9, *207*
    smoked slaw, 202
Salmon:
    candy, 189–91, *190*
    cold-smoked, like they make it
        in Denmark (Bornholm lax),
        183–84, *185*
    kippered, *186,* 187–88
    smoke times, 178
Salsa, smoked tomato-corn,
    39–41
Salt:
    flavoring raw food with, 16
    how to smoke, 204
    smoked, adding flavor with, 37
Sandwiches:
    lamb belly banh mi, 132
    smoked mozzarella panini, 44
Sauces:
    burnt sugar, 238
    chipotle-orange cocktail, 177
    hot, how to smoke, 204

hot, sriracha-lime, 131
    lemon-dill, *181, 182*
    mayonnaise-based, serving with
        seafood, 18
    mustard vinegar, 118
    sweet mustard-dill, *181, 182*
    three hots horseradish, 78
    vinegar, Carolina, 91
    see also Barbecue sauces
Sausage(s):
    and bacon fatty (Tulsa torpedo),
        143–45, *144*
    preparing, tips for, 147
    smoked bratwursts, 146
    smoking chart, 138
Sawdust, 9, 12
Schwarzwälder Schinken, 119
Scotch whisky:
    adding smoke flavor with, 37
    blood and sand, 258
Seasoning, jerk, 157
Sesame seeds, how to smoke, 205
Shallots, how to smoke, 204–5
Shanks, smoke-braised lamb, with
        Asian seasonings, 128–30,
        129
Shellfish:
    bacon-crab poppers, 55
    doneness tests, 30
    oysters smoked on the half
        shell, 174, *175*
    shopping for, 18
    smoked seafood dip, 45
    smoked shrimp cocktail with
        chipotle-orange cocktail
        sauce, *176,* 177–78
    smoked shrimp with two Danish
        dill sauces, 180, *181*
    smoke times, 178
Shop vacuum, 13
Shoulder, pork, smoked, pulled, and
        vinegar-sauced in the style of
        North Carolina, 88–90, *89*

STEVEN RAICHLEN

Author, journalist, lecturer, and TV host, Steven Raichlen is the man who redefined modern global grilling. His 30 books include the international blockbusters *The Barbecue! Bible, How to Grill,* and *Planet Barbecue*. He hosts the popular PBS TV shows *Steven Raichlen's Project Smoke, Primal Grill*, and *Barbecue University*. (He also hosts two French language TV shows—*Le Maitre du Grill* and *La Tag Barbecue*.) Raichlen's books have won 5 James Beard Awards and 3 IACP-Julia Child Awards, and been translated into 17 languages. He has lectured on the history of barbecue at the Smithsonian Institution and Harvard University, and founded *Barbecue University* at the Broadmoor resort in Colorado Springs. An award-winning journalist, he has written for *The New York Times, Le Journal de Montréal, Esquire, GQ*, and the major food magazines. In 2015, he was inducted into the Barbecue Hall of Fame. Raichlen holds a degree in French literature from Reed College in Portland, Oregon, and studied medieval cooking in Europe on a Thomas J. Watson Foundation Fellowship. He and his wife, Barbara, live in Miami and Martha's Vineyard.

641.616   Raichlen, Steven.
RAI
          Project smoke.

$37.50

DATE			